An Onslaught
of Spears

An Onslaught of Spears

THE DANISH CONQUEST OF ENGLAND

JEFFREY JAMES

Front cover: Viking longship at sunset. *Courtesy of and copyright of Mark Milham*; Back cover: The Aberlemno stone.

First published 2013

The History Press
The Mill, Brimscombe Port
Stroud, Gloucestershire, GL5 2QG
www.thehistorypress.co.uk

© Jeffrey James, 2013

The right of Jeffrey James to be identified as the Author
of this work has been asserted in accordance with the
Copyright, Designs and Patents Act 1988.

British Library Cataloguing in Publication Data.
A catalogue record for this book is available from the British Library.

ISBN 978 0 7524 8872 1

Typesetting and origination by The History Press
Printed in Great Britain

Contents

Introduction

England fell under Danish control around 1,000 years ago, in 1016. The motive of the invaders was not to settle land but to gain riches, wreak revenge and establish political and military hegemony over a rich and prosperous country. For the best part of three decades, successive Danish kings ruled in England as well as Denmark and much of Norway. Had each king not been short-lived, an Englishman's national heritage might now be considered in large part Scandinavian.

Viking attacks on England had been an overriding menace for more than 200 years. Historians identify two discrete Viking ages: the first (*c.* 793–954) when three of the four old Anglo-Saxon kingdoms of England fell for a time under Viking control, before being won back; the second spanning much of the reign of Aethelred II (978–1016), when sustained attacks from successive, voracious Scandinavian warlords toppled English rule altogether. The first two chapters of this book cover the 'first Viking Age'; the rest of the book focuses on the second. The narrative spans a period of our history when the way armies were organised and how they fought is not fully understood; the locations of even the larger battles are unknown or disputed. Assandun, the culminating battle of Cnut's campaign of conquest in 1016, was fought in Essex, but whether at Ashdon, on the borders with Cambridgeshire, or at Ashingdon, in the south-east of the county, is unclear. Some battles are not referenced in the mainstream chronicles. Only tantalisingly brief mentions occur in little-known Celtic annals or in later Icelandic sagas of dubious provenance. Over fifty known battles were fought between Anglo-Saxons and Vikings in England from the late eighth century up until 1016, approximately one every four years on average, but they often arrived in clusters. Outside of unusually eventful years such as 871, 893 and 1016, battles were uncommon, and only a few were major cataclysms (see the Appendix 1 Battle Chronology 796–1016).

Encounters could be quite formal affairs. A lengthy period of religious observance, including the hearing of Mass, took place on the Christian side before the Battle of Ashdown (871). Large communities of monks accompanied the English army into battle at Assandun. An Old English poem known as 'The Battle of Maldon' (991) describes the English leader Byrhtnoth allowing a stronger Viking force to cross a causeway unopposed, enabling both sides to fight on an equal footing. Although rarely sought, set-piece battles at this time seldom appear to have been rushed.

If the military history is elusive, the geography of the time is no less so. Forests were more extensive than today; roads across mountainous districts, such as the Pennines, almost non-existent. Extensive regions of marshland curtailed or funnelled movement. Areas such as the Humberhead Levels (circumscribing the borders of Yorkshire, Lincolnshire and Nottinghamshire), Romney Marsh in Kent and the Somerset Levels (all now dry land), were in early medieval times permanently or seasonally waterlogged and subject to regular inundation from the sea. The political term Northumbria attests to the Humber being a major barrier between North and South, splitting the country geographically. The sinuous course of the Thames (demarcating the boundary between Wessex to the north and Mercia to the south) underwrote the importance of heavily garrisoned fords at flashpoints such as Wallingford, Oxford and Abingdon. Seaways and navigable river systems such as the Trent and the Severn often afforded the safest and quickest mode of travel for raiding armies, and islands such as Mersea in Essex, Sheppey and Thanet in Kent, and the Isle of Wight became important Viking strongholds.

The most densely populated areas of England in early medieval times were parts of Lincolnshire, East Anglia and east Kent. Other, lesser concentrations of peoples existed in south Somerset and along the South Coast. Population estimates range from 1.25 to 2 million people in the late eleventh century, a marked decline from more prosperous and secure Roman times, when the population is estimated to have peaked at as many as 4 million. It would not be until the 1300s that numbers would again reach such levels; only to decline again with the arrival of the Black Death in the Middle Ages.

Early English chroniclers routinely described Viking invaders up until the eleventh century as 'raiding-armies', and sometimes used the same terminology to describe local forces striking back. In its mildest form raiding might equally well be termed foraging, the procurement of forage and supplies being (as in any period of history) an on-going requirement for large armies, and one needing to be undertaken ever further afield, for obvious reasons. But Viking raiding armies were not noted for their mildness. If contemporary accounts are to be believed, their sorties were aggressively undertaken, with local peasant communities bearing the brunt of the violence; men were killed and women and children enslaved. Such Viking depredations resulted in untold misery for captives sold on in the slave marts of Dublin and Rouen. Harrying of an opponent's land differed only in motivation. It was an overtly warlike activity which both sides engaged in, designed to deny resources to an enemy or to punish transgression. Areas harried were systematically destroyed by fire and sword. Villages were razed to the ground and inhabitants indiscriminately slaughtered.

To the early English chroniclers, the Vikings were simply referred to as 'heathen men' or, more often, Danes. Only later was the term Viking commonly used, thought variously to mean sea pirate, trader, traveller or men of the fjords. Irish chroniclers made a clear and early distinction between the Norse 'Finngaill' (white foreigners) and Danish 'Dubhgaill' (black foreigners), whose fierce, hereditary rivalry turned all Ireland into a battleground in the ninth and tenth centuries, and whose depredations resulted in enormous losses to the Irish in destroyed manuscripts and precious religious objects. The route from Oslo fjord to Dublin became known as the 'sea road' and the islands and archipelagos of northern Britain became established settlement points and stopovers for seagoing Viking communities. Seafaring acumen and fierce fighting skills gave the newcomers mobility and martial advantage capable of overwhelming the relatively flimsy, static defences of much of Christianised Europe. Even the mighty Carolingian Empire was rocked by the severity of their attacks, and kings such as Charles 'the Bald' and Charles 'the Fat' were forced to pay tribute to avoid protracted warfare in the same way as a number of Anglo-Saxon kings, including Alfred 'the Great' (d. 899) and Aethelred II. River systems and estuaries which acted as buffers between rival petty kingdoms in Ireland, Britain and on the Continent were highways for the invaders, whose shallow-drafted boats were able to penetrate deep into the interior before disgorging raiding parties, forerunners of full-scale armies.

As early as the eighth century, warships are thought to have been quite different from other mercantile craft, and were designed to be distinctively long in proportion to their width. Eight knots was a likely maximum speed for a typical longship under oars, though it was not a pace likely to be kept up for long, and would have been impossible to achieve against a swift tide. Size mattered. The number of warriors on board determined the ship's combat potential and speed. King Olaf Tryggvason of Norway (d. 999) is credited with having a flagship capable of carrying 500 men. Such enormous ships were presumably quite rare; their size was also likely exaggerated for dramatic effect. More typically, longships are thought to have carried around forty to forty-five men when at full complement – three men to an oar, depending on space – allowing for one or more relief crews, an important consideration in wartime or when undertaking long-distance voyages.

Though renowned as seafarers, with a good knowledge of rudimentary astronomy, early medieval mariners did not take unnecessary risks. They stayed well in sight of land whenever possible, making use of estuarine islands and inlets as safe havens. Also, the need to regularly take on fresh water and re-victual would have necessitated frequent stopovers. Even so, disaster sometimes struck. Just a year after the Vikings first appeared off the north-east coast of England, in 793, the twelfth-century chronicler Simeon of Durham reported how a violent storm shattered, destroyed and broke up the Viking's vessels – 'the sea swallowing up very many of them', while others were cast ashore and speedily slain without mercy by the locals.

Sandwich and Thanet are often mentioned as the first landfall for raiders from Scandinavia and northern Europe, indicating that the Vikings sought to minimise sailing time by crossing the English Channel at its narrowpoint.

The construction of simple but effective fortifications and supply depots in the territories invaded indicates a strong sense of forward planning among early Viking leaders. Their trademark D-shaped defensive enclosures exist today as ghostly, barely discernible earthworks, notably at places such as Repton in south Derbyshire. Garrison sites such as these served as centres for domestic and commercial activities as well as warlike ones.

Though fierce and uncompromising, the majority of Vikings were not as keenly impatient for death and glory as popular mythology would have us believe. Danish settlement north of the Thames and in East Anglia was in large part driven by the requirements of a retired Viking warrior class, exhausted by campaigning. Having seized overall control and stripped an area of its riches, Viking leaders were often content to coexist with compliant Anglo-Saxon kings, sometimes puppets set up by the Vikings themselves. When faced with strong opposition they would look elsewhere for plunder.

Once an initial period of raiding and fighting was over, there appears
to have been no great barrier to coexistence of Anglo-Saxons and
Scandinavians. The campaigns fought in the second half of the ninth century, which saw the demise of three of the four Anglo-Saxon kingdoms
of England, paved the way for future prosperity. York and Chester became
booming commercial centres for Scandinavian trade; the former is thought
to have been able to support a population in excess of 20,000 by the close
of the tenth century.

Whereas chronicled accounts of Alfred the Great's time are both objective
and immediate, such objectivity is rarely found in the narratives of Aethelred II's troubled reign. Failure in battle for the latter attracted criticism
more on moral grounds than material ones, the assumption being that God
was punishing the loser for good reason. By the end of the tenth century,
chroniclers had become increasingly judgemental of their rulers. As a result,
the accounts of campaigns fought against a succession of Viking invaders in
the first decade of the tenth century were systematically contaminated by
the frequent scapegoating of Aethelred's ministers and commanders.

Despite the fact that he reigned for significantly longer than any other
early medieval king, and is one of only two English kings ever to win back
his throne by force of arms (the other was Edward IV), Aethelred's military
reputation has, as a result of this bias, become irrevocably tarnished, leading
to the indictment of him as being 'ill-counselled', a ditherer, unprepared to
face his aggressors. The accounts of Aethelred's reign in the *Anglo-Saxon
Chronicle* were written some time after the king's death, and were based (it
is thought) on a single history of his reign written by an anonymous and
judgemental author. The writer knew the fateful outcome for the English
and backdated portentous events for dramatic effect, including ominous
red clouds appearing at midnight and unexplained routs and mutinies
afflicting his countrymen.

The historian Pauline Stafford has stated in her book *Unification and
Conquest* that the 'bleak picture of incompetence, arbitrariness and treachery' painted by this writer, plus 'the fullness and compulsion of his narrative'
has resulted in future historians being unable to free themselves from his
influence. Building on this early gloss, twelfth-century historians embellished their own histories with dubious acts of treachery, of decapitated
heads changing the course of battle and of assassins lurking in the shad-
ows. Being the work of monks (writing was a clerical monopoly – laymen
could often read, but could seldom write), such authors were hampered by

having access solely to classical or biblical works for descriptions of how men might fight or overcome their enemies.

Earlier accounts from Alfred the Great's time are generally crisper and more detailed, implying they were dictated by someone who actually witnessed the fighting. The first version of the *Anglo-Saxon Chronicle* (known as the Winchester manuscript) may even have been sponsored by Alfred directly, the accounts of battles and campaigns fought by him and his commanders being written during his lifetime. Later histories, such as those written by Florence of Worcester (referred to in this text as Florence), William of Malmesbury, Simeon of Durham and Henry of Huntingdon – all written in the twelfth century – also provide valuable insights, being based, it is thought, on versions of the *Anglo-Saxon Chronicle* that are now lost. Other important sources include Bishop Asser's contemporary *Life of Alfred* – Asser was a monk of St Davids in Pembrokeshire who entered Alfred's service and eventually became the Bishop of Sherborne – and the *Encomium Emmae Reginae*, written 'in praise of Queen Emma' (the wife of both Aethelred II and Cnut) by an anonymous author around the year 1040, less than thirty years after the Danish Conquest. Nevertheless, the Maldon battle poem is by far the most detailed written account of men facing battle in the so-called Dark Ages.

Although a literary undertaking first and foremost, the Maldon poem is not thought to be a work of fiction, despite some important aspects of the narrative owing more to classical history than late tenth-century reality. Though not intended to be precisely accurate, the poem must have contained sufficient factual detail for it to have been believed by a contemporary audience. Moreover, the absence of retrospective statements indicates it was penned before the full impact of the Viking onslaught was recognised. In the second half of the eleventh century, the Bayeux Tapestry (a 77yd-long embroidered account of the campaign and the battle at Hastings) provides a more direct visual insight to medieval warfare, showing not only the way warriors were armoured and equipped, but also how William of Normandy's invasion was launched and how armies of the period fought. But no such tapestry exists to help the military historian seeking to understand the time of Swein Forkbeard's and Cnut's invasions and equally hard-fought campaigns fifty years earlier.

First Onslaught

Reports in twelfth-century histories of 'horrible lightnings and flashes of fire, glancing and flying to and fro' heralded the first appearance of the Vikings in England. They invoke images of fierce, heavily armed and opportunistic freebooters arriving in shield-bedecked longships, slaughtering and plundering at will. But this highly romanticised view is unlikely to be true. Norse raiders, who arrived in three ships – the first recorded raid – and who bludgeoned a king's reeve (customs officer) to death on Portland beach, Dorset, in 789, had been mistaken by their victim for commonplace traders. Viking appearance cannot therefore have been in any way remarkable.

At the religious centres at Lindisfarne, Jarrow and Iona (all in the far north), raiders knew beforehand that their victims were rich and undefended, having had commercial dealings with them in the past. At each, the Viking marauders are said to have dug up the altars and plundered the church treasures: gold, silver and other precious objects. In the case of Iona (off the west coast of Scotland) the religious community there was attacked several times in the space of a decade. On one occasion sixty-eight of its monks were slain. On another the abbot was killed when he refused to disclose the location of the hidden shrine of St Columba. A letter sent by the cleric Alcuin to the King of Northumbria bewailed, 'Never before has such terror been seen in England as we have suffered from heathen people.'

Further fierce 'heathen men' – both Norse and Danes – began arriving in ever greater numbers on the coasts of England at the turn of the ninth century. Viking war-bands were campaigning in Kent as early as 804. When confronted by a resolute defence, these forays could be driven off and the Vikings defeated and destroyed, but not always. King Egbert's West Saxons were defeated at Carhampton in Somerset in 836. Carhampton was one of several Saxon royal estates located between Minehead and the estuary of the River Parrett. Others included Williton and Cannington. Carhampton was also at one time a Celtic monastic site; its name is thought to derive from little-known St Carantoc. Other monastic centres lay nearby at Porlock, St Decumans, Timberscombe and Cannington. Two years later Egbert got his own back, crushing a combined Viking and Welsh army at Hingston Down beside the River Tamar. Southampton and Portland were assaulted in 840; the men of Wessex prevailed at the former, but were defeated at the latter. The terrified inhabitants of Romney Marsh in Kent were slaughtered or enslaved the following year. London and Rochester were both broken into and sacked. Then, in a repeat encounter at Carhampton, thirty-five shiploads of Vikings raided the royal estate there in 843, defeating King Aethelwulf's Devon array. But when the Vikings struck the South-West Coast later in the decade, the West Saxons butchered them in a bloody encounter at the mouth of the River Parrett.

Main battle sites between 836 and 860.

The West Saxon royal tomb at Sherborne Abbey: the bones of kings Aethelberht and Aethelbald lie nearby.

The great victories won at the midpoint of the century stemmed the tide of Viking attack for a decade of so. One occurred at Wigborough in Somerset, where the men of Devon came out on top; another took place in the South-East at the unlocated battlefield of Aclea (Oak Leigh). On this second occasion the locals were faced by an exceptionally large army of Vikings arriving up the Thames in 350 ships, ten times the number that assaulted Carhampton in 843. Once they had plundered London and Canterbury, the invaders travelled into Surrey, where King Aethelwulf of Wessex and his son Aethelbald faced them. The hardy West Saxons are said to have made the greatest slaughter of any heathen army ever heard of at that time. The Battle of Aclea was a major encounter by the standards of the day. King Aethelwulf was a formidable leader, just as his son Alfred would become.

Three ambitious brothers – Ivar (known as 'the Boneless'), Ubba and Halfdan – fronted the first successful and concerted Danish onslaught on England, dismantling the old Anglo-Saxon kingdoms of Northumbria, East Anglia and Mercia within a decade of their arrival in 865. They had been militarily active in Ireland and on the Continent for some time; the motivation of these particular men and others of their kind was the forcible occupation and exploitation of lands richer and more fertile than their own. The term 'great' used by the chroniclers to describe their army differentiates it from many of the earlier war-bands plaguing England throughout the first half of the ninth century. Only the Viking army at Aclea and perhaps another which devastated Winchester in 860 can have rivalled it in living memory. Behind a protective screen of spears, Scandinavian settlement proceeded apace between the years 865 and 870, and the 'great army' gained military control over much of the north and east of the country.

In Northumbria a puppet king was established and whole swathes of territory east of the Pennines fell under Viking control, later to be settled by Scandinavian incomers. The northern and eastern lands were not occupied without a fight, and much savagery was enacted. Two Anglian claimant kings of York and eight northern ealdormen were slain attempting to wrest York back from heathen clutches in the spring of 866. One of the kings – Aelle – was reputedly 'blood-eagled' by Ivar – sacrificed to the Norse god Odin; the dying king's ribcage was shattered, and then his lungs drawn out in a cruel parody of an open-winged bird. Legend has it this was done to avenge the death of Ivar's father – the semi-mythical Ragnar Hairybreeks – who had earlier been thrown alive into a Northumbrian snake pit on Aelle's command.

Three years later, Ivar's mounted war-bands are described as 'falling like wolves' on King Edmund's East Anglian kingdom, while Ubba with the Viking fleet harried the coastline. Villages were burned and monasteries destroyed. At the religious centre at Peterborough the abbot and all his monks were brutally killed. Edmund, retrospectively lauded as 'the most saintly and glorious King of the East Angles', having fallen at the Battle of Hoxne (*c.* 870), suffered martyrdom. Although variously alleged to have been blood-eagled, decapitated or tied to a tree and executed by a firing squad of archers in the manner of St Sebastian, more likely he died fighting. Whatever the manner of his death, the East Anglian king had made the mistake of withholding his submission and any tribute demanded by

Heavily decorated Viking sword hilt and pommel.

the Vikings until Ivar and his brothers accepted Christianity. Unfortunately for Edmund it was a tactic that worked better for Alfred the Great, and later for Aethelred II, when faced by opponents less committed to a pagan way of life than the sons of Ragnar.

Ivar's name disappears from Anglo-Saxon records around this time. The chronicler Aethelweard claims he died in 870, shortly after martyring King Edmund of East Anglia. Yet someone called Imhar (Norse for Ivar) is recorded in the *Annals of Ireland* as having ended his days in Ireland in 873. A decade or so earlier this same Imhar is said to have won a great victory against rival Scandinavians and their Irish auxiliaries in Munster. After further battles, he descended on the rich Boyne valley in the company of a mixed band of plunderers and looted the revered royal tombs of Knowth, Dowth and Newgrange. The outrage this engendered forced him out of the country and the Irish chroniclers lose track of him at this point.

If Imhar was the same person as Ivar 'the Boneless', he spent the next few years dismantling the kingdoms of Northumbria and East Anglia. He then switched his attention to Strathclyde and the Scottish lowlands. After capturing the stronghold of Dumbarton, on the Clyde, he is claimed to have brought away with him into captivity 'a great prey of Angles and Britons and Picts', and to have arrived back in Ireland in 200 ships. He died soon after. Whether he enjoyed a natural death or suffered a violent one is not known. What fate awaited his captives, sold on in Dublin's bustling slave marts, can only be imagined, and such unsavoury activities should serve as a salutary reminder of the appallingly destructive nature of Dark Age aggression at this time. Ivar was hailed grandly as 'king of the Norsemen of all Ireland and Britain' and many of the kings at Dublin and York in the first half of the tenth century would claim to be directly related to him, later becoming known as Clan Ivar. Slave trading and tomb raiding aside, his activities represented an astonishing and unique achievement. The Dublin–York axis he helped to create would prove to be a long-standing and powerful political counterweight to later English unification attempts; this is testament to Ivar's restless energy, and, if the traditional stories about him are to be believed, to his unbounded cruelty.

Having first occupied London, the great heathen army – now led by Ivar's brother Halfdan – marched against the kingdom of Wessex and set up their winter camp at the West Saxon royal manor at Reading, in Berkshire, in the winter of 870–71. Situated on an island at the confluence of the Thames and Kennet, the Viking base there benefited from strategic attributes beloved of Vikings. Naturally moated, with good communications eastwards to the sea and a rich hinterland to plunder, it was an ideal site. During the year that followed – sometimes referred to as Alfred the Great's 'year of battles' – the men of Wessex are described as often 'riding out' on horseback against the enemy. The Vikings did the same, in their case on horses seized or bartered from the terrified locals. The seizure of horses had been a feature of Viking warfare in Europe for some time. Once they were unable to penetrate further inland by ship, the raiders used stolen or purchased horses to travel deeper into the interior. For this reason the Frankish king, Charles the Bald, having seen his lands almost overwhelmed by Viking incursions, forbade the sale of horses to the Northmen on pain of death.

The Battle of Ashdown – January 871

After suffering an initial setback outside the gates of Reading, the Wessex forces, led by King Aethelred I, met the Vikings in battle a day's march to the west, at Ashdown in east Berkshire. A day's march westwards from Reading is Lowbury Hill, the highest point on the East Berkshire Downs, and a likely rallying point for the West Saxon forces. The momentous battle which followed would in large measure determine the fate of the kingdom. Though no battle plans from this period exist, accounts in the *Anglo-Saxon Chronicle* and Asser's history agree that both sides formed up two divisions apiece, squaring up to each other across a shallow valley. King Aethelred was opposed by forces led by the Danish kings Halfdan and Bagsecg; Aethelred's younger brother Alfred faced a force led by a number of 'jarls'. Asser deliberately embellished Alfred's role in the battle, while at the same time downplaying Aethelred's. He portrayed the king as reluctant to fight immediately, stubbornly waiting to hear Mass in his tent until battle was joined, leaving his younger brother to make the first move against the heathens.

Attending to spiritual needs was an essential adjunct to martial preparedness in medieval times. Yet surprisingly Asser – a churchman – appears to make this a point of criticism. Both Aethelred and Alfred must have taken considerable time preparing themselves prior to the battle, and it is much more likely Mass was over and done with when they – together – co-ordinated their efforts against the Viking divisions, closing with them simultaneously. The stronger of the two Danish units would have been the kings' force. Even the biased Asser admitted the 'core' of the army had been assigned to the command of the two heathen kings; the rest were assigned to the jarls confronting Alfred.

Aethelred I's army would have comprised his own and Alfred's war-bands, embattled together with the armed retainers of other noblemen and prominent landowners from the shires of Wessex, the latter levied based on formalised military obligations. The call-up rate was based on one fighting man per five 'hides' of land – a 'hide' being a measure based on a quantity of land capable of maintaining a family unit. The absolute size of the army is difficult to gauge, but must have been at least equivalent to the Viking army opposing them; the latter comprised a large part of the force which had already overrun Northumbria and East Anglia, and which may have been reinforced since then. Some idea of its size can perhaps be gained from another better-documented Viking force that arrived in south-east England from the Continent in the 890s in two fleets. Frankish chroniclers reckoned the smaller of the two fleets to contain around 400 warriors. The other force, described as a 'great army', was larger still. The two fleets comprised vessels of all shapes and sizes, the craft having been procured in an emergency triggered by famine and the threat of Carolingian retribution. Some were described as merely light 'barks', transporting not just warriors but also horses, womenfolk, children, weaponry and provisions. If the army arriving in eighty ships was 400 strong (much of the space on board being taken up by dependents and belongings), the other Viking force, arriving in 250 ships, might have fielded 1,250 warriors on the same basis, making the size of the combined army around 1,650 – a not unreasonable number for the time. The complement of a Viking longship in wartime might normally be in the region of forty men, but the two fleets which arrived in 892 were not war fleets, and might better be described as 'boat people'. The Viking forces at Ashdown may have numbered little more – 2,000 men perhaps. That the West Saxons defeated them implies their numbers to have been at least comparable, if not greater.

If it was made up of semi-professional soldiers, Aethelred and Alfred's army might have been assembled at short notice. If the participants also worked the land, they would take longer to be gathered, as they would be spread out across the countryside. Additionally, farmers could only be relied upon to fight outside of the busy planting and harvesting seasons, otherwise everyone would starve. Society was broadly split between those who prayed, those who laboured and those who fought. Common shire-folk could hardly be expected to down tools and ride the length and breadth of the countryside when the need arose, although locals might on occasion have acted as gofers, fetching supplies for the army and tending the wounded after battle. Terms such as 'the great *fyrd*' have been used in the past to describe the way Anglo-Saxon and later English armies were called up. Countering this, David Sturdy, in his book *Alfred the Great*, asserts that the belief that peasants and small farmers ever gathered to form a national army or *fyrd* is a strange delusion dreamt up by Victorian antiquarians; he argues instead that such armies comprised the henchmen and bodyguards of noblemen (landowners).

Both Anglo-Saxon and Viking armies throughout the ninth and tenth centuries appear to have routinely dismounted before battle, and tethered their horses to the rear; they remounted only to pursue or flee. Leaders emulated their men, demonstrating their resolve to stand and fight. Cavalry in the strictest sense of the term, with drilled units of horsemen charging together in open or closed order, did not feature in English warfare until the arrival of the Normans, mainly because the wherewithal in terms of suitable mounts, training and accoutrement was lacking. Tactical units – war-bands or divisions – comprised discrete groups of men owing allegiance to one or more nobleman or leader. Larger musters were led by a king or by his delegated appointee. For the Anglo-Saxons this was often a grandee known as an ealdorman, the equivalent of a regional overlord, sometimes called a 'half-king', later an earl.

When the king or his ealdormen took the field, mailed thegns were required to follow them into battle. Noblemen and landowners in their own right, thegns were first and foremost battle-hardened warriors. Post-Norman Conquest, they would become better known as knights or barons. Viking armies followed a similar organisational structure, with kings and sub-kings, jarls and housecarls mirroring the Anglo-Saxon pecking order. Alfred the Great's will made reference to payments to 'the men who serve me', and a sixth of all Alfred's revenue was paid to his well-armed fighting retinue. Warriors such as these 'rode out' with the king on a day-to-day basis.

The combat dress of a well-equipped Anglo-Saxon or Viking warrior might have comprised a conical helmet made from a framework of metal (iron or bronze) bands, strengthened by a leather cap with or without a nasal guard, with a studded or ringed leather byrnie over a padded jacket known as a '*gambuson*' or '*aketon*', plus leather greaves to protect the legs. Only the nobles and their bodyguards would have been so well equipped. Many of the rank and file would likely have worn just a simple leather coat or jacket, and may have lacked body and head protection altogether. It was not until the early eleventh century, in response to Viking aggression from better-armed and -equipped warriors – many clad in mail – for whom fighting had become a vocation, that armour and helmets became more commonplace among the English. King Aethelred II's militarisation programme during the latter part of the first decade of the eleventh century laid the groundwork for this, and the Bayeux Tapestry illustrates the way warriors had evolved by 1066, with full-length mail tunics, iron helmets and kite-shaped shields.

Leaders and their bodyguards wielded good-quality swords; the common fighting men did not. Weapons reflected status. The rank and file relied on javelins, spears, axes and daggers. Ownership of a finely worked double-edged sword – the supreme weapon of war – is thought to have been almost completely restricted to the nobility in England in early medieval times, something probably true for the Vikings as well. An example of such a sword was discovered deep in the bed of the River Frome at Wareham in 1927. Its guard was decorated with copper and silver; its handle grip was made of antler horn. An incomplete inscription in Old English on the handle read 'Æ[something] owns me'. Æ being a prefix restricted to the West Saxon Royal Family, the sword most likely belonged to a Wessex nobleman of some standing, and was probably lost later than Alfred's day, during fighting around the turn of the millennium, or even later in 1015.

The Wareham sword found in the River Frome. *(By kind permission of Dorset County Museum)*

Circular shields, larger ones just under 3ft (90cm) in diameter, made of leather-bound wood and centred with a 6in (15cm) iron boss, were carried by the warriors of the time until superseded by kite-shaped ones originating from the Middle East. A formidable weapon in its own right, the shield boss could be used as a knuckleduster when fighting in close order to topple an opponent before despatching him with spear or dagger. Javelins (sometimes called 'darts') launched at a range of around forty to fifty paces were designed to embed themselves in shields, which bent under the weight, rendering the shield useless. They could even penetrate mail at a depth sufficient to disable an armoured warrior, and were sometimes barbed, hindering their removal from an unarmoured victim's torso, causing

Anglo-Saxon shield bosses and partial sword. (*By kind permission of Hampshire County Council*)

frightful wounds. Throwing axes and slingshots were also hurled during the preliminary exchanges, and archers appear to have figured too.

Circumstantial evidence points towards the use of bows being more prevalent among Viking armies than Anglo-Saxon ones. The bows in question were longbows between 5 and 6ft in length, and a grave find containing twenty-one arrow heads might be taken to represent a typical quiver load. Snorri Sturluson's *Heimskringla* – a collection of sagas written in the first half of the thirteenth century – recounts, with reference to Eric Bloodaxe, how 'the prince bent the yew, and wound bees flew', and how 'the yew bow twanged when swords were drawn'; this vividly illustrates how archery preceded hand-to-hand combat in battle. The Scandinavian-inspired Old English heroic poem *Beowulf* tells how, 'the rain of iron when a storm of darts, sped by bowstrings, came flying over the shield wall'. The Frankish chronicler Regino of Prum described a Viking army seeing off a Frankish attack by, 'rattling their quivers, raising shouts and joining battle'. The lower margin of the Bayeux Tapestry shows William the Conqueror's diminutive archers supporting their cavalry by 'shooting in' the deciding charge of the day at Hastings in 1066.

Bowmen shown in this way are sometimes explained as reflecting an archer's low social status in comparison with other warriors. At odds with this notion, Viking arrows have been uncovered in numerous high-status graves in Ireland and elsewhere. Because it needed strength and a high degree of proficiency, archers were much valued in Scandinavian armies, and probably in Anglo-Saxon ones too. Longbows excavated at Hedeby, at the southern end of the Jutland peninsular, and at Ballinderry in Ireland, unless one-offs, indicate that the bows carried by their Viking owners would have been very considerable weapons. Norwegian law listed bows as among the items to be brought to an army's muster by those summoned. Casting doubt on assertions that English armies made do without archers, outlines of decomposed bows of more than 5ft in length have been found in pagan Anglo-Saxon graves, predating the Alfredian period. Since weaponry does not appear in Christian graves, it could well be that Anglo-Saxon bowmen continued to feature in Alfred's wars and the wars of his successors, even though they get scant mention.

Fighting spears, known variously as '*francas*' or '*aescs*', named for their geographic origin (*Francia*) or wood type (ash), comprised the most commonly employed melee weapons in both Anglo-Saxon and Viking armies. Some were fitted with wings part way down the shaft to prevent over-penetration of the victim's torso, thereby facilitating its reuse. The wings might also deflect an enemy's weapon, or be used to hook around an opponent's shield. Spear heads were either spiked or leaf shaped: the former for piercing, the latter for inflicting lateral blows. When a spear was lost or broken, the '*scramasax*', a widely used Frankish dagger, or the '*seaxe*', a long knife that gave the Saxons their distinctive name, became invaluable secondary weapons. Spears were later supplemented by the two-handed broad axe – a weapon introduced into England by Scandinavians around the turn of

Anglo-Saxon spears heads and axe head. (*By kind permission of Hampshire County Council*)

the millennium and shown wielded by the English to good effect against Norman cavalry on the Bayeux Tapestry.

Virtually all accounts of battle from early medieval times are brief and formulaic, with little or nothing of the course of the action described. Common terminology includes phases such as 'place of slaughter', medieval shorthand for locating the dreadful aftermath of battle. Where a decisive result was gained, the death toll from Viking Age battles could be very high, with the bulk of the killing occurring when one or the other side turned in flight. The experiences of modern-day re-enactors indicate that someone who fell in battle would never have seen the face of the opposing warrior who killed him. Even if facing to the front, each man would tend to crouch to the right in a reflex to fear, seeking to shelter his unshielded side securely behind the warrior beside him.

The two Saxon divisions, or 'bands' as they are described in the *Anglo-Saxon Chronicle*, attacked simultaneously at Ashdown; the opposing lines clashed violently with loud shouting from all sides. Greek warriors, half a millennium before the birth of Christ, are said by Plutarch (d. 120 BC) to have worn their body armour for their own use, but carried their shields for the entire army. This same co-operative principal still applied more than 1,000 years later during 'Alfred's wars'. Commanders such as Aethelred I and Alfred must have reminded their warriors to maintain their formation and stay closed up in rank for the good of all, in much the same way as any successful Spartan general might have done. At the Battle of Ellendun (*c.* 825), fought in Wiltshire between rival Anglo-Saxon armies, the opposing battle lines are described as meeting 'head on', having first drawn up some few hundred yards apart. At an unnamed battle fought in Ireland in 867 a unit escaped the slaughter meted out to their friends by forming themselves into close order. Troops failing to get into order – taken by surprise or unable to do so – were quickly seen off or destroyed.

Drawn up in close order, a unit facing its enemy, holding its ground and maintaining cohesion was unlikely to be immediately broken. Attackers would sensibly baulk at the prospect of closing to hand-to-hand combat; especially if their own shuffling lines of spearmen remained disordered. Not until both sides had dismounted and formed up into opposing solid and impenetrable arrays – had faced each other for some time, nerving themselves to close in combat – might one or both sides do so. Whether or not there was a period of mounted skirmishing between rival noblemen is not clear, though late seventh-century cross slabs in Scottish churchyards indicate that this might have been the case. One in particular, from

The Aberlemno stone, showing mounted battle scenes from the Battle of Dunnichen fought between the Picts and Northumbrians in 685.

Aberlemno in Angus and thought to depict scenes from the Battle of Dunnichen, fought between the Picts and Northumbrians in 685, shows warriors fighting in this way. But whether Anglo-Saxons and Danes followed such a practice is not known.

Based on the evidence of the Aberlemno stone, Nick Aitcheson, in his book *The Picts and the Scots at War*, argues that seventh-century battles may have begun with a cavalry charge, and that the protagonists comprised largely or exclusively of mounted nobles in, or in advance of, the front rank of the army. True or not, the sight of uninterrupted lines of brightly painted shields and rows of levelled spears may have inspired sufficient terror to make men bolt without the need for either side to close. Otherwise, battles might be joined in a gradual way, with undisciplined or over-eager troops launching sudden rushes, hurling their javelins and threatening to bring on a more general engagement. While a close-order unit – sometimes referred to as a shield wall – remained ordered, neither volleys of spears nor throwing axes, nor repeated surges forward could break it. In all likelihood such skirmishing would become protracted, and might even constitute the sum total of the battle unless one or other side resolved to charge and fight hand-to-hand. Then only through close co-operation, one man with another, could such formations do battle effectively. Discipline and cohesion were crucial; long-standing ties of kinship fostered and strengthened the determination to fight. Deep formations made for unyielding lines and the lack of combat specialisation kept things brutally simple. Survival in battle – especially in its later stages – relied as much on aggression and strength as on weaponry.

Alfred the Great was described by Asser as charging like a wild boar at Ashdown. The description could simply have been meant to flatter the future king. Emblematic of virility, the wild boar is a regularly occurring Dark Age motif. The famous Sutton Hoo helmet (one of only four helmets discovered in England) has representations of a boar above each cheek guard, and was thought to endow the helmet wearer with semi-magical qualities. Another, found at Benty Grange Farm in Derbyshire, is topped by a wild boar crest. At the ninth-century Viking encampment at Repton in Derbyshire, among the individual burials was the skeleton of a man nearly 6ft tall, an officer or nobleman who died in battle. A wild boar's tusk had been placed between his thighs. Warriors of old clearly viewed a charging boar as something to emulate.

Roman writers sometimes describe ancient Germans as charging *en masse* in a 'boar's head' formation – a column of men, narrower in front and wider in the rear. The unique aspect of the 'boars head' appears to have been that the shape of the attacking horde started out in column, but became progressively distorted into a wedge by the effect of its leaders and their retinues pulling and encouraging the mass of more-reluctant fighting men along with them. The term 'wedge' is derived from the Latin word *cuneus*, which means column, a standard deployment up until as late as the twentieth century, which enhanced both the psychological and physical shock of attack; where the depth of the unit is either equal to or greater than the width.

Almost nothing is known of the course of the Battle of Ashdown: but as it was fought in midwinter, the ground would have been churned up by hundreds of marching feet, and so the soldiers there must have had a hard time of it. Asser reports that when both sides had been fighting 'resolutely and exceedingly ferociously' for quite some time, divine judgement told against the heathens. Unable to withstand the Saxon onslaught, with a great part of their force already fallen, they fled. Possibly the death of the pagan King Bagsecg started the Viking collapse. Unnerved by the calamity, his war-band broke in panic. Many were cut down by pursuing Saxon spearmen as they attempted to regain their horses. The killing is said to have continued until darkness fell. The tenth-century chronicler Aethelweard recounted how all the nobler youth of the barbarians died at Ashdown, and how never before had such slaughter been known. Though something of an exaggeration, it represented nonetheless a fitting tribute. Should the two West Saxon brothers have lost the battle, and the hope of eventual success, a Viking Conquest of England might have been brought forward by almost 150 years. Certainly Alfred must have viewed the battle as important. Asser claimed he had the exact spot where the future king proudly fought pointed out to him by his hero – its location was marked by a lone ash tree.

1.2

The first half of the year 871 is littered with battles fought in Wessex. Nine are mentioned and six are named: Englefield, Reading, Ashdown, Basing, Mereton and Wilton. Despite victory at Ashdown, the men of Wessex became dangerously overstretched. The robust defensive policies of the Frankish king, Charles the Bald – including the fortification of places such as Dijon and Le Mans – had resulted in the displacement of large numbers of Vikings to the east coast of England at around this time, swelling the ranks of Halfdan's army. King Aethelred I was just one of the many Saxon fighting men who lost his life, dying from wounds received in battle at Mereton, probably Martin, near Cranborne in Dorset. As at Ashdown, the Saxons formed up in two divisions at Mereton. For some time they held the edge over their opponents. But coincidental with the king's mortal wound, and the death in battle of Heamund, Bishop of Sherborne, the Wessex men gave way. Aethelred was taken to the nearby monastic site at

Wimborne and later died and was buried there.

Severe fighting also occurred at Abingdon, an important crossing place on the River Thames. A camp to the north-east, called Serpen Hill, is reputed to have been the scene of a battle fought between Saxons and Danes. Perhaps this is one of the three unnamed fights in 871 mentioned in the *Anglo-Saxon Chronicle*. Monastic buildings at Abingdon were

The brass at Wimborne Minster of Aethelred I, buried nearby after being mortally wounded at Mereton in 871.

destroyed and the dozen or so monks they housed scattered as a result of the conflict. Despite the damage having being caused by the Danes, the religious authorities afterwards accused Alfred of violently seizing their monastery and all of their lands close by. It had been an action forced on him in a desperate effort to put the area into a fortified state in the lull after Ashdown. Even so, the monks appear to have found it hard to forgive their future king for further disrupting their monastic routine. Alfred was perhaps feared by his own people for his ruthlessness as much as he was later praised for his courage. What is more, he made no later effort to restore the ancient monastic site. It was not until the reign of King Edgar (d. 975) that the monastery was re-established, and not until even later, in the early twelfth century, that work on a new church was started.

Although only two of the battles fought in 871 appear to have been won by the men of Wessex, the others were not decisively lost either; this despite Halfdan's best efforts and a supply of fresh troops arriving from the Continent. Nonetheless, the combination of Aethelred's death, defeat at Mereton and the arrival of reinforcements, plus a further defeat at Wilton, forced Alfred to make a holding treaty with Halfdan, probably with the payment of a hefty tribute. The Danish host fell back on London in the autumn of 871. Coins minted there from this time proudly bear the name Halfdan.

The traditional Alfredian narrative is of the young king (he was still in his early twenties) facing an overwhelming threat, unprepared, with his back to the wall. But Halfdan may not have seen it that way, the impetus of his campaign wrecked on successive Wessex battlefields, where one Danish king, nine jarls and (according to Asser) countless heathen men were killed. As a result, he opportunistically reassessed his options and looked elsewhere for conquest. The *Anglo-Saxon Chronicle* relates how the raiding army went from Reading to Lindsey (Torksey), and then on to Repton, where they took up winter quarters. The next year they attacked and drove out the Mercian king, Burhred, who fled to the Continent, and eventually to Rome. All of Mercia was apparently subdued by them.

Repton was a high-status monastic centre like Wimborne, serving the Mercian royal dynasty since the seventh century. Here, on a cliff top above the then swift-flowing Trent, the Vikings built a large D-shaped defensive enclosure, including a rampart and ditch. St Wystan's church and its tower were used as a gatehouse and command centre. Having Vikings in residence must have been enormously humiliating for the proud Mercians – the 'men of the march'.

Contained within the famous church's (still-existent) crypt were the bones of several of their kings, queens and princes. The relics of the venerated Wigstan (Wystan) – a prince of Mercia, murdered during a family dispute in 849 – claimed pride of place. His bones had long been credited with miraculous powers, making the mausoleum a magnet for pilgrims. Nearby, the remains of more than 250 individuals have been uncovered in a two-roomed subterranean basement area 15ft square. Though the bones were originally neatly stacked, by the time formal exhumation commenced in the nineteenth century they had become jumbled. These men (and some women) must have formed part of 'the great heathen army', which overwintered at Repton in 873–74; their deaths were probably due to contagion – camp fever. The numbers of those buried helps establish the Viking army as numbering in the low thousands – assuming roughly 10 per cent died and were buried at the site.

No record of fighting between Danes and Mercians survives, and it is tempting to assume Halfdan overran the kingdom without facing serious opposition, but this is unlikely to have been the case in reality. Mercia, encompassing much of England's rich heartland was, if anything, stronger militarily than Wessex, and had already beaten off earlier attempts by Ivar's forces to overrun it. At that time Aethelred I's forces had marched to King Burhred's assistance, laying siege to the Danes at Nottingham. But when once again requested by Burhred to rally to Mercia's support six years later, Alfred turned a blind eye. Prior to the Battle of Ashdown, the Mercian king had refused to come to the assistance of Wessex when requested to do so. Overawed by a strong and growing Viking presence in London, the Mercian king had refused the request from Wessex. In retaliation, *quid pro quo*, Alfred ignored Burhred's appeal when Mercia was invaded by Viking armies in the late autumn of 873. Halfdan's renewed onslaught on Mercia led to a terrified Burhred's hurried departure; the king fled to the Continent, and was supplanted in a bloodless coup by a Viking surrogate named Ceowulf II. Halfdan seized hostages and imposed himself as overseer of Mercia in much the same manner as his brother Ivar had done in Northumbria and East Anglia.

Many of Halfdan's veterans split away from the 'great army' at around this time (*c.* 874); some settled in the Vale of York. Halfdan, instead, determined to stake his claim to the kingship at Dublin and travelled overland across lowland Scotland before embarking for Dublin Bay. Along the way he overwintered with his men on the Tyne, finding time to terrorise the unfortunate monks of Lindisfarne Island, driving them into exile on the mainland. Predictably, control at Dublin did not pass smoothly from brother to brother. Fighting soon broke out on Halfdan's arrival. The *Annals of Ulster* state that a certain Oisten, the son of Olaf the White, King of the Norsemen, was 'deceitfully killed by Albann' (an Irish variant of Halfdan). Having overcome immediate opposition by fair means or foul, Halfdan was then driven off when a coalition of Irish and Norse rose up against him. He returned to Northumbria, licking his wounds, before disbanding the remnants of his battle-weary retainers. Like their colleagues earlier, many settled down to a life of farming in the North-East. Halfdan's end was more in keeping with a brother of Ivar the Boneless. After a year spent completing the settlement of his men, he set out once again to win back the kingship of Dublin, but was killed in battle against his Norse rivals and their Irish allies at Strangford Lough in 877.

The Battles of Cynwit and Ethandun – 878

If Ashdown prevented England from being overwhelmed by the sons of Ragnar on their first attempt, the Battle of Ethandun – probably fought at Edington, near Westbury in Wiltshire – memorably turned the tables on the invaders. In doing so it underpinned the survival of Wessex and the eventual reconquest of Anglo-Saxon England. Because of this, Ethandun stands among the handful of truly decisive battles ever fought in England.

The campaign against the Danes.

Having arrived in England in the summer of 871 and overwintered with Halfdan at Repton in 873–74, forces led by the Danish warlord Guthrum moved eastwards to a base at Cambridge, overwintering there in 875–76. The following year – 'leaving Cambridge by night' – the army travelled overland and linked up with another in the West, establishing successive coastal bases at Wareham and Exeter. Alfred's men overawed them each time, aided by storms which swept the South Coast in the autumn or winter of that year. One hundred and twenty Viking longships are recorded as being destroyed off Swanage. As a result, Guthrum's forces were driven back into Mercia. But at midwinter 878 – 'after twelfth night' – the Dane organised a surprise offensive by falling on Wessex 'by stealth', occupying Chippenham (which became his base of operations) and conquering and settling land, driving a great part of the people across the sea. Some historians consider 'overseas' to specifically mean the Bristol Channel: the émigrés departed for Wales. Others interpret it more broadly to mean the English Channel. Guthrum's warlike concentration at Chippenham implies a more localised threat, mainly affecting north Somerset and west Wiltshire. Yet the evidence – such as it is – indicates that his forces overran much of Wessex, including large tracts of Dorset and parts of Hampshire.

Even though winter campaigns were nothing new (Ashdown had been fought in midwinter), Alfred had been caught unprepared by Guthrum's strike. Having ejected the Dane from Wareham and Exeter and taken hostages, it seems the West Saxon king cannot have been anticipating an attack.

That Wessex was so quickly and comprehensively overrun seems at first surprising. Nevertheless when set beside the collapse that occurred in Mercia in 874 and the earlier toppling of Northumbria and East Anglia, it should not be any great surprise that the Danes remained – militarily – quite capable of bringing Wessex to its knees; a fact that should be borne in mind when considering Aethelred II's longer, much maligned campaign against even stronger forces after the turn of the millennium. Nevertheless, Alfred the Great's reputation relies less on the results of the battles he fought (several of which were lost) than on his dogged determination to fight back and not to give in. Even during these, his darkest hours, assaulted by Guthrum's army and driven back into the remote 'swamp-fastness' of Somerset to his island stronghold at Athelney – 'the Isle of Princes' – it is clear he was planning a comeback. His men remained safe on elevated ground, moated by marshy reed beds and flanked by natural bastions such as the pyramidal outpost of Burrow Mump. Like other Iron Age hill forts in Wessex, Athelney had been brought back into use by the West Saxons when they were first threatened with invasion in 870. Further fortified, the stronghold provided Alfred with a secure base to rally the men of Wessex during the crisis of 878.

To support his growing army and to strike back, Alfred launched a series of raids against the Danish outposts. The king was relatively secure from Guthrum's mounted infantry based to the north, and operated in this way with some impunity. Even so, his embryonic army was dangerously vulnerable to a strike from Vikings travelling down the River Parrett from its estuary in the Bristol Channel. Detailed to launch such a venture with his fleet – estimated variously as comprising either twenty-three or thirty longships – Ubba (the last of the trio of brothers who had first arrived in 865) set off from South Wales for the north Devon coast. He had spent the summer and autumn of 877 ravaging Dyfed, where, according to Asser, many Welshmen were slaughtered. Ubba's intention was to travel down the River Parrett, strike inland and then to harry the areas abutting Alfred's refuge with the 1,200 men at his disposal. Conservatively, each ship's crew must have numbered around forty men, including one or more relief crews per ship – an important consideration when establishing the size of ship armies. In times of war, or when embarking on longer journeys, additional crews on hand provided a fleet with the ability to maintain a constant speed, disgorge a substantial raiding party, and provide for a strong boat party (ship guard).

The Parrett provided ready ingress for Ubba's fleet to threaten Alfred's base. But rather than make an immediate sortie upriver, Ubba unaccountably settled down to prosecute a winter siege of the Saxon citadel at Cynwit (Countisbury, near Lynmouth), located several miles further to the west. His approach and landing on the north Devon coast was most likely spotted by lookouts on the heights between Porlock and Lynton. Led by a West Saxon thegn named Odda, the outnumbered defenders quickly sought refuge at the broken-down and windswept Iron Age hill fort on Wind Hill at Countisbury. Meanwhile, the Vikings moored their ships further down the coast and scouted out the area.

Odda's hilltop refuge was only approachable from the east, across a narrow neck of land from Countisbury. According to Asser, the refuge was wholly 'unprepared [a reference to a lack of provisions – food and water] and altogether unfortified'. Only the crumbling ramparts of the ancient fortress would stand between the defenders and the Vikings. Attack from the east was the sole option available to Ubba's men. Any attempt from the south, up the precipitous and heavily wooded slopes from the Lyn valley, tumbling down from Exmoor in a series of rapids and falls, would have been too dangerous for the Vikings to contemplate. To the west, daunting slopes down to Lynmouth Harbour were too steep to mount an uphill assault; to the north there was a sheer drop to the sea over rugged cliffs, to a boulder-strewn beach below. Asser later visited the battlefield and saw for himself the lie of the land, and stressed in his *Life of Alfred* the absolute security the position enjoyed, save from attack from the east.

Leaving an intact garrison in his rear, while proceeding further down the coast to the Parrett estuary, must have been considered unwise by Ubba. But, since the West Saxon refuge had no fresh water, and could not be provisioned, rather than launch an immediate and costly assault across the narrow neck of land from Countisbury, the Viking warlord sensibly decided to lay siege to the defenders on the hill, allowing hunger and thirst to do the work for him. Precisely where the Vikings moored their fleet of long-ships is unknown. If at Lynmouth, Odda's men would have been stationed between Ubba and the Viking ships. Much too risky! More likely, the ships were moored further down the coast at Porlock and Ubba's army marched or rode the 15 miles or so to Countisbury to besiege the locals.

According to Florence, the pagans were 'disappointed in their expecta-tions'. Without a water supply, 'nerved thereto by Divine inspiration, and preferring either to die or conquer', Odda's men launched an unexpected sally upon the pagans at their encampment at Countisbury. Overthrowing them 'at the very first onset', few Vikings reached the safety of their boats. Many of the Danes may have been slaughtered as they slept. Ubba's great raven banner (stitched by his three Danish sisters) was captured during the battle. Florence goes on to relate how Ubba and his followers were 'in the midst of their wickedness, miserably slain by the king's thegns'.

An alternative battle site for Cynwit is beside Cannington Camp in the Parrett estuary, close to the settlement and ford at Combwich, from which the name Cynwit might derive. Being closer to Alfred's base at Athelney is a major point in its favour. But though championed by a number of recent authors, *The Place-Names of Devon* (Cambridge: 1931) appears to conclu-sively identify Cynwit etymologically with Countisbury. Also the defences of Cannington Camp are not markedly secure on three sides, as is said to have been the case by Asser.

Operating from his base at Chippenham, Guthrum must soon have become aware of Ubba's demise. The invaders had lost the initiative and Guthrum should have fallen back behind more secure defences. Instead, he concentrated his forces within striking distance of Alfred's army, inviting attack. What he cannot have known was that Alfred had been heavily reinforced by contingents of fighting men arriving from as far afield as Hampshire. By underestimating his opponent he may have failed to take adequate precautions against a surprise attack. Converging trackways to the south of Warminster, in Wiltshire, focused a concentration of Alfred's forces from far and wide. An eighteenth-century folly known as King Alfred's Tower on Kingsettle Hill, to the east of Selwood Forest, is said to mark the spot where the Egbert's stone once lay, and where Alfred addressed his army.

Military historians have somewhat tentatively estimated that if just half the military personnel from the shires not overrun by the Danes were present at Ethandun, the king's army might have numbered as many as 4,500 men, and may have outnumbered the Vikings in excess of two to one – almost certainly making it the largest battle of the age. Richard Brooks, in his *Cassell's Battlefields of Britain and Ireland*, states that two full-strength counties might have fielded 4,000 men, plus several hundred more from Hampshire. He remarks that Guthrum's strength is incalculable but must have been at least 1,600 men to have defended Wareham's walls, based on one man per every 4ft of wall. Shipwreck had since taken a toll, but fresh reinforcements were probably gained in Mercia.

Once preparations were complete, the West Saxon king led his men into battle against Guthrum's host at the nearby royal manor of Edington. Asser describes how Alfred fought with a 'compact shield-wall' against the entire 'serried ranks' of the Viking army. He speaks of battle being fought for a long time, until 'at length [Alfred] gained the victory through God's will, destroying the Vikings with great slaughter'. The *Anglo-Saxon Chronicle*, on the other hand, fails to mention a protracted fight, or indeed much loss of life occurring as an immediate result of the battle, which is unusual. The implication is that – unable to form up in good order before coming under attack, and heavily outnumbered – Guthrum's warriors fled at the onset. Perhaps just a few isolated groups of Danes managed to put up a fight. The fact that the primary source (a reliable one at that) fails to mention significant casualties (compared to Ashdown, where many thousands of Danes were reputed to have been killed by the same Winchester chronicler) implies – despite Asser's claims of a protracted battle – that the fight was soon over, and that the bulk of the Danish host fled back to their fortified encampment.

The location of the Danish stronghold is not specifically identified in any of the sources, but military historians consider it most likely to have been at

Chippenham, to the north. Tradition, however, locates it at or near Bratton Camp, an Iron Age hillfort 750ft above sea level on Salisbury Plain, near Edington. A small memorial stone there commemorates the battle fought below, and the famous White Horse of Westbury is etched into the chalk escarpment nearby.

Alfred launched an immediate mounted pursuit, cutting down stragglers and seizing everything he could outside the gates of their fortress, including men, who were immediately killed, plus horses, sheep and cattle. The Vikings within their camp are said to have surrendered to him two weeks later 'in hunger, cold and terror'. Driven to the lowest depths of despair, they granted the king hostages and promised they would leave Wessex never to return. Guthrum, described as the 'king of the Northmen', together with thirty of his officers, was baptised in Alfred's presence at Wedmore, near Athelney, three weeks later; he then feasted for almost a fortnight. Thus was a pagan prince subdued – by sword, fine food and holy water.

2

Confronting the Danelaw

The brief hiatus in Viking activity in the south of England which followed his victory at Ethandun provided Alfred with the opportunity to recover, entrench and even recapture lost land. He also set in motion work to strengthen the walls of old Romano-British cities and ordered a series of strongpoints across Wessex, known as burhs, to be built.

Alfred's prestige had increased enormously after his victory in Wiltshire. Chroniclers ascribed his success to divine providence: it being viewed as no less than a miraculous event. Had the campaign been lost, with Alfred killed or driven into exile, Wessex would not have been able to resist partition or takeover. Even so, Guthrum's submission came with strings attached. Alfred – like Aethelred II later – was forced to make some concessions, though none of the details survive. The threat Guthrum posed – his forces remained poised on Wessex's frontier – indicates that (though decisive in preventing the Danes from overrunning Wessex) the battle at Ethandun left the Viking army largely intact, and still potentially dangerous. It was not until the end of the decade that a formal treaty was drawn up between the two kings (*c.* 879–81); followed by another, sometime later in the mid-880s.

This latter agreement established a boundary between the English and the Danes, demarcating the two men's respective spheres of operations. The frontier followed the north bank of the Thames to its confluence with the River Lea; then from there to Bedford, and then along the Ouse to Watling Street. North of this became known as the Danelaw, an area where Danish law held sway. Underlining the importance of the treaty, Guthrum's army at Cirencester – a threat to Alfred while it remained there – moved eastwards and settled land in East Anglia. Another wing of the army – based at Fulham, on the Thames – departed from England altogether, crossing the Channel and occupying Ghent. Worn down by more than a decade of fighting, Guthrum's veterans peaceably settled down to a life of farming. Guthrum ruled East Anglia from then on as any other Christian king. He died in 890. There is no indication that he and Alfred ever crossed swords again.

Mercia's new king, another Aethelred, allied himself to Alfred in the early 880s by marrying Alfred's daughter Aethelflaed (*c.* 887). Aethelred ruled over the remaining Anglo-Saxon-controlled half of Mercia (partitioned with the Danes), having succeeded Ceowulf II. A closer union with Mercia had been a long-standing aim of successive Wessex kings, and its eventual accomplishment represented one of Alfred's greatest achievements. The combined military strength of Wessex and Mercia would in large measure serve to underwrite future successes. The capture of London in 886 was another major accomplishment; the Wessex and Mercian allies are said to have gloriously stormed its defences with much burning and slaughter. Coins minted afterwards by Alfred, rightly lauded by Asser as 'England's hero and darling', proudly display the London monogram.

Four years of relative peace ensued in Wessex, while on the Continent Viking armies ravaged unabated, leaving desolation and famine in their wake. Finally defeated by the Bretons, then again by a combined army of Eastern Franks, Saxons and Bavarians, the continental Viking host was forced westwards, where their leaders – opportunistically seizing an offer of ships and supplies to be gone – set their sights across the Channel towards England.

Arriving from Boulogne in the year 892, accompanied in the night skies by an ominous 'haired star' (*cometa*), the Norse warlord Haesten and another unnamed commander created two strongholds in south-east England. Haesten led the smaller of the two fleets, estimated at around eighty ships, and set up his base at Milton Regis, near Sittingbourne, in Kent. Known as the Loire Vikings, his men had operated independently on the Continent for more than a decade, until forced westwards across the Channel. The other force – 'a great army' – is said to have arrived in 250 ships, making landfall on the east Sussex coast, before traversing an isolated and flooded interior from Lympne. Rowing 4 miles inland, they then stormed an unfinished and lightly defended earthwork at Appledore in the Weald. The siting of the two camps and the mutual support they afforded enabled the Vikings to threaten destructive raids into the open countryside of Kent and Surrey at will.

To counter this new threat, Alfred and his son Edward (known as 'the Elder', to differentiate him from later kings of that name) gathered an army together the following year (893), and set up their main camp between the two enemy strongholds. Contemporary accounts describe how the West Saxon leaders formed their men into 'gangs' and 'mounted troops', relatively small units, the equivalent of foot patrols and cavalry piquets. Later Napoleonic tactical doctrine would identify this sort of arrangement as operating on 'interior lines', an advantageous strategy when a commander needed to respond quickly to a variety of contingencies.

The immediate danger from Haesten's army at Milton Regis was curtailed by Alfred coming to terms with its leader by making him generous gifts of money and provisions, and persuading him to cross the Thames into Essex; in effect moving the problem elsewhere. Even so, the West Saxon king could not prevent a sudden concerted sortie by the stronger enemy in the Weald. At Easter time the Vikings based at Appledore 'went out through the forest' and fell on Wessex, devastating Hampshire and Berkshire. While attempting to transport their 'war booty' northward, seeking a juncture with their ships, now moored up in the Thames, their force – with men, women and pack animals strung out over several miles – was intercepted by Edward. Riding his men around in front of the Viking column and bringing them to battle at Farnham in Surrey, Edward put them to flight. Survivors of the rout were then besieged at an unlocated islet on the Colne, a tributary of the Thames, in Hertfordshire.

The unfolding scale and complexity of the campaign of 893 – if accounts are accurate – is astonishing. With Haesten (despite having come to terms earlier with Alfred) busy extricating his erstwhile allies and kinsmen on the Colne, and being seriously wounded in the process, the Danes of Northumbria and East Anglia launched their own ship-borne forays against Wessex. With Guthrum dead, the East Anglians – who had earlier provided Alfred with six 'prime' hostages – broke their truce, possibly at Haesten's prompting. The focus of their attacks was along the Devon coast, where Exeter and an unidentified stronghold in the Bristol Channel were targeted. One hundred and forty shiploads of fighting men are said to have taken part. If true – at forty men per ship – this works out at a staggering 5,600 warriors. Half this number would have comprised a force in excess of most estimates for Guthrum's army in 878 or Halfdan's in 871. Even accepting the numbers to have been exaggerated, the fact that the Anglo-Saxons eventually emerged victorious underlines the importance of the alliance sealed between Alfred and Aethelred of

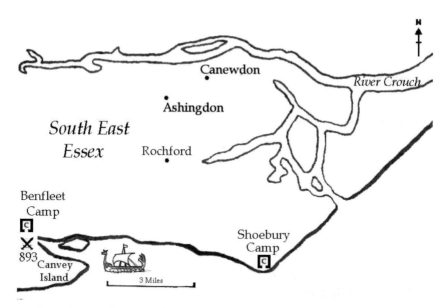

South-east Essex in the 890s, at the time of Haesten.

Mercia. Had Alfred faced such numerous opponents alone, Wessex would doubtless have fallen to the invaders.

The effect of this western-focused onslaught was to draw the bulk of Alfred's forces away from the South-East, leaving just a residual force – supplemented by the garrison of London – to deal with the remaining Viking threat in the Thames. Having, sometime earlier, created a base at Benfleet on the north bank of the estuary, Viking forces, probably under Haesten's command, were by this time regularly raiding into Mercia as well as into Essex; this despite Aethelred, the province's overlord, having earlier agreed to stand as godfather to one of Haesten's children. Such Christianising acts apparently failed to pacify the warlike Vikings. Another of Haesten's offspring could even boast Alfred as his godfather.

Located in the area of the modern churchyard, close to the water's edge, the encampment at Benfleet was naturally moated on two sides and housed boats, a garrison, women, children, supplies and animals. Perhaps the guard was inadequate and the camp only lightly defended. In any event, the place was devastated when it came under attack from the West Saxons, reinforced by the Londoners. Charred remains of longships and many skeletons are said to have been uncovered nearby in the 1890s – bearing silent witness to the savage and unexpected onslaught. Florence details how:

A severe battle was fought with the Pagans [at Benfleet] and the Christians put them to flight at the first onset, demolishing their works, taking whatever they found there, carrying their [the Vikings'] wives and children to London [including Haesten's], sinking some of their ships, burning others, and transporting some to London and Rochester.

Meanwhile, Haesten appears to have concentrated his remaining forces at Shoebury in Essex and to have been later reinforced by others arriving from East Anglia and Northumbria. The combined force then abandoned the camp and headed west. The geographic scale of this second phase of the campaign, like the first, was extensive. Numerous ship-borne pagan armies are described as plundering first on the banks of the Thames and then along the banks of the Severn. In response, Alfred's son-in-law, Aethelred of Mercia, assembled a large force from the western shires, augmented by Welsh auxiliaries. The *Anglo-Saxon Chronicle* names the other ealdormen involved as Aethelhelm of Wiltshire and Aethelnoth of Somerset, along with all the thegns manning the fortifications (burhs) east of the River Parrett and west and east of Selwood Forest; also, those north of the Thames and west of the river Severn. Additionally, Welshmen allied themselves with the Anglo-Saxons, having sometime earlier submitted to Alfred.

Travelling on horseback, the coalition of forces led by Aethelred succeeded in trapping the main body of the raiders inside their temporary encampment at Buttington, near Welshpool, beside the River Severn. They then systematically attempted to starve them out. Many Vikings died, with others surviving only by eating their horses. In a desperate bid to escape, the enfeebled remnants broke out, but were brought to battle on the east bank of the river and mercilessly cut down. Florence later recorded that many thousands of the pagans were killed there and that the rest were put to flight. Skeletal remains, including around 400 skulls, discovered in the churchyard at Buttington in the nineteenth century, attest either to the ferocity of the fighting or a brutal aftermath. Writing at the end of the tenth century, the chronicler Aethelweard claimed that the events which occurred at Buttington in 893 were still talked about by the old men of his day.

Haesten may have been among those Vikings who found himself besieged at Buttington. If so, it appears he survived the slaughter and later made peace with Alfred. The Viking king's wife and children were even returned to him by the West Saxon king as a gesture of goodwill. Once again, this feting of an allegedly defeated opponent begs the question as to how successful, militarily, the campaign really was. The inherently biased

West Saxon sources may have downplayed the impact of the Viking offensive and its on-going potency. Whatever the truth of it, Haesten's name disappears from the records at this time, so it seems likely he settled down somewhere in East Anglia or Northumbria. Other Viking leaders nevertheless continued their raids. One group, bottled up by Aethelred in Chester, were deprived sustenance by the Mercians, who took all the cattle that remained in the immediate area and indiscriminately killed anyone who might have assisted the besieged – presumably local Scandinavian settlers as well as stragglers from the Viking raiding army. The Mercians are said to have burned the crops and allowed their horses to 'eat up the whole neighbourhood' – a classic description of ravaging an area to deny sustenance to the enemy. A further setback for the Viking forces occurred in parallel to this in west Sussex, where another of their raiding armies, possibly part of the army driven from Exeter by the earlier arrival of Alfred's relief force, was crushed by the men of Chichester at Kingly Vale in the South Downs. The death toll is said to have stretched into the hundreds.

The following year (894), the raiders at Chester broke out and plundered North Wales, before returning eastwards, encamping on Mersea Island at the head of the Blackwater estuary in Essex. Later that year, they are recorded as vacating their sanctuary, 'pulling their ships up the Thames and then up the River Lea' towards Hertford, where they built a fortification 20 miles upriver from London. In doing so, they threatened both the city and an imminent corn harvest. Four of Alfred's thegns were killed when the West Saxons attempted to intervene to prevent them from establishing a permanent presence. The king's response was twofold: first to make camp nearby, to protect the harvest; second to order the construction of two forts to be built downstream, to deny the Viking ships an outlet to the Thames. Finding themselves trapped, the Vikings abandoned their longships in the Lea, sent their womenfolk and children for safekeeping into Danish-controlled East Anglia, and then travelled overland to Bridgnorth on the Severn, where they overwintered. The next summer (896) the army dispersed. Some men returned to their families in East Anglia, others to Northumbria or to the Continent.

It was not only on land that successes were realised. At sea, too, Alfred appears to have emerged the stronger. Anglo-Saxons and Vikings were both seafaring people. Wessex had probably not been a naval power at the commencement of Alfred's reign, but the young king had been quick to realise the need to become one. In the summer of 875 he is recorded as having gone out to sea with a raiding ship army and fighting against seven ship-loads of Vikings (around 300 warriors), capturing one ship and putting the others to flight. Shipbuilding efforts must have been urgently progressed in the years following Ashdown. It was this policy of using sea power as an alternative means of going on the offensive that would later earn the West Saxon king fame as the father of the British navy.

Alfred's naval forces clashed with four shiploads of Danish men in 882; they captured two of them and killed all the men on board. Two years later, his fleet surprised and defeated sixteen Viking ships at the mouth of the Stour in Essex. He then suffered a crippling setback when his ships were set upon by a much larger Viking fleet on the return leg down the coast.

Frisian crews are specifically mentioned among the casualties of a later Alfredian sea battle in 896. Hiring foreigners to fight on behalf of the English was later something held against Aethelred II, but was clearly a well-established practice in Alfred's day – continuing a formerly wide-spread Romano-British practice of employing federate troops in Britain. The king even commissioned new, larger ships. These ships, ordered by King Alfred, are described as being twice as long as the earlier ones and also higher above the waterline. Some had sixty oars; others, even more. They are said to have been neither strictly of Frisian design, nor of Danish, but encompassed the best attributes of each. By combining the best features of foreign models, but with bigger crews, the new ships would have been faster and more formidable than opposing Viking ones – known as '*askrs*'. Assuming two fighting men per oar, the crew of one of these ships might have been in excess of 100 men – twice the size of a typical Viking longship of the period. But being bigger also meant having a deeper draught, making them less effective when manoeuvring in shallow waters. Offsetting this, the higher freeboard of Alfred's ships enabled the crews to fight more effec-tively from elevated decking.

Nine of these ships saw action in 896 – the year they were launched – having first blockaded a prowling Viking squadron from East Anglia inside an unidentified harbour mouth along the South Coast. The squad-ron is recorded as having based itself on the Isle of Wight and to have raided as far to the west as the south Devon coast. The fight may therefore have occurred anywhere along the coast between Exeter and Shoreham. Portsmouth Harbour is a possibility. Poole and Chichester harbours must also be strong contenders.

In a fierce fight, they succeeded in destroying three of the opposing Viking vessels and sufficiently weakening two others to ensure they never regained their base. The whole squadron might have been destroyed out-right had not the Viking ships proved handier in the shallow waters of the harbour, giving them an edge when escaping on an incoming tide. Sixty-two English and Frisian allies were recorded as being killed during the fighting, including two named Frisian noblemen: a king's reeve named Lucumon and a member of the king's household named Aethelfrith. One hundred and twenty Danes were killed, not including captives picked up later in Sussex, who were marched to Winchester, and then hung as pirates on Alfred's orders. In all, twenty Viking ships were destroyed along the South Coast that summer.

The crushing defeats inflicted on the Vikings by land and sea during the 890s – when (according to dispassionate Irish chroniclers) countless hea-thens were killed – ended Scandinavian aspirations of conquest, for the time being at least, allowing Alfred's successors to consolidate and hit back. It is in this respect that Alfred's 'greatness', and, arguably, Aethelred of Mercia's too, becomes apparent. Had the two men failed to contain what appears (if the numbers quoted in the accounts can be taken at anything like face value) to have been an equally great threat as that posed by Halfdan and

Guthrum, all England would have fallen under pagan sway. The first great onslaught on Wessex and Mercia had been checked. Even so, large swathes of land to the north and east remained under Scandi-navian control, yet to be confronted.

The statue of Alfred the Great at Winchester.

2.2

Alfred died on 26 October 899, 'six days before the Feast of All Hallows'. He is said to have ruled over the entire English race by the time of his death; all except those areas under Danish control. His son Edward the Elder succeeded him and was crowned at Kingston upon Thames in Surrey. Whether Edward enjoyed the same level of geographic control as his father is not clear; his sister Aethelflaed, known as the Lady of the Mercians, with her husband Aethelred, appears to have operated independently of her younger sibling throughout the first two decades of the tenth century. Moreover, Edward's was a disputed succession. Aethelred I's surviving son, Aethelwold, had immediately thrown down the gauntlet in open revolt upon Edward gaining power, setting himself up as a Lord of the Danelaw.

Britain in the tenth century.

His actions were not merely those of a tinpot rebel. He reigned at York for two or three years, secure enough to have coins struck bearing his name. Described as the 'king of the pagans', Aethelwold posed a much greater threat to his cousin than any Norse or Danish warlord at large in England at the time, and his later invasion of the south at the head of a composite army undermines the idea that ethnicity can ever have outweighed naked ambition during the Viking Age.

A twelfth-century definition of the Danelaw specifies an area around York, plus fourteen shires to the south, including five Danish bulwarks in the East Midlands: Derby, Leicester, Lincoln, Nottingham and Stamford, better known as the Five Boroughs. Alfred's children – like the great man himself – relied on strategically located fortified sites to guard against aggression from the Danelaw; they carried on a policy first begun in the 870s, by constructing new strongholds in close proximity to Danish ones. These burhs were located on defensible sites – often high ground. Previously abandoned Iron Age hill forts were reoccupied and brought back into play. In some instances the remains of Roman walls were patched up and reused – as at Chester in 907. Though not castles in the Norman sense, the burhs were effective nonetheless, being protected by ditches, earth walls and palisades.

A number of the burhs were sited at important crossing places over larger rivers, such as Wallingford on the Thames, and Langport on the River Parrett in Somerset. A series of other burhs protected vulnerable points along the southern and western coasts. The areas enclosed by these defences varied in size, but could sometimes exceed 20 acres. The largest garrisons were at Wallingford, Warwick and Winchester. The smallest was at Lyng in Somerset. The occupants of the burhs were warrior chiefs and their henchmen – the strongholds being military outposts first and foremost. Local nobles owning land nearby occupied them with their armed retainers. During the fighting against Haesten in the 890s Alfred sent one half of his army home while retaining the other half on campaign. This partition of his forces did not count those who held the burhs, implying a large part of the king's overall soldiery was dedicated to their defence at all times.

The historian Nicholas Brooks, in his book *Communities and Warfare 700–1400*, has calculated that the necessary manpower to construct, maintain and defend the burhs would have committed one in every five or six of the adult male population of Wessex; as many as 27,000 men overall. There was – in theory at least – a close correlation with the worth (hidage) of an area and the number of men charged with a burh's upkeep and defence. One 'hide' was the value assigned to a parcel of land capable of maintaining one family unit, and one man from each hide was responsible for approximately 1¼yds of wall, the equivalent of four men to a 'pole or perch' – old-style measures equating to about 5½yds. When garrisoned, a burh rated as being worth 1,000 hides required 1,000 soldiers to defend and maintain it. Winchester and Wallingford, both rated at 2,400 hides, therefore had very substantial garrisons. The walls of the West Saxon capital at Winchester may have set the model; its 3,300yds of Roman wall being equivalent to 600 poles or 2,400 hides.

The geographic siting of the burhs of the original Burghal Hidage of Wessex was first planned by Alfred after Halfdan's warriors withdrew north in the autumn of 871. Towards the end of Alfred's reign nobody living in Wessex would have been more than half a day's march of a burh. Their siting was planned this way. Of the original burhs, the defences are arguably best preserved today at Wareham – the place fortified by 893 – where the modern town's still-impressive earthen walls stretch for more than 2,000yds, east, west and north, anchored by the River Frome in the south (see Appendix 2).

The River Frome at Wareham in Dorset.

Vikings were also responsible for fortress building, and with the refortifying of still-defensible British strongholds – York being a prime example. The city's Roman walls were strengthened and a great defensive bank built alongside the River Foss. The famous Coppergate district – laid out in the early tenth century – soon became a densely populated commercial centre. Equivalent urbanisation occurred in the other Danish-occupied regions, in particular the Five Boroughs of the East Midlands, as well as other Danish-occupied sites in East Anglia, such as Thetford and Norwich.

Throughout the second half of the ninth century and the first half of the tenth, Danish armies, of necessity, had to be gathered without delay in an emergency. Means of concentrating their forces were readily at hand: the existing network of old Roman roads. Roads such as Watling Street, running south-east from Chester, and the Fosse Way, traversing the country from Exeter to the Humber, plus numerous other interlacing routes across the countryside were ready-made highways for opposing armies to march and counter-march right up until the eleventh century and beyond. Evidence for this is found in the many Scandinavian place names along Roman roads in southern Yorkshire and Lincolnshire.

The early part of the tenth century witnessed a dramatic flowering of Anglo-Saxon success against the Danelaw, seeded by an apparent defeat and a major victory. The defeat in question occurred at the Battle of the Holme, fought on the borders of East Anglia in the spring of either 903 or 904, when a Kentish rearguard was annihilated by an Anglo-Danish coalition led by Edward the Elder's renegade cousin Aethelwold, who – as described earlier – had set himself up as an overlord in Northumbria. A settlement in Cambridgeshire bearing the name Holme has been identified as the most likely site of the fighting. But the coalition's victory was pyrrhic at best. Aethelwold fell in the fighting, ending any immediate threat to Edward's royal line. The pretender died along with a host of notables, including Eohric, the Danish King of East Anglia, and a Mercian renegade named Brihtsige. Despite claiming a victory, the eastern Danelaw had been dealt a severe blow, with its leadership dramatically culled.

The other decisive military encounter was a great English victory won at Tettenhall near Wednesfield six or seven years later, on 5 August 910, when Mercian forces, supplemented by reinforcements from Wessex, destroyed the main Viking army of the Danelaw, led by the kings Eowils and Halfdan II. Both Danish kings were killed, together with a large number of other Danish noblemen. With jingoistic relish, the chronicler Aethelweard

Main battles fought in the danelaw in the first half of the tenth century.

recounted how the Danes – having earlier harried throughout Mercia and over the Severn into the West Country – were set upon by squadrons of Mercians and West Saxons and were defeated at Woden's Field; the pagans thereby 'hastened to the hall of the infernal one'.

The Holme and Tettenhall left the Danelaw rudderless and vulnerable to reconquest. Even so, only through a sustained encroachment into Danish territory – a kind of chequerboard advance – was Viking military control south of the Humber successfully confronted. Local populations, previously under Danish control, were in this way brought to heel. A third crucial battle was fought at Archenfield, in the Wye Valley, in 914, where English forces defeated two troublesome Viking commanders – Jarl Hroald and Jarl Ohtor. The fusion of Wessex and Mercian forces under energetic siblings proved irresistible. Key strongpoints in East Anglia were assaulted and fortified by Edward, while Aethelflaed aggressively infiltrated the Midlands. She led an army to Tamworth and built a stronghold there, and then later another at Stafford. Earlier she had fortified Bridgnorth. Extending her control northward, she established burhs at Eddisbury (a hill fort beside Chester) and Warwick. Further fortresses were constructed at Chirbury in Shropshire, at Weardbyrig (Warburton, on the Mersey) and at Runcorn, in Cheshire. The important Danish stronghold of Derby fell in 917. Leicester succumbed to Aethelflaed's forces the following year, shortly before her death.

In a belated attempt to regain the initiative, the Danes from Leicester and from further afield responded by launching raids against Anglo-Saxon burhs at Towcester and Aylesbury. Others built camps and forts in Bedfordshire, using the Great Ouse as a means of striking inland. Navigating the Ouse was a practical proposition for the shallow-draughted Viking boats. Forward bases for their ships were built within striking distance of one of Edward's newly established burhs at Bedford. Their main base appears to have been at Tempsford, which, as at Repton, boasted strong ramparts and a distinctive D-shaped ditch and enclo-sure. Edward responded to these encroachments by launching a furious, retaliatory offensive. The defences at Tempsford were assaulted and broken down. Florence describes how Edward's warriors systematically, 'besieged, assaulted, took, burned, and razed it'. They slew the pagan king Guthrum II (the King of East Anglia), as well as several jarls and all others who offered any resistance. Edward followed up this success by advancing into East Anglia and capturing Colchester. He then marched on Stamford, where he fortified the high ground to the south of the River Welland, forcing the Danes on the opposite bank to surrender.

Aethelflaed died in the summer of 918, and Edward immediately rode at the head of his army to Tamworth, annexing Mercia to Wessex. Nottingham also submitted to him at this time. The *Anglo-Saxon Chronicle* states that all the nation of the land of Mercia – earlier subject to Aethelflaed – now 'turned to him' as their king. They had little choice – even the Welsh kings, Clydog, Hywel Dda and Idwal, under threat of invasion, submit-ted to the English king. The surrender of Danish-occupied Lincoln is not recorded specifically, but it is likely to have occurred just after the fall of Nottingham. Only the Northumbrian kingdom of York remained firmly under Scandinavian military control, and even there a holding treaty was hurriedly negotiated with the triumphant Englishman.

2.3

Even while Edward the Elder and his sister Aethelflaed were busy placing the Danelaw in check in the first decades of the century, other regions of Britain were caught up in less well-documented wars of their own. The Norse king Ragnall overran Bernicia in 914, defeating an unlikely Anglo-Scottish coalition at Corbridge, on the Tyne. He then won a second battle at Corbridge four years later. In the decades to come, Norse kings from Dublin and Norway would pose serious problems for Edward's succes-sors, and the wars fought between the Anglo-Saxons and the Norse might reasonably be considered an important catalyst for English unification – an achievement usually credited to Athelstan (r. 925–39).

Acclaimed on coins as *Rex Totius Britanniae*, it was Athelstan who first brought together all the nations of Britain under his overlordship – achieving this within just a few years of coming to power. Northumbria was annexed by him in 927, and as a result the rulers of Bernicia (East Lothian and Bamburgh) and the kings and princes of Alba, Cornwall, Gwent, Gwynedd and Strathclyde all submitted to him the same year. Not all was achieved peaceably. Athelstan is said to have forcibly deported a large group of unassimilated Britons from their ghetto in Exeter – 'purging it of its contaminated race' – resettling them across the border into Cornwall. William of Malmesbury, writing in the twelfth century, claimed that Athelstan 'obliged them to retreat from Exeter, which until then they had occupied with equal privileges with the Angles'. The king then fixed the boundary of their province on the other side of the Tamar River. He had earlier done much the same with the Welsh, setting the border between Saxon and Celt to the west of the River Wye. A contemporary poem celebrated these events, proclaiming 'this England now made whole'.

Predictably, Athelstan's expansionist policies stirred up enmity against him. Constantine II, the Scottish King of Alba – a political area also referred to as Scotia, roughly encompassing the central lowlands of Scotland and the land to the east of the Highlands, between the Moray Firth and the Firth of Forth – had particular cause to be alarmed. Athelstan's annexation of Northumbria meant the two men now shared a common frontier. Tensions mounted and war followed. As a result, the English king marched north with an army described as being from the whole of Britain, laying waste to land as far north as the Pictish fortress of Dunnottar on the Aberdeenshire coast. His navy struck even further north, harrying coastal settlements in Caithness, then part of the Norse kingdom of Orkney. The raids were launched to punish the Scottish and Orkney kings for taking sides over Northumbria; they had allied themselves with the main Viking pretender to York, Olaf Guthfrithsson, King of Dublin.

Olaf Guthfrithsson's father had been ousted from York by Athelstan some time earlier, and Olaf was determined to win it back. With Constantine's support, the Dubliner attracted substantial backers. Among them was the Scottish king's nephew Owain, King of the Strathclyde Welsh. Olaf's plan was to re-establish his family's rule at York and ravage nearby English territory, bringing on confrontation with Athelstan. Its execution would have required considerable planning; the impressive build-up of forces in Dublin

Bay would have been time-consuming, stretching over many months. The invasion fleet comprised Olaf's own ships from Ireland – hauled across lowland Scotland from the Clyde to the Forth – plus others from Strathclyde, Alba and the Kingdom of Orkney. Viking forces journeying back and forth from Dublin and York in the tenth century are known to have routinely manhandled their longships across Scotland's narrow waist, following a route drained by the Kelvin and Carron rivers. In doing so, their ships might remain afloat for long periods without the need for excessive manual effort. Such journeys were not isolated or exceptional events. In 936 – the year before Olaf's invasion of Northumbria – other Vikings in Ireland are recorded as hauling their ships from Lough Erne over Breifne to Lough Ree in midwinter, a distance of approximately 40 miles. Given Olaf's close ties with Owain and Constantine, manpower would have been plentiful for such a journey, and an echo of this event is contained in the following verse from a poem quoted in William of Malmesbury's twelfth-century *History of the Kings Before the Norman Conquest*:

> Then Olaf the briny surge forsakes,
> while deeds of desperation urge.
> Her king consenting, Scotia's land receives
> the frantic madman and his horde of thieves.

Further corroboration for this is found in the accounts of Florence of Worcester and Simeon of Durham – both of whom claim Olaf arrived off the east coast of England, in the Humber, in 937. Targeting the East Coast would have made sense if Olaf's intention was to occupy York and to rally or coerce the Northumbrians to his banner before ravaging further afield.

The Battle of Brunanburh – 937

That Athelstan won a resounding victory over Olaf's coalition at a place called Brunanburh is evident from the various annals, although the precise location of the fighting is unknown. The name Brunanburh is thought to mean either Bruna's stronghold or the fort by the burn. Despite strong claims by historians that it was fought in the North-West at Bromborough in the Cheshire Wirral, a battlefield in the North-East or the East Midlands seems more likely. Contemporary sources stress the magnitude of the event, and the scale of the slaughter. The number of combatants was very large by the standards of the day, numbering several thousand on each side, with Viking mercenaries bolstering Athelstan's numbers. The sheer diversity of the combatants may have been unprecedented in Britain, with war-bands from Alba, Dublin, Mercia, Northumbria, Strathclyde, Wessex and the Western Isles massed around their individual banners. William of Malmesbury describes how:

> The youth [Olaf], overbold and hoping to his heart forbidden things, advanced far into England, when at last he was opposed at Brunefeld [Brunanburh] by leaders of great skill [Athelstan and his brother Edmund] and by a strong force of knights.

Other accounts relate how the English king initially held back from confronting the invaders while Olaf raided inland, giving battle only when convinced he had the numbers to win. He then determinedly challenged the forces ranged against him, and in a hard-fought battle he is said to have 'laid low an endless host of the invaders', winning 'undying glory at the sword's edge'. An anonymous poet quoted in the *Anglo-Saxon Chronicle* vividly describes how the West Saxon horsemen:

> Pressed on the loathed bands; hew'd down the fugitives, and scattered the rear, with strong mill-sharpened blades.

Strewn with the bodies of the dead and dying – carrion for the 'greedy war-hawk' – the battlefield ('the meed of death') witnessed the greatest slaughter since the coming of the Anglo-Saxons. Five young Norse kings and seven jarls, along with countless common Scots and Norse warriors, were slain. Among them were Owain of Strathclyde, and Gebeachan, King of the Western Isles, along with two Viking princes from Dublin. The English also suffered notable losses, including two of Alfred the Great's grandsons and the Bishop of Sherborne.

Both Olaf and Constantine fled from the field of battle. Constantine headed back north on horseback, outpacing his pursuers. Olaf escaped with a few followers by boat before departing for Dublin. Constantine returned safely to Alba, and several years later relinquished control to a cousin, before retiring to live a cloistered life at St Andrews, where he died in 952. Perhaps he never recovered from the trauma of defeat at Brunanburh, where many of his kinsmen had died, and where his son lay among the fallen, 'mangled by wounds'. Athelstan died childless on 27 October 939, having been

The tomb of King Athelstan at Malmesbury Abbey.

lauded while he lived as 'the pillar of dignity in the western world'. His half-brother, the 18-year-old Edmund, a youthful veteran of Brunanburh, succeeded him.

Although widely acclaimed as the most momentous and decisive military encounter of the age, the victory that was won at Brunanburh failed to prevent Olaf from launching yet another invasion of England two years later, upon Athelstan's death. Olaf lost little time in establishing himself in Northumbria this second time around, and was ruling at York by the end of the year. Coins minted there at this time show his raven motif, honouring Odin, the Norse God of War. He invaded Mercia the following year. Many Northumbrian Danes rallied to his banner. Only with great difficulty did English forces succeed in halting them at Northampton. Repulsed there, Olaf headed north-west, stormed Tamworth and took hostages. King Edmund's army, belatedly coming up from the South, finally cornered him at Leicester. In the resulting peace treaty Olaf appears to have gained most of his territorial objectives, including the five important fortresses of the eastern Danelaw. The old Watling Street boundary, previously demarcating Scandinavian and Anglo-Saxon territory to the north and south respectively, was reinstated.

In return, Olaf agreed to be baptised into the Christian faith. Edmund stood sponsor. But within a year the incorrigible Viking once again commenced hostilities, this time in Anglo-Saxon Bernicia, raiding northward into East Lothian where St Baldred's church at Tyninghame was torched by his marauding war-bands. He died soon after. Three years later, in 944, Edmund brought the East Midlands and Northumbria back under English control. He also settled relations with Alba's new king, Malcolm, and subdued the troublesome Strathclyde Welsh, blinding the sons of Owain's successor in the process. The 'Song of Edmund' in the *Anglo-Saxon Chronicle* praises the young king's achievements, proclaiming Edmund as 'a protector of kinsfolk, and beloved doer of deeds'. Such praise was well deserved, recognising the king's success in gaining military control over those parts of Mercia and the East Midlands which had fallen to Olaf, 'redeeming the Danes', until then held, 'in bonds of captivity', by the Norse.

Despite Edmund's successes, his brother Eadred had to do it all again when yet another fierce Norseman – Eric Bloodaxe – gained control of Northumbria in the second half of the 940s. The Icelandic skald Egil Skallagrimsson chillingly describes Eric as keeping the Northumbrians in their 'dank land' cowed 'under the helmet of his terror'. Egil was being overly dramatic. Submitting to southerners such as Athelstan, Edmund or Eadred was, in all probability, more galling to the Northumbrian nobility than to a Scandinavian, no matter how fierce. Quite what Eric's credentials were is hard to gauge. The son of Harald Fairhair, King of Norway (d. 930), he is credited with earning his nickname by successfully killing off all but one of his rival brothers after the death of their father. Only the youngest – Hakon – survived, safely ensconced at King Athelstan's court in England. Eric appears then to have failed to retain a firm hold on Norway – a bleak, mountainous land of remote, semi-autonomous chiefdoms. The region needed effective central control – something Eric, due to unpopularity, was unable to provide. Instead, his younger brother, Hakon, established himself there with Athelstan's help, and with the support of the main Norse power broker, Sigurd, Earl of Lade. The young king was ruling in Norway as early as 933. Eric is thought to have possibly gained temporary control of Northumbria as part of this deal. He may even have been forcibly displaced by Olaf Guthfrithsson in 937; may, credibly, have fought at Brunanburh alongside Athelstan and Edmund.

Bloodaxe – with his wife, children and entourage of warrior chiefs – was accepted as king at York more formally around 947–48, and was baptised into the Christian faith by Wulfstan, Archbishop of York, to seal the arrangement. The English King Eadred viewed Eric's return with dismay and immediately launched raids into Northumbria to punish the northerners for breaking faith with him. The Northumbrians had earlier submitted to Eadred at Pontefract in 947. John of Wallingford, writing in the late twelfth century, described the terror tactics employed by the English, who burned down towns, razed fortifications, flattened walls, slaughtered opposition and arrested suspects. The most outrageous act committed by Eadred's forces was the destruction of the glorious seventh-century minster at Ripon, and the seizure of the relics of its founder, St Wilfred. These acts represented an expression of southern vandalism, likened by Michael Wood, in his book *In Search of the Dark Ages*, to the German shelling of Reims in 1914. The Northumbrian saint's remains were an important spiritual focus for the Northumbrian separatists. Archbishop Oda of Canterbury, who led the raid on Ripon, later defended himself by arguing that the bones of St Wilfred were seized by him to preserve them from 'the innumerable upheavals of the English kingdom'. But more likely the theft, like the burning of the minster, was enacted in spite.

Eric Bloodaxe, as his nickname would suggest, was not one to be easily intimidated. Still with a tenuous hold on York, despite its defences being destroyed by the English, he stubbornly refused to leave the province without a fight. His forces followed hard on Eadred's heels as the English army withdrew from the devastated city. Overtaking their rearguard by using another road, he surprised and defeated them at Castleford, where Ermine Street bridges the River Aire. It was an act of defiance made by a rash and desperate man. Despite this victory, and now once again threatened by further punitive attacks from Eadred's forces, the council at York found ways of deposing the Norse tyrant, placating Eadred with payments to compensate him for his losses in battle.

Saga evidence has it that Eric, having been driven from the province, buccaneered for a time in the Irish Sea before, once again, regaining power at York. Irish sources speak of a great battle being fought, and of Norsemen (perhaps Eric's forces) defeating an alliance of Bernicians, Scots and Strathclyde Welsh. If true, Eric's recovery of Northumbria was achieved at the point of the sword. It appears that the fierce Viking had retained the support of Archbishop Wulfstan, who continued to hold out for Northumbrian independence. At some stage, Eadred engineered the archbishop's arrest, and Wulfstan was taken under escort northwards to the fortress of Jedburgh in modern Roxburghshire. He was later transferred to the former Roman Saxon shore fort of Othona – located near

Bradwell-on-Sea in Essex, where the famous seventh-century chapel of St Peter still stands. He died in 956. Wulfstan's removal sounded Eric's death knell. Having been chased off once again, the Norse king attempted to escape back to his ships in the Solway Firth, but was ambushed on Stainmoor by a force of Bernicians from Bamburgh led by a shadowy assailant named Maccus. The resulting melee (more in the nature of a running fight than a formal battle) occurred 10 miles west of Barnard Castle, where the remains of a Roman camp straddled the road. Eric, along with five other Norse sub-kings, was killed. Two sons of the Jarl of Orkney also fell in the fighting.

> Kings five, Eric said,
> Their names I will tell;
> I, the sixth, at their head
> In the gory fight fell.
>
> (Egil Skallagrimsson)

Even after Eric Bloodaxe's demise, Northumbria continued to maintain its own distinct identity. The region's bid for independence might have been crushed – with political control passing to Oswulf, Lord of Bamburgh – but Danish legal customs continued to be recognised at York, as well as in the Five Boroughs of the East Midlands, right up until the second half of the tenth century; this despite future kings asserting rights to legislate for the whole nation – whether Briton, Dane, Saxon, or Norse. Though it was not apparent at the time, Bloodaxe's death had largely completed the regional map of England as we know it today. All the same, Northumbria – described by the historian Richard Fletcher in his book *Bloodfeud* as 'distant, dangerous, difficult of access, poor of soil and inclement of weather' – would continue to be a rock against which the aspirations of English kings would sometimes be dashed. Distrust between the North and the South would remain an entrenched political issue. Tellingly, as late as the reign of Edgar 'the Peaceable' (d. 975) a good deal of latitude had to be given to the region, allowing its leaders 'such good laws as they best decide upon'. These concessions, rationalised as a reward for the loyalty shown to Wessex overlords, owed more to the underlying political reality of the times. Edgar's government must have known that any attempt to force Anglo-Saxon legal norms or personalities onto the Northumbrians would get short shrift, and would likely result in another incursion from some fearsome and unwelcome Scandinavian usurper.

2.4

Eulogised by the chroniclers as reigning over a land so strongly defended that 'no fleet so proud, or raiding army so strong, fetched itself carrion among the English race', England, by all accounts, enjoyed a period of hiatus from troublesome Viking attacks during Edgar's relatively short reign; in large part this was a reflection of political turmoil in Scandinavia and on mainland Europe, plus a consequence of the expired energy of his expansionist predecessors. In 973 the king was afforded a highly ritualised second coronation at Bath, where the still imposing Roman remains provided a dramatic backcloth of imperial majesty. His queen, Aelfthryth, was formally crowned and anointed during the ceremony, and granted a far higher status than was usual as 'legitimate Queen', sowing the seeds for a future succession dispute. The king then travelled north to Chester to be feted by a number of sub-kings from Scotland, Wales and the Western Isles. As a show of might – designed to intimidate as well as to impress – he brought with him his whole naval force. English reliance on sea power from Alfred's time onwards had become paramount; the naval might on display in the Dee estuary represented an immediate and powerful foundation for Edgar's continued claims to overlordship. It is even asserted that Edgar's fleet made annual circumnavigations of the British Isles throughout his reign to demonstrate his naval power.

In what appears to have been an elaborately choreographed political statement, Edgar is then said to have been rowed along the Dee by the retainers of his client kings. Conviviality, drinking and feasting were enormously important in medieval times. Kings and nobles carousing together enhanced friendship and goodwill. The pageant on the Dee confirmed this friendship, underpinning the alliance's unity of purpose and shared values. Edgar is said to have been so pleased with what was achieved at Chester, he boasted aloud that his successors would now be truly able to call themselves 'kings of the English'.

It should be stressed, however, that the chroniclers of the summit were 'southerners'; their accounts were written to glorify the southern-based English king. In all likelihood, Edgar's client kings would have been a good deal less subservient than portrayed, with pressing agendas of their own. They were substantial rulers in their own right: powerful men such as Kenneth II of Scots, Malcolm of Strathclyde and Maccus Haroldsson, King of Man and the Hebrides, described disconcertingly as 'a Prince of Pirates'. Instead of the event being seen as one of submission (as the pageant would suggest) it is more likely Edgar spent his time arbitrating between powerful rivals: twisting arms to tease out gritty compromise agreements.

There had been internecine fighting going on in Wales between sparring princes for some time. Westmorland and Lothian – in the north-west and north-east of England respectively – had also recently witnessed clashes between rival warlords. A certain Thored Gunnarsson's ravaging of Westmorland in 966 is a good example of this. Though his motives are obscure, the relative prominence given to his actions in the *Anglo-Saxon Chronicle* suggests a protracted conflict – part of an on-going and somewhat fraught English campaign to halt the southwards encroachment of King Malcolm's Strathclyde Welsh. Kenneth II of Alba was also a man with expansionist intent, having raided across his borders into England immediately prior to the summit. Kenneth's main objective at the meeting with Edgar may have been to agree the formal handover of the rich Lothian coastal territories between the Forth and Tweed, then part of Anglian Bernicia – an area periodically annexed by the Scots since the 950s. Nominally ruled by Eadulf Yvelcild of Bamburgh – whose son lay hostage at the Alban court following one of Kenneth's earlier raids – the region was an important bargaining counter. One of the outcomes of the summit may have been to agree the ceding of the province to the Alban king and to secure the release of Eadulf's son.

It was not only in the North that trouble was brewing. The *Annales Cambriae* (Welsh Annals) tell of English war-bands ravaging the kingdom of 'the sons of Idwal [Gwynedd]' in the year 967. The English protagonist was Aelfhere of Mercia – Edgar's, and later his son Aethelred's, right-hand man. Also mentioned in the histories of the time are raids on Anglesey launched by the piratical Manxman Maccus Haroldsson and his brother Godfrey, which resulted in the island's subjugation to the Norse. Edgar (and later his son Aethelred) held no God-given right to rule the tributary territories over which they progressively came to exert overlordship; no more so than had Athelstan, Edmund or Eadred.

Even as late as the 970s the lands north of the Humber remained largely isolated from the politicking of the king's court. Dangerously unstable places such as Northumbria, Cumbria and the Scottish borders had to be held at the point of the sword against resurgent Norse and Danish kings, Celtic war-bands and recalcitrant nobles. A king's first duty was to defend the people, and he had to be seen to do so. Any weakness or vacillation would be rewarded with revolts at home or unwelcome incursions from abroad. Quite clearly there had been more to discuss at the summit in Chester than the quality of the local mead and the inclement weather. If it included a growing Viking threat, it is nowhere mentioned.

Even so, predatory Scandinavian warlords – freed from internal bickering – were soon once again looking west for an outlet for their aggression, where England – a rich and prosperous land – lay ripe for the plundering. Edgar's early death at the age of 29 or 30, and the murder of his eldest son shortly after, meant it would fall to the youngest of his sons, Aethelred – known inaccurately to history as 'the Unready' – to face Scandinavian challengers even more dangerous than Olaf Guthfrithsson and Eric Bloodaxe.

3

Dawn of the Second Viking Age in England

3.1

Ominously straddling the millennium, a time of heightened apocalyptic import, the thirty-seven-year reign of Aethelred II (the longest of any English medieval king) began with the assassination of his half-brother King Edward 'the Martyr' at Corfe, in Dorset, in the year 978. The deed was probably carried out by supporters of Queen Aethelfryth (Aethelred's mother and Edward's stepmother). The chroniclers of the time bewailed that 'no worse deed for the English race was done than this since the English first sought out the land of Britain'. The following year chroniclers reported the sighting of 'a bloody cloud seen in the likeness of fire, spied at midnight' – a meteorological display retrospectively interpreted as portending God's anger on the English. Unfortunately for young Aethelred – still a minor – not only was he faced by a wrathful God able to conjure up disturbing weather patterns, he was also heir to an uncompromising martial legacy and would be faced by a Viking threat as devastating as any in the past.

Up until the death of Aethelred's father in 975, the kingly succession from Alfred's time had passed, in the main, from brother to brother, or father to son, without bloodshed. With the exception of Aethelwold's challenge to Edward the Elder, armed disputes had been avoided (see Appendix 3). Willingness to compromise, rather than immediately resort to force had become – or perhaps already was – a hallmark of Anglo-Saxon politics. In the recent past, Edgar and his elder brother Eadwig had ruled Mercia and Wessex separately – if not amicably, at least peaceably – maintaining rival courts and avoiding open warfare. Only upon Eadwig's death in October 959 did Edgar assume the overall kingship of England. His son Edward the Martyr's murder in 978 – after just three years of rule – was therefore unusual. Even more unusual was the fact that the deed went unpunished. There is no record of anyone being formally charged with the crime. Little wonder that the almost simultaneous recurrence of Viking raids attracted the retrospective attention of the chroniclers.

Born to King Edgar's first wife or concubine, Edward was the eldest of the king's three recognised sons. The other two, Edmund and Aethelred, were born to Edgar's third wife, Aelfthryth. Edmund died in 971 at the age of 5 or 6. Upon King Edgar's unexpected and untimely death four years later, the 12-year-old Edward was elected king. Though allegedly of an unstable and aggressive temperament, and despite the existence of good grounds for a counterclaim on behalf of his half-brother, Aethelred, the young Edward received the dying king's blessing to succeed him. As if auguring a profound change in England's fortunes, the period immediately following Edgar's death and Edward's consecration in 975 was marked by the three-month passage of a baleful comet across the night skies, and the following year by a disastrous famine throughout the land.

Edward's murder was committed high in the Purbeck Hills of Dorset, near the royal stronghold at Corfe, a fortified wooden or stone structure known as a *burhgeat*. Built on the same elevated, rocky site as the later Norman castle – the impressive ruins of which still dominate the surrounding landscape – the bastion there had been strengthened by Edgar to control unwarranted access inland from Swanage. Returning from a hunting expedition, Edward is claimed to have been set upon by Queen Aethelfryth's supporters and stabbed to death while dismounting from his horse. The site of the murder is associated in legend with 'the Martyr's Gate' at Corfe – a later Norman construct on the site of Edgar's original gatehouse.

If the allegations are true, and there is no good reason to think they are not, the event has compelling parallels with the later murder of Archbishop Thomas Becket: armed retainers getting carried away, convinced they are acting in the best interests of their masters. Rather than a planned assassination, the murder may have been committed on the spur of the moment, the result of an accident, or the outcome of an angry confrontation; a not unlikely scenario given the young king's violent and unstable personality. Exactly what occurred after the king's death is also something of a mystery. Commoners are said to have discovered the king's corpse some considerable time after his death through the agency of ghostly light. The remains

– if they were in fact Edward's remains – were then buried unceremoniously at Wareham before later being dug up and taken to the nunnery at Shaftsbury for formal burial in February 979, almost a year after the murder.

Aelfhere, Ealdorman of Mercia and a close relative and ally of the queen, was the man responsible for making the final funeral arrangements. Belatedly getting the dead king's corpse interred with due ceremony was necessary to facilitate the consecration of the boy king, Aethelred. Historians have since speculated that Aelfhere, with the queen's connivance, may have been the mastermind behind Edward's murder. The twelfth-century chronicler William of Malmesbury even went so far as to name him as the killer. On the day of the interment, legend has it that the queen's horse would not budge when the funeral procession got under way, and that further attempts with other horses fared no better. Even attempts to proceed on foot are said to have proved impossible for her. Credulous locals soon spread tales of further unexplained events occurring at the tomb. Predictably, the place the bones were laid to rest became a busy pilgrimage site. Later, in the dark days of 1008, with England under threat from overseas, Aethelred would agree for his murdered half-brother to be sanctified. Churchmen viewed the unavenged killing of Edward as shameful – worthy of God's wrath. The issue had never really been laid to rest up until then. With the State facing enormous economic and military trials, pandering to popular sentiment and having his brother proclaimed a saint and martyr made political sense. The country was by then on a permanent war footing, in need of a boost.

Described augustly as the 'Prince of the Mercian people', Aelfhere had been the most powerful of King Edgar's nobles, and the first to witness the king's charters (quasi-legal pronouncements, conferring rights and privileges). His accession to the ealdormanship of Mercia owed much to the crisis which had occurred in 957 when Mercia and Wessex were for a time divided between Edgar and his brother Eadwig. Mercian nationalism may have been behind the split; upon assuming overall kingship Edgar was quick to create an ealdormanry of Mercia as a sop to separatists. He appointed Aelfhere – already by that time a trusted ally – to rule there. With other leading men such as Dunstan, Archbishop of Canterbury, and Aethelwine, Ealdorman of East Anglia, the Mercian lord became an important and influential member of the king's inner circle of advisors.

During Edgar's reign and Aethelred's later minority, Queen Aelfthryth's signature also appears regularly on charter witness lists, implying she too played an active role at court. But during the short reign of her stepson Edward

The millennium plaque in Corfe village, commemorating the murder of Edward 'the Martyr'.

her signature does not appear at all. Either she was excluded by him, or she removed herself from public life at this time. Edward's murder and Aethelred's succession provided Aelfthryth and Aelfhere and their supporters with almost half a dozen years of unfettered power before Aethelred reached an age fit to govern. Was this motive enough for murder?

Aethelred II was described by twelfth-century chroniclers at the time of his coronation in 979 as being 'a noble prince, and [a youth] of fascinating manners, handsome countenance, and graceful appearance'. Great things were hoped from him. One of the reasons many of the noblemen of the land preferred Aethelred over his murdered brother was because – according to Florence – 'he appeared to all gentler in speech and deeds'. Edward, on the other hand, is said to have inspired not only fear, but even terror. The literal meaning of the name Aethelred was 'noble counsel'. Later, pundits made of it a play on words, adding the sobriquet 'un-*raed*', denoting no counsel – in modern parlance poorly or ill advised – a criticism of the king's ministers as much as the king himself. Only later did the noun 'un-*raed*' get changed to the adjective 'un*redi*', providing a new meaning and implying the king himself was somehow always unprepared or unready – an indecisive, vacillating man – one who could be easily led and manipulated.

Supporting this characterisation, the noted historian Frank Stenton concluded that Aethelred's acts of spasmodic violence, and the air of mistrust which overhung relationships with his nobles, were signs of something more than an incapacity for government; rather they were suggestive of the overreaction of a weak king struggling to come to terms with the fact he had gained power through what was regarded by contemporaries as the worst crime committed in Anglo-Saxon history. In his classic trilogy, *The Lord of the Rings*, Tolkien uses this stereotype to good effect in his portrayal of the bewildered and war-weary Theoden of Rohan, King of the Golden Hall, who is held back from confronting his enemies by an evil spell cast by his treacherous chief advisor, Grima Wormtongue. But it is unlikely a king such as Aethelred, who ruled England for the best part of four decades, was as sleepy and inactive as this defamatory image of him suggests. On the contrary, what we know of Aethelred's early years suggests an energetic, forthright and at times arrogant personality; he asserted his authority militarily on at least one important occasion during the first decade of his rule in Kent, when in dispute with the Bishop of Rochester.

Prevented from accessing the well-fortified Medway town, the young king ravaged the surrounding area, his scouts and incendiaries torching villages and destroying crops. The reasons for the problems between the king and the bishopric of Rochester are obscure, but may have stemmed from a disputed or illegal land grant made by the young king, then overturned by the bishop. The earliest account of the raid, written almost 100 years after the event by the chronicler Sulcard of Rheims, describes how Aethelred – 'in a fit of insolent rage' – set fire to the city of Rochester and the Church of St Andrew. By burning and ravaging, he is said to have laid waste all the lands belonging to the bishop of that city. It was only on Archbishop Dunstan's intervention, with his warning to Aethelred not to irritate St Andrew – 'ever ready to pardon [but] equally formidable to avenge' – along with the payment to the king of £100, that Aethelred's forces were withdrawn. St Andrew had appeared in visions more than once to the archbishop, a fact widely known. So the threat this posed would have appeared to Aethelred as a very real one in a markedly superstitious age.

In later years Aethelred is said to have regretted his conduct against Rochester, claiming he had acted not so much in cruelty, as in ignorance, having been incited into action by a certain Aethelsige, a later discredited favourite. With Aelfhere dead, and with his mother's influence on the wane, the teenage king had by this time turned to a new and younger set of advisors, among whom Aethelsige may have been a leading light. Some see this episode as representing an early example of Aethelred's random cruelty, a character trait which appears to reoccur again and again in his reign. Because he was so easily led astray by a worthless favourite while young, claims that in later life he continued to display poor judgement are given added credence. His apologists on the other hand stress his youth, and see the affair as representing the healthy assertion of a fledgling Dark Age warrior prince. Aethelred's biographer Ryan Lavelle has stated that rather than see the incident as one in which the young king was led astray – it could, conversely, be seen as a 'perfectly legitimate exercise in the assertion of royal authority'.

3.2

The Danish invasions of England in the second decade of the eleventh century came after a period of mounting Viking attacks stretching back almost thirty years. The incursions varied from hit-and-run raids on vulnerable and undefended coastal settlements to large-scale sorties launched by ship-borne armies from the Continent. They were well-led and sustained assaults, likely to test the mettle of any medieval king. From 980 onwards the *Anglo-Saxon Chronicle* highlights the increasing occurrence of Viking attacks on England. Small in scale, but widespread, they appear to have been launched by a mix of raiders from Cumbria, Denmark, Ireland, the Isle of Man and the Western Isles – the Danish raiders operating from safe havens in Normandy. Southampton was the first place to be raided; many of its inhabitants were killed or enslaved when seven ships' crews descended on what was then an unfortified town. The Isle of Thanet and Cheshire were ravaged the same year. Vikings then destroyed the monastery at Padstow in Cornwall in 981 and raided extensively along the Devon and Cornish coasts.

Returning the following year in three longships, they pillaged the Dorset coast and sacked Portland. Based on an estimated forty warriors per ship (in line with the ratio of ships to men when Ubba's army attacked north Devon in 878) the three Viking ships that sacked Portland might have carried 120 attackers; the seven ships which sacked Southampton the year before, just over twice as many. Although small in comparison to earlier ship armies, these raiding parties were nevertheless sizeable enough to inflict enormous damage to life and property if not resolutely confronted.

Aethelred was barely in his teens at the time, so can have had little or no involvement in planning countermeasures. Localised in nature, these attacks were the responsibility of English regional leaders. Possibly the king remained largely unaware of their occurrence until their increasing scale made the problem they posed more pressing. The great fire that consumed London in 982 and the news that the Saracens had been defeated in a battle fought in Italy by the Emperor Otto were of more import that year to the king and his nobles than these isolated Viking forays. Moreover, the deaths of a number of important men in the kingdom, notably Aethelred's chief mentor, Aelfhere of Mercia, in 983, and Bishop Aethelwold of Winchester the following year, overshadowed such concerns.

By the end of the 980s, if not before, English commanders had organised themselves sufficiently well to intercept the marauders and bring them to battle. Viking raiders who clashed with local forces under the command of Goda at the harbourside town of Watchet in Somerset in 988 never made it back to their ships. With a number of monastic sites and royal manors nearby, Watchet was a prime target for the Vikings. Although the defenders arrived too late to prevent the surrounding area from being pillaged, they were able to confront the raiders before they could escape. The thegn Goda and his second in command, Strenwold, were nevertheless among the fallen.

Viking attacks towards the end of the decade appear to have occurred alongside a flurry of diplomatic activity between Aethelred's government, the Normans and the papal authorities in Rome. The raids on England – some of which must have emanated from bases in Normandy – were seen by this time as sufficiently serious to warrant English reprisals. Pope John XV sent his emissary, Bishop Leo, to England in the summer of 990 to broker peace between Aethelred and Richard, Count of Rouen. Negotiations later held in Normandy proved successful, and in March 991 an agreement was announced 'to all the faithful' that peace between Aethelred and Richard should remain forever unshaken. The treaty may have formally outlawed Viking fleets from utilising Norman harbours and using commercial centres such as Rouen and Caen to offload their booty. It is no coincidence, therefore, that one or more rootless Viking fleets, denied berths in Normandy, should descend on Aethelred's England a few months later. More in keeping in scale with the large ship armies of Alfred the Great's time, a fleet of ninety-three ships arrived off Folkestone. Its onslaught marked the start of what would later become popularly known as the 'second great Viking Age in Britain'.

The Viking ship army which assailed the Sussex coast in 991 was a mix of Scandinavian war-bands raiding under the banner of the Norse leader Olaf (Crowbone) Tryggvason, a future king of Norway and the great-grandson of Harald Fairhair (d. 930), founder of the first Norwegian ruling dynasty. Olaf's nickname, 'Crowbone', was earned through his penchant for reading the omens. Known to have been active off the British coast at around this time, he was probably responsible for some of the earlier raids throughout the 980s too. Icelandic sources claim he completed an impressive circumnavigation of the British Isles: raiding Scotland, the Hebrides, the Isle of Man, Ireland and Wales, before setting up a base on the Scilly Isles – an ideal anchorage for launching forays into Cornwall and along the South Coast. Of the other named leaders who arrived in 991, Jostein is thought to have been Olaf Tryggvason's uncle, whereas another leader, named Guthmund, remains obscure. Swein Forkbeard, King of Denmark, may also have been present in England that year, though none of the primary sources mention him specifically.

Having harried shipping outside Folkestone Harbour and plundered the surrounding countryside, Olaf's fleet travelled up the east coast of England to Ipswich, which they sacked. The Vikings then coasted back down to the Blackwater estuary and encamped on one or more of the large estuarine islands in the area. Such islands made ideal short-term bases for the Vikings, removing the need for them to construct earthen enclosures to protect their ships and belongings. Over the course of centuries, changes in sea levels and on-going riverine and coastal sedimentation have altered the local geography of this area of the Essex coastline. There are today three large islands in the Blackwater estuary: Mersea, Northey and Osea. Mersea is the largest of the three, and is located at the estuary mouth. It had previously hosted a Viking army in 896, towards the end of Alfred's reign, and had a reliable supply of fresh water. Most likely the Viking fleet moored here again in 991 and set up their main encampment on the island. Mooring further up the Blackwater estuary would have been a dangerous undertaking for them, risking their ships becoming trapped by a blockading English fleet. Both Osea and Northey may, instead, have been used as forward bases of operations for launching raids against the mainland.

Northey, the smallest of the islands, lies furthest up the estuary, closest to the fortified town of Maldon. A narrow causeway between Northey Island and the mainland is still passable today, but only at low tide, and then just by a few men abreast. The distance across the channel is now too far for sound to carry clearly, casting doubt on whether a Viking herald – who was claimed to have shouted across warnings to the English host on the mainland – would have been heard. However, modern geological techniques have established that the channel between Northey and the mainland was narrower and deeper at the time of the battle of Maldon, so a shouted message – if indeed one were ever really made – would have been heard and understood. Osea, closer to the estuary mouth, also boasts a causeway but it is thought to have been too long, even in the late tenth century, for an

Northey Island in the Blackwater estuary near Maldon – the causeway to the mainland is clearly visible. (*Courtesy of and copyright of Terry Joyce*)

army to safely cross. Maldon was located close by, at the upper tidal reach of the estuary. It was a well-fortified site as far back as prehistoric times. A substantial ditch enclosing 20 acres of high ground at the west end of the High Street has been uncovered in modern times, indicating that the burh built here by Edward the Elder in 916 may have been based on a pre-existing Iron Age structure. The town's northern and eastern approaches were secured by extensive tidal marshes at the confluence of two rivers, the Blackwater and the Chelmer. Both rivers drained into the estuary directly beneath the town's walls.

Ipswich's defences had been breached by the Vikings without the necessity of a siege. Failure to maintain essential wall work may have been a factor. Folkestone's defences, on the other hand, appear to have held. Assuming Maldon's walls were still intact too, a direct assault on the town, or the mounting of a formal siege, would have been a substantial undertaking for the raiders. Defended walls were a 'force multiplier', negating any numerical advantage enjoyed by attackers. Without battering rams and siege engines, Olaf's commanders would have been loath to expend time and energy attempting to undermine the town's defences. More likely, their aim was to set up a base in the Blackwater estuary from which to harry the surrounding countryside; then loosely besiege the town, and attempt to persuade the local authorities to buy them off.

The man charged by Aethelred with defending the east coast of England was Ealdorman Byrhtnoth, a nobleman of immense wealth and prestige, the second-ranking ealdorman of England, and one of the most prominent men of his generation. Delegation of military affairs appears to have become well established by Aethelred's time. Byrhtnoth shared joint control of the eastern counties with the 'Half-King' Aethelwine of East Anglia, who lay ill at the time of the Viking attack. It is possible his responsibilities extended further north into regions of the Danelaw. Over 60 years of age, Byrhtnoth was described at the time of his confrontation with the Viking force as still strong in his power, of the greatest physical size, indefatigable in warfare. This was no exaggeration. When renovations were made to the north wall of the choir at Ely Cathedral in 1769, a skeleton, thought to be that of Byrhtnoth, was unearthed and discovered to belong to a man well over 6ft tall.

The Essex nobleman had received the shocking news of Ipswich's fate shortly after it was pillaged. Warning beacons stretching inland from the coast would have alerted defenders of the arrival of the Viking fleet. Byrhtnoth's scouts would then have tracked the fleet's passage down the coast to the Blackwater estuary. Approaching from the north, the English force must have arrived just in time to prevent a strike against Maldon's hinterland. The ealdorman may have recently travelled to Northumbria to gauge the mood of the local nobility of the region; may even have fought against forces owing allegiance to Swein Forkbeard, the warlike King of Denmark. Forkbeard's brother is thought to have been active in Northumbria at around this time.

The northern lords posed a potential threat during periods of heightened Viking activity, and Byrhtnoth may have taken hostages to secure their loyalty. The restless spirit of Eric Bloodaxe, dead for almost forty years, still haunted the North.

Quickly covering long distances by using the still-existing and extensive network of old Roman roads, Byrhtnoth's men rode on horseback to confront the Vikings. Travelling with them were monks from nearby Ely Abbey. Byrhtnoth, a patron of the abbey, had likely lodged there during his journey south, holding a hurried council of war within its monastic confines. The English leader may have considered his best tactic to be to interpose his forces between the raiders and their ships, bringing on a battle, in much the way as Goda had at Watchet. As it turned out (according to the battle poem), his men arrived before the Vikings had time to debouch onto the mainland.

Essex men accounted for the bulk of Byrhtnoth's army, supplemented by men from the Maldon garrison, and from neighbouring Cambridgeshire. Reckoned at 1,000 strong, this would have been a very large army by tenth-century standards. Nonetheless, they were probably outnumbered by the Vikings. Arriving in over ninety ships, packed with warriors (not families and possessions, as had been the case in Alfred's day) they may have outnumbered the English three to one. English armies of the late tenth century cannot have differed substantially from those of earlier times. The principle of one soldier for every 5 hides of land may still have been the foundation for military obligations in 991. The contemporary chronicler Aethelweard described the men of Wiltshire as being raised in this way a few years later, and tells us that £1 was paid for two months' service. Up until this time during Aethelred's reign, raiders may have generally shunned confrontation, preferring to make a hasty getaway with their plunder. The Viking ship army faced by the fighting men of Essex and Cambridgeshire in 991 was, however, of a different order of magnitude – large enough to overwinter in England and to accept battle if necessary as a way of achieving its objectives.

The Battle of Maldon – August 991

According to the Maldon battle poem, the English army formed up on the shoreline of the estuary. Opposite – on an island (possibly Northey) in clear view – separated by the narrow flooded causeway, the Viking army massed; eager warriors vied for the honour of being the first to cross once the tide ebbed. A Viking envoy shouted warnings and threats from the island, demanding a tribute be paid to avoid bloodshed. Byrhtnoth scorned their demands, making it clear he intended to stand his ground; that he would with a few chosen men repel their attacks across the narrow causeway. Should the Vikings manage to make it over in any numbers, Byrhtnoth reckoned on them being disadvantaged with their backs to the channel, unable to effectively deploy. Should they fail to gain a bridgehead, they risked being cut off at high tide, leaving part of their force trapped on the mainland once the causeway became submerged.

While the two armies waited for the flood tide to subside, bowmen skirmished, shooting off their arrows, some of which found their mark. As the tide ebbed, Wulfstan, one of Byrhtnoth's most trusted lieutenants, was detailed to hold the land bridge. He fiercely held off the Viking attempts to cross, assisted by two other warriors – Aelfere and Maccus – described in the poem as 'a mighty pair'. The first Norse raider to venture over was brought down by Wulfstan's lance. Those that followed met a similar fate. The resolute English defence held out, hurling back the Viking rush. Many of the attackers, driven from the causeway, were slaughtered as they wildly floundered in the black ooze of the estuary.

The Viking leaders, thwarted by Wulfstan's dogged stand, urged Byrhtnoth to allow them to cross unimpeded. They are said to have cunningly played on the Englishman's sense of fair play, claiming the right to fight on an equal footing. Byrhtnoth apparently acceded to their request, shouting across the watery expanse for the Norsemen to come over, saying 'there is room enough for you now'. The English leader must have known what he was up against. The Viking fleet had been tracked along the coast for several days. Reports from his scouts had provided him with intelligence of the enemy's strength. The quantity of Viking longships confirmed this: accounts spoke of more than ninety ships. At an average of forty men per ship (as had been the case with Ubba's fleet in 878) the Viking army can be reckoned at 3,600 strong. Even if only half were engaged at Maldon, Byrhtnoth took a massive risk accepting battle. To face a Viking host on roughly even terms and prevail would be hard enough – for Byrhtnoth

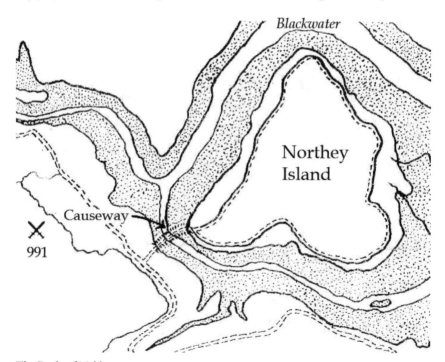

The Battle of Maldon.

to take on a force twice his size, on ground of the enemy's choosing, was tantamount to folly.

Having persuaded Byrhtnoth to allow them across, the English army probably fell back to cover the Maldon road. The poem then relates how the fierce Norse 'blood wolves' advanced through mud and water – 'west over the land-bridge' – to confront them. As the first Vikings arrived on the shore, the ealdorman embattled his army to receive them. He personally oversaw the marshalling of his men, demonstrating how they should stand, bidding them 'hold their shields a'right firmly with their hands and not to fear'. The ranks of English fighting men were drawn up in close order, with each warrior's shield presented so as to form a continuous and unbroken front to the enemy. Half a century later at Hastings, William of Poitiers noted that along the English 'shield wall' the dead could scarcely fall nor could the wounded remove themselves from the fight, so tightly were the ranks packed. This must have been equally true – if not more so – at Maldon, where the warriors were armed with traditional round shields rather than the later, narrower kite-shaped ones depicted on the Bayeux Tapestry. The battle poem mentions an English 'war-wall', or 'war-hedge' specifically – a clear reference to this same defensive deployment.

Byrhtnoth's bodyguard comprised an elite force of well-armed and trusted retainers. They were the ealdorman's personal 'hearth-troop', fused together by bonds of fealty and patronage. A quarter of a century later at the Battle of Sherston, such men were described by a contemporary chronicler as the 'Optimates', or the best troops. They fought in the front rank of the army, absorbing the first shock of combat with the Vikings. Less experienced men formed up to the flanks or behind in support. Byrhtnoth is likely to have employed similar tactics – deploying his most experienced warriors in his front line, with his own 'hearth-troop' gathered together around him in the centre of the array.

The Vikings formed up opposite, their standards featuring the black raven (symbol of Odin, God of War), which fluttered in the breeze. As pointed out by the historian Cyril Hart in his book *The Danelaw*, it is unrealistic to assume they simply poured across the causeway and formed up their army without first having sought out favourable terrain on which to deploy. Byrhtnoth's acceptance of battle must therefore have allowed for a period of 'joint reconnaissance' to establish a suitable battlefield. Choosing good ground to fight on was important in a set-piece encounter – in particular the avoidance of facing directly into the sun, or having to cross boggy ground to make contact.

The statue of ealdorman Byrhtnoth at Maldon. (*Courtesy of and copyright of Brian Medhurst*)

Although a qualitative comparison of armour and weaponry used by the two sides at Maldon is impossible to make, Olaf Tryggvason's men, warriors by vocation, seem to have had the edge. Byrhtnoth cried out 'stand fast against the foe – battle is near'. Birds screeched overhead. Standing over 6ft tall, with his banner raised, the English nobleman would have been immediately conspicuous – a dominant figure bedecked in mail, sword in hand – at once an inspiration to his men and a cause of dread to the enemy.

The initial phase of fighting involved the firing of missiles by both sides. The poem tells of 'bows being busy' and of warriors launching their 'hard, sharp pointed spears'. Once the discharge of arrows and javelins was completed, the Vikings surged forward, crashing against the defensive English 'war-wall'. Men on both sides fell wounded and dying. Byrhtnoth's nephew was among the first to be killed. At this pivotal moment in the fight, the English war leader cried out above the din of battle, seeking to instil courage in his men, urging them to fight on bravely and prove their valour against the invaders. Leading by example, Byrhtnoth threw himself into the fray but was immediately struck down. A spear had penetrated his shield, wounding him. The giant warrior managed to break the shaft, removing the spear point, and then launched his own missile, sending the javelin clean through his unfortunate assailant's throat. He launched another javelin, which also found its mark. The poem recounts how the 'deadly spear-end' was thrown with immense force, penetrating the opposing Viking warrior's mail shirt, killing him outright.

Like other noblemen, Byrhtnoth had several fighting men in close attendance – possibly spear carriers. The poem mentions two in particular: Aelfnoth and 'a youth' named Wulfmaer – son of Wulfstan, the brave defender of the causeway. When Byrhtnoth again fell wounded, impaled by a second javelin, Wulfmaer is said to have drawn the fatal dart from his master's body and hurled it back into the enemy ranks. A heavily armoured Viking then rushed forward, seeking to put an end to the English leader. Somehow Byrhtnoth retained enough strength to strike back at his aggressor, but was almost immediately beaten down; his shoulder was shattered by another assailant's sword or axe. His 'golden hilted' sword tumbled to the ground, leaving him defenceless. He was then hacked to death. Aelfnoth and Wulfmaer died with him.

As the news of Byrhtnoth's death spread, many Englishmen turned and fled. Among them was a warrior named Godric, son of Odda. In the poem, Godric becomes the scapegoat for the defeat; he leaped upon Byrhtnoth's steed and rode off in panic westwards, towards the refuge of the woods. Other men fled with him, among them his brothers Godwine and Godwig. The anonymous poet castigates Odda's sons, mockingly recalling how they had been among those who spoke so manfully at the council of war, but whose deeds on the battlefield failed to match their brave words. But not all behaved so cravenly. Some among Byrhtnoth's 'hearth-men' remained defiant, resolutely determined to fight on, regardless of their fate. With them was a Northumbrian hostage named Ashferth. Byrhtnoth had – as mentioned earlier – recently travelled to Northumbria to gauge the mood of the local nobility. Ashferth may have been taken hostage to ensure their loyalty, and have travelled back south with Byrhtnoth's army. Despite the circumstances he found himself in, the young Northumbrian proved to be an adept warrior, firing off a stream of arrows, 'again and again wounding men'.

This prominence afforded to a lone Northumbrian may have been symbolic; an attempt perhaps by the author to place the battle in the context of a national epic rather than a regional one, which in reality it was. By the end of the tenth century, the term Englishman had become widely used to describe the polyglot mix of peoples settled in the country – indicative of the first stirrings of national identity.

The final stand of Byrhtnoth's 'household' troops is vividly narrated by the poet. Individual warriors are named, their last heroic moments preserved in Old English verse. They include Edward 'the Tall', Aetheric 'the Excellent' and 'Grim-Fighting' Offa. Their resolve to avenge the death of their lord has echoes of much earlier Germanic martial traditions, leading some to doubt the event's authenticity. But for the poetic account to be credible and be accepted by a contemporary audience, a warrior surviving his leader in battle, without having avenged him, must

Effigy of Byrhtnoth at All Saints' church, Maldon.

still have been seen as a disgrace as late as the tenth century.

The poem ends abruptly with Aethelgar's son – another Godric – hurling a spear into the ranks of the Norse raiders, before launching himself into their midst, hacking and hewing at them until he too fell. Had a full version of the poem survived, no doubt the demise of the remaining 'hearth-men' would have been recounted, along with the return of the Vikings to their base, bloodied but victorious. The monks from Ely, who had accompanied Byrhtnoth into battle, later recovered his body, but not his head. The decapitated nobleman had been the abbey's benefactor. His remains were interred at the abbey church – a ball of wax substituted for the missing head. When examined in the nineteenth century, the skeleton was found to have had the collar bone nearly completely cut through by the downward strike of a battle-axe or sword – cold case corroboration of the poetic account.

3.3

The crushing defeat at Maldon and the shocking news of Byrhtnoth's death persuaded King Aethelred's government to buy time and pay off the Vikings. The ealdorman's demise and the destruction of his army had left East Anglia at their mercy. Even having inflicted losses on the raiders, the Viking threat to the East Coast must still have been considerable. Sigeric, Archbishop of Canterbury, was among those who counselled the king to agree to the Viking's financial demands. He even sold property of his own to help raise the necessary amount – an enormous sum of £10,000. The whole of the south-east of England may have been under threat by this time, adding credence to the notion that Byrhtnoth's motivation in allowing the Vikings across the causeway was – in part at least – to bring them to battle in an attempt to prevent such an outcome. The gallant ealdorman may earlier have been present when reports of Goda's fight in

Somerset were recounted to the king's council (Witan). A reluctance to pass up an opportunity for equal glory may also have been behind the decision to fight. Supporting this supposition, a reference in the poem to the leader's pride getting the better of him is an indirect reflection of this.

Without a similar epic poem, the Watchet battle gets scant attention today. But since both battles receive only brief mention in the *Anglo-Saxon Chronicle*, the fight on the Somerset coast may have been every bit as fiercely fought as the one is Essex. The contemporary chronicler Byrhtferth, a monk from Ramsey Abbey, took great pains to mention two major battles being fought at around this time – 'one in the east, and one in the west'. The western one was almost certainly Goda's battle at Watchet.

Intriguingly, the anonymous poet relied on a combination of native arrogance and an Englishman's innate sense of fair play to explain the decision – stereotypical attributes more commonly associated with the nineteenth century. What is more, the battle may have been a more straightforward affair than the version in the poem – the fight on the causeway echoes mythical tales from antiquity. Rather than admit to the English forces being soundly defeated, the anonymous poet – enhancing the dramatic tension – substituted Viking guile for overwhelming numbers and martial prowess.

Archbishop Sigeric was not alone is advising the king to meet the Viking's demands. Aethelred's other close advisors, Aethelweard, Ealdorman of the Western Shires, and Aelfric, Ealdorman of Hampshire and Wiltshire, also urged Aethelred to quickly settle the matter of tribute, presumably to preempt the Vikings launching further raids along the South and West Coasts. It is often assumed that these payments – made after the defeat at Maldon – were the first of their kind to be extorted by the Vikings. But this was not the case. Payment of tribute was a long-standing practice.

The Frankish king Charles the Bald was forced to pay the Vikings tribute at least six times in the years between 845 and 877. King Eadred's will, drawn up almost forty years before the Battle of Maldon, left £1,600 to the English people as insurance against attacks by heathen armies. Almost 100 years earlier, the men of Kent had made a temporary truce with a Danish raiding army based at Thanet, offering them money in return for peace. Though not explicitly stated in the accounts of the period, Alfred the Great most likely had to pay the Danish warrior lord Halfdan some form of tribute to secure a truce shortly after the death of his brother Aethelred I in 871. Another payment may have been made by him to broker a cessation of hostilities with Guthrum's forces both prior to, and possibly after, the Battle of Ethandun – details are lacking. Though not called tribute, monetary gifts are mentioned as being made by Alfred to the Norse leader Haesten on at least one occasion in the 890s. On the Continent, the Emperor Charles the Fat found that the use of force alone could not prevent Vikings from placing a stranglehold on Paris in the 880s – and that only the threat of encirclement, along with the payment of 700 livres of silver could persuade the invaders to disperse.

As early as the end of the second century, the Romans are recorded as buying off the wild northern tribes from beyond the Antonine Wall with great sums of money. Coin hordes discovered in Scotland bear this out. Writing in the sixth century, the Welsh historian Gildas describes, 'foul hordes of Picts and Scots emerging like dark throngs of worms, wriggling from narrow fissures in the rocks when the sun is high'. These were not mere painted savages. Their leaders wore armour, and the warriors themselves carried square shields, spears, swords and axes into battle. A hail of slingshot preceded their attacks, and war chariots, like those at one time employed by their Celtic cousins in the South, formed the vanguard of their charge.

The practice of buying off these fierce tribes fared no better for the Romans than it would for Aethelred. The emperor Caracalla (d. 217) was forced to launch a series of punitive campaigns against them in an attempt to stem their troublesome attacks. But it was only after his legions were withdrawn back behind the security of Hadrian's Wall, with strong fleets patrolling the coasts, that the problem was resolved. Maintaining a strong fleet was also important for the English in Aethelred II's day – something that would become more apparent in the coming years, as the military crisis deepened. Aethelred's government was therefore not the first Dark Age administration to purchase security, but this is what it has become best known for.

Alfred the Great's enemies in the ninth century had been primarily intent on settlement. Once settled, they developed a stake in England's future. The objective of the late tenth-century raiders – men such as Olaf Tryggvason and Swein Forkbeard – was, instead, to gain treasure as a means of furthering their political ambitions back home in Scandinavia. Both men's sole objective was to squeeze the English for all they were worth. For warlike but economically marginalised Scandinavian leaders, plunder – in the form of loot, enslaved captives, monetary tribute and precious metals – was very much an end in itself. Only later, with England brought to its knees, would conquest become their objective.

The immediate threat of attack from the Viking ship army that fought at Maldon (though others may have been active against the English too) appears to have been limited initially to Essex and Kent, both shires being rich and accessible for raiders arriving from across the Channel. Agreeing to make the payments must have seemed a sensible short-term solution to a problem which everyone hoped would simply go away. But of course the problem did not go away. Over the coming years, regular sums of money had to be paid out to the raiders; apparently 36 million silver pennies were minted during Aethelred's thirty-seven-year rule to meet Viking demands. The first payment of £10,000 in 991 or 992 was followed by another in 994 of £16,000 – this time with the additional supplement of food and clothing, plus permission for the Vikings to overwinter beside Southampton Water. Such settlements and provisions were not, however, made unconditionally. The Viking force in 994, for example, had to sign up to help protect the English against future marauders.

Rather than simply encouraging the Vikings to clear off (though many may have done so), a more complex set of relationships appears to have been at work, whereby Viking war-bands were actively encouraged to stay to bolster the country's defences; they were sometimes formally placed under treaty to do so. Indemnities for earlier misdemeanours were also granted. This symbiotic relationship would continue in fits and starts right up until the start of the second decade of the new millennium. Reliance on foreign mercenaries was unpopular and had proved problematic in the past, notably for the Romano-British when placing their trust in the Angles, Saxons and Jutes for their defence upon the departure of the Roman legions; much of England had fallen under Germanic control as a result.

Historians have since questioned the almost logarithmic progression of the value of payments made to appease the Vikings. They started in 991 with £10,000, and rose to £16,000 in 994, £24,000 in 1002, and £36,000 in 1006; they dipped to £14,000 in 1014, but then rose to a staggering £72,000 in 1018. The historians argue that the amounts are more representative than real, and that the chroniclers were more intent on emphasising the increasing pressure put on the kingdom during the latter part of Aethelred's reign than engaging in accurate accounting. True or not, there can be no reason to doubt that significant sums of money were involved, and that the demands made by the Vikings represented a serious drain on Aethelred's financial and material resources, though not a crippling one. During the first decade of the eleventh century, as the military situation in England worsened, the associated tax, known variously as Danegeld (Dane's money) or Heregeld (Army money), was levied on all land. Failure to make the required payment resulted in forfeiture of land to the crown. In a climate such as this, with an unpopular tax being levied and draconian penalties being exacted, the Maldon poem, glorifying the English defence, might well, some consider, have been written as an admonishment of Aethelred's policies as much as a nationalistic rallying call for the English to resist Danish aggression.

3.4

Whether the bulk of the large Viking ship army which defeated Byrhtnoth in 991 remained encamped on the English coast, or sailed back whence it came, will never be known for sure. But it seems likely some part maintained a continuous presence in the country for several years – well into the new millennium – augmented from time to time by newcomers from Scandinavia. A year or so after the Battle of Maldon, either the same or a new hostile fleet is reported to have been moored in the Thames, where numerous large estuarine islands, such as those at Sheppey and Grain, provided excellent bases for raids into Kent and Essex. Following the accepted paradigm of Aethelred II's reign, we might expect the king to have hurriedly sought ways to once again raise funds to buy off the marauders. Instead, his government's response was aggressively militaristic. By penetrating the Thames estuary, threatening London and its trade links with the Continent, the Vikings appear to have 'upped the ante'. Drastic measures were called for, and the English fleet was immediately ordered to concentrate against them. By attacking in two flotillas – one from London, the other from East Anglia – the objective may have been to trap the Vikings within the estuary, forcing a decisive naval action.

Dismissively described as involving only those ships 'worth anything', the inference is that Aethelred's government had too few serviceable warships at their disposal to respond effectively to this call to arms. Either that or the English had neglected the fleet's maintenance, and had allowed the ships to rot at their moorings. It has sometimes been argued that the relative 'peace' of Edgar's reign (that of Edward's and Aethelred's, too, up until the late 980s) had a negative knock-on effect on England's military preparedness. But this is far from proven. Indeed, it would be surprising that a mere sixteen years from the death of King Edgar, when the reputation of the English fleet was at its height and something to boast about, that it should now be in such a sorry state. Aethelred's earlier threat of war against the Normans must presumably have been made with the backing of a fleet.

His order for all serviceable warships to concentrate in the Thames would not have been made if lack of numbers made the operation impractical. Also, a major naval campaign was launched by him against pirates operating off the Cumbrian coast at the turn of the millennium. Earlier, during the Maldon campaign, the fleet had had little time to concentrate, and attacks made further north, along the Northumbrian coast, may have had the effect of diverting forces away from the South-East. The notion, therefore, that the country was militarily unprepared is overstated. Only later, when the increasing scale and regularity of attacks (not just from Vikings, but also from Scots and Welsh) came close to overwhelming the country's defences, did the necessity of a major re-militarisation programme become pressing.

Notwithstanding the readiness of the fleet to do battle, the naval campaign that followed was a complete failure, apparently decided by what was to become a recurring theme during Aethelred's reign – treachery. The king's council had recently been weakened by the deaths of Archbishop Oswald of Worcester and Ealdorman Aethelwine of East Anglia – the latter after an illness that had prevented him from fighting alongside his colleague Byrhtnoth at Maldon. The overall command of the fleet was entrusted jointly to Ealdorman Aelfric of Hampshire and Thored of Northumbria, the king's father-in-law. Bolstered by prayer and potent relics, the warlike bishops Aescwig and Aelfstan also accompanied the expedition. The English plan appears to have been to catch the Vikings in a pincer movement: one squadron of English ships attacking westwards down the Thames from London, led by Aelfric; another, from East Anglia (comprising the fleet that had recently returned from the North-East), commanded by its Northumbrian earl, Thored.

For reasons that are unclear, Aelfric, in command of the London squadron, was accused by the chronicler of treacherously warning the Danes of the coming battle. On the eve of the intended attack, he is said to have fled, 'scurrying away by night, to his own great disgrace'. Forewarned of the impending attack, the Danes were able to avoid the trap laid for them, with all but one of their ships escaping. What fighting occurred appears to have been focused on the capture of Aelfric's flagship. Of course, true naval warfare in the sense we understand it today was impractical in Aelfric's day. Fights such as the one on the Thames in 992 and the one described during Alfred's reign on the South Coast took place in sheltered harbours or on adjacent strands. Engaging another ship with missiles over any great distance was impossible with the weaponry available, and opposing vessels needed to be laid close alongside each other for spears and arrows to be effective; both having to be firmly locked together for hand-to-hand fighting. Like during any land battle, care was taken to block the enemy from manoeuvring through gaps in the line or against open flanks. Fighting took place from the forecastles or sterns of opposing vessels, with ships acting as floating fighting platforms for warriors to slug it out. On the high seas none of this was possible. Instead, fleet commanders ranged their ships in line across the mouths of estuaries. At a better-documented battle in 999, the opposing fleets were described in the *Heimskringla* as being lined up for battle in just such a way, 'spread over the bay with thin beaks gaping'.

With respect to the sea fight (or lack of a fight) in 992, it seems the same gloomily retrospective Englishman was at work when penning these events. Rather than warning the Vikings of the coming attack, Aelfric was more likely attempting (almost certainly with the approval of the king's council) to make a last-ditch effort to persuade the marauders to honour the agreements made the previous year, and for them to leave the area peacefully. Presumably these negotiations failed to resolve the crisis and may, inadvertently, have served to alert the raiders to the likelihood of an English attack, putting them on their guard. Because we have so few facts, the sequence of events and motivations of the players remains opaque.

Described as one of Aethelred's new men, and someone the king placed much trust in, Aelfric had risen to prominence during the early part of the king's reign. With Archbishop Sigeric and Ealdorman Aethelweard, he was among those who had urged Aethelred to purchase peace the year before, after the Battle of Maldon. It may have been for this reason that he was vilified by the chronicler, the author viewing him as someone more likely to parley with the heathens rather than to confront them. Whatever the truth of the matter, Aelfric remained a close ally and trusted advisor of the king throughout Aethelred's long reign – this despite his son, Aelfgar, later being blinded on Aethelred's orders. Tradition has it that Aelfgar was punished for his father's part in the fleet debacle; a deed which provides Aethelred's critics with a further example of the king's random cruelty. But for this claim to be credible, Aethelred must have already harboured doubts about Aelfric's loyalty, an assumption at odds with statements that he was among those whom the king trusted most. Most likely, pecuniary matters lay at the heart of the altercation between Aelfgar and the king. Aelfric had earlier been involved in the purchase of the abbacy of Abingdon, and was censured for encouraging the king to make the abbey's lands available to speculators, including his ill-fated son. This could have been reason enough for the chronicler to defame him. Financial scandal probably led to Aelfgar's blinding, the draconian punishment having nothing to do with the disastrous fleet action. Had Aelfric acted treacherously, the king would have accused him directly. At the very least, he would have lost his ealdormanship, possibly his life. Instead, he remained one of the king's closest advisors, remaining loyal to Aethelred and to his successor, Edmund; he fell to a Danish blade on the field of Assandun in 1016.

The other fleet commander, Thored of Northumbria, the king's father-in-law, may have been the same Thored Gunnarsson who had ravaged Westmorland during Edgar's reign in 966. The evidence points to him travelling south from Northumbria with part of the fleet in 992, having beaten off attacks launched by Swein Forkbeard or his surrogates in the spring of the preceding year. He regularly witnessed Aethelred's charters throughout the 980s, and his disappearance from the records after 992 coincides with the sea fight in the Thames. He may have died at or shortly after the battle, or resigned as a result of the failure to entrap the Vikings, or after a series of further defeats suffered in his earldom the following year. None of the chroniclers specifically mention what became of him, so we can only speculate as to his demise.

Aethelred's marriage to Earl Thored's daughter, Aelfgifu, was (if the number of children he sired by her is a good indicator) a very successful one; this fact must have greatly strengthened Thored's position at court. The marriage arrangement also provided Aethelred with a vital familial link to the nobility of Northumbria, where English kings always needed friends as a buffer against foreign incursions, and as a means of keeping control over the important Anglo-Danish population centres there. Aethelred sired six sons and three daughters by Aelfgifu over a fifteen-year period. His sons were named after former kings, with the name Aethelstan given prominence; followed by Ecgberht, Edmund, Eadred, Eadwig and Edgar. Later sons by his second wife, Emma, would be called Edward and Alfred. That Alfred is the last named indicates no special preference was afforded to such an illustrious ancestor, and it has been argued that the so-called cult of Alfred did not really get under way until later in the twelfth century, when Asser's works became incorporated into the histories of the time. Because of her almost continuous confinement, the queen played little part at court, and did not attest any of the king's charters in the later 980s or 990s. There is also reason to believe that some of the royal children were raised by a foster mother; others, among them Athelstan (Aethelred's heir) and Edmund, were raised by their notorious paternal grandmother, Aelfthryth.

3.5

The entry in the *Anglo-Saxon Chronicle* for the year 993 somewhat innocuously states, 'Bamburgh was broken down, and much war-booty taken there'. That the raid on Bamburgh is mentioned at all is significant, given the normal southern bias of the chroniclers. Built high on an imposing outcrop of dolerite rock, dominating the land and sea approaches along the Bernician coast in modern-day Northumberland, the frontier settlement there had enjoyed a turbulent history long before the devastating Viking attack of 993. Located at the extreme northern edge of the Roman Empire, Bamburgh had once been in the front line against raids by the wild Votadini tribes of the region. The surrounding countryside was then, and still is, naturally well drained and fertile – an important consideration in ancient and medieval times, before the introduction of modern drainage methods. Fertile land and high crop yields meant wealth and power for the region, making Bamburgh a particularly important stronghold. It became the capital of Anglo-Saxon Bernicia, an entity comprising a coastal dukedom stretching northward from the Tees to the Forth. That Bamburgh was overrun and destroyed by the Vikings was therefore a matter of some consequence.

The historian Nennius records the early British name for the fortress town of Bamburgh as Din Guyardi – a name dating back to at least the sixth century. At this time Bamburgh, like Edinburgh and Dumbarton, was an important regional centre, the stronghold of a local British king. The early Anglo-Saxons, led by King Ida, first built a citadel here in 547. The bastion they erected was enclosed by a stockade, and then later by wooden walls or palisades. King Ida was, by tradition, the founder of the main royal line of Northumbrian kings. The site became known as 'Ida's seat', and was later renamed 'Bebban's burh', after a queen from the area. Tradition has it that when the Mercian king Penda assaulted Bamburgh in 651, he attempted to burn down the wooden defences, but was foiled by a miraculous wind, conjured up by prayers to St Aidan, which blew the flames back into the faces of the besiegers. St Aidan was the founder of the nearby monastic centre on Lindisfarne, which was destroyed by the Vikings in 793.

Anglo-Saxon domination of the region had been secured by Ida's grandson Aethelfrith, in battles fought at Catterick in Yorkshire (598) and Dawston Rigg on the Scottish borders, (603). Described by the historian Bede as the king who 'ravaged the Britons more extensively than any other English ruler', through the subjugation and slaughter of the indigenous population, he consolidated the English hold on the North, creating a

Northumbrian overkingship which included lands to the south as far as the Humber and to the north as far as the Forth, in Lothian.

It followed a pattern common across England. Elsewhere too, wherever Anglo-Saxon incomers successfully overcame local British opposition, they appear to have ruthlessly displaced them, with the indigenous populations being driven away, assimilated or simply bypassed – leaving isolated British enclaves intact at places such as Elmet, in the West Riding of Yorkshire; Rheged, in north-west England, and Strathclyde, on the west coast of Scotland. There are accounts of peoples fleeing westwards or overseas to Brittany to avoid the horrors of frontier life, and of belea-guered Britons seeking military help from Roman forces on the continent – despairingly claiming that the Saxon barbarians were intent on driving them headlong into the sea, only for the sea to drive them back again, into the arms of the barbarians.

At a battle fought somewhere in England around AD 496, the westerly progress of the Anglo-Saxons had been halted for a time by the Romano-Britons at the Battle of Mount Badon. The victor is maintained to have been the mythical King Arthur. Though embraced as a hero jointly by the English, Welsh and Scots, recent academic opinion favours him to have been Irish. The only contemporary source for the battle fails to mention Arthur at all, but does describe the fighting as protracted (*obsessio montis badonici*), implying a siege of some sort, with the possibility of a battle being fought between the besieging Saxons and a combined British gar-rison and relief force. The Roman Empire had been a vast melting pot. Federate troops, auxiliaries and mercenaries, from far afield, had made up the bulk of the Imperial front line in Britain, before later settling down and marrying into the local population. Even as early as the fifth cen-tury the bipolar distinction between Anglo-Saxon and Briton must have been becoming blurred. But the evidence is inconclusive. The absence of Anglo-Saxon archaeological finds from Romano-British settlements such as Lincoln could be held to indicate the locals sometimes kept the invaders at bay. On the other hand, it may simply mean the newcomers preferred to stay outside of such forbidding and largely ruined Roman garrison towns. Though extensive genocide is thought improbable, atroci-ties were committed nonetheless. Alfred the Great's ancestors, the warlords Stuf and Wihtgar, put to death the few native British they could find on the Isle of Wight at a place called Wihtgarabirig (Carisbrooke – the site of a Roman fortress). The rest of the inhabitants of the island had previously been slain, or had fled in terror.

By the end of Aethelfrith's period of rule in the North, his kingdom of Northumbria comprised two distinct regions: Bernicia, made up of modern Northumberland and Lothian, with its centre at Bamburgh; and Deira, an area roughly equivalent to modern Yorkshire, centred on York. Bernicia would later escape the large-scale Danish settlement of the last half of the ninth century, remaining predominantly Anglo-Saxon – the Bernicians famously becoming known as 'the Angles of the North'. Deira, on the other hand, would become heavily settled by Danish migrants; York, as we have seen, became at one time, with Dublin, the twin capital of a large Danish trading and military bloc. The wars waged by the English against the Vikings in the first half of the tenth century had prevented a long-standing Norse political administration putting down firm roots in the north of England, but it was only upon the deaths of Eric Bloodaxe and Archbishop Wulfstan, with control at York passing to Oswulf of Bamburgh, first Earl of Northumbria, that an on-going bid for Northumbrian independence was finally crushed. Even so, the region remained remote, with its own distinct customs. Little wonder Aethelred chose to marry a woman of Northumbrian stock. It was an astute political move.

Having plundered the Bamburgh area, the Viking fleet (possibly the same one that escaped from the Thames estuary the year before) headed south, entered the Humber, and raided into Lindsey (modern Lincolnshire) and the area around York. An English army was raised to bring the invaders to battle. Aethelred can have had little immediate influence on the events that followed. Being based in the South, he placed his reliance on his father-in-law, Thored, and the northern nobility to muster local forces and to confront the Viking host. A 'great army' was gathered, jointly commanded by three leaders – Fraena, Frithugist and Godwine. Godwine is an English name; the other two are Scandinavian, but according to Florence all three were descended on their father's side from Danes. When they squared up to the Vikings, according to all accounts, the three leaders galloped away in panic – 'setting the example of flight' – the rank and file followed hot on their heels. It was an ignominious end to what had started out as a potentially glorious northern replay of Maldon or Watchet. But whereas Byrhtnoth and Goda bravely stood their ground, the northern lords caved in.

Commentators have since suggested that the failure of English forces to confront the Vikings in Northumbria reflected unwillingness among the northerners to put their lives on the line for a king and administration they held in low esteem. This is to retrospectively overstate the case against the king, and to understate the immediate and overwhelming threat facing the northerners, who were probably outnumbered and may never have had to confront a formed and resolute army before. Attempts to steady the English war-bands may have failed in the face of the enemy. Without Earl Thored on hand (he is not mentioned again in the chronicles after 992), resolve may have been lacking. Another possibility is that the English force remained mounted for longer than was wise, facilitating flight. In circumstances such as these, an army disintegrating in the face of the enemy is in no way remarkable. But that their leaders initiated the flight, despite the accusatory tone of the chronicler, is less credible. None of the leaders appear to have been censured as a result of the defeat. A thegn called Fraena – most likely the same Fraena who commanded part of the army in 992 – continued to witness royal charters during the following years, so remained active in public life. Godwine – later Ealdorman of Lindsey – bravely fought and died fighting alongside Edmund 'Ironside' at Assandun in 1016. Despite Florence's reference to all three having paternal Danish ancestry – implying treachery – sharing a Scandinavian heritage would not have prevented their lands from being pillaged by the raiders. They stood to lose as much as anyone else from the Viking onslaught.

The failure of the fleet to entrap the Vikings in 992, the sacking of Bamburgh a year later and the dramatic collapse of resistance that followed in the North had far-reaching consequences politically and militarily for Aethelred. In particular, the failure of his father-in-law's forces in the North to confront the Vikings may have served to encourage previously dormant separatist feelings among its nobility – the consequences of which the Danish king, Swein Forkbeard, and his son Cnut would later take full advantage of. A king's first responsibility was to defend his people. With Aethelred ensconced in the South, this was not always easy when fighting broke out in the North, but kings such as Athelstan, Edmund and Eadred had managed it in the past. A good case can be made in asserting that the sense of alienation and betrayal felt by many in the North suffering loss at this time may have facilitated the later bloodless annexation of the region by the Danes in 1013. Indirectly, it may also have served to reinforce fears among the southern nobility of a dangerous 'fifth column' developing in the northern Danelaw.

'The Insolence of the Danes'

4.1

London was the next place to be attacked by the Vikings. The large Mercian river port on the Thames had by this time become the most important town in the kingdom, with a population estimated at around 8,000 by 1017. Aethelred is known to have held a number of meetings of his council (the Witan) there, and appears to have favoured the bustling commercial centre as a political capital. The Vikings are described as returning up the Thames from the Humber in ninety-four ships – the same number as are said to have first arrived off Folkestone three years earlier – implying either it was the same fleet, or that the chroniclers were muddling up one event with the other. Florence dates their attack on London as occurring on the 8 September 994 – a day celebrated throughout the Christian world as the nativity of St Mary, Mother of God.

Olaf Tryggvason, the likely victor of Maldon, together with Swein Forkbeard, the King of Denmark, led the assault. This first direct mention of Swein being at large in England implies that he was part of the raiding army all along, had recently joined them or had been operating independently in England up until this time. It may well have been Swein's army which had scattered the Northumbrians the previous year after sacking Bamburgh. Given the paucity of information, one can only speculate. Since there appears to have been no great love lost later between Olaf and Swein, the union of their forces may have been purely opportunistic. The Danish king had by this time consolidated his hold on Denmark, as well as parts of Norway. Olaf may technically therefore have owed him his allegiance, although there is no evidence to suggest he ever formally submitted to the Dane. The two men would later become mortal enemies.

Whatever the truth of the matter, to the Viking's surprise and dismay, the defenders of London (the '*burhwaru*', or burh warriors) put up a spirited defence – aided, it is said, by the supernatural intervention of the Blessed Virgin Mary, bountifully manifesting her partiality to the Londoners on this day of her nativity. Standing firm, they thwarted the heathens. In somewhat jingoistic manner, the anonymous chronicler of Aethelred's reign (possibly a Londoner himself) gloried in reporting that the attackers suffered more harm and injury than they ever imagined possible from mere town-dwellers. Manning the walls, the defenders used javelins, arrows and slingshots to deter attacks – as well as bucketfuls of boiling wax, tar and urine to foil the Vikings from making any attempts to undermine the walls. Large rocks and iron-tipped beams – the latter capable of smashing through the wooden keels of Viking river craft – might also have been employed, cast down from fighting platforms on London Bridge.

The first mention of a bridge at London in post-Roman times is from around the middle of the tenth century, when a woman accused of 'pin-sticking' is reputed to have been thrown from the wooden structure into the river. The bridge acted not only as a thoroughfare, but also as a buffer against hostile ships attempting to penetrate up the Thames. An enemy fleet occupying the river would be forced to moor up well downstream. But even so, river-borne trade would be brought to a standstill, placing an economic chokehold on the city. London had been sacked and pillaged by the Danes in 842 and 851, and was again attacked and occupied by Halfdan's army in 870–71. Alfred the Great later recaptured the town in 886, before putting work in place to strengthen its walls. The original Roman walls are thought to have been 20ft high and 8ft thick, so the restored fortifications may have been even more formidable. The settlement sprawled for approximately 2½ miles along the north bank of the Thames. The boggy river valleys of the Lea and Fleet and the marshy wasteland of Moorfields protected its northerly approaches. On this side, a great defensive ditch had also been cut, stretching for approximately 2 miles, providing additional protection. The riverside was also fortified. Near the area known today as Southwark (Suthringa Geworc), on the south bank, where underground trains now thunder past on the Bakerloo line, a great bastion, or 'Borough', had been established to protect London Bridge. Manned by the indomitable Londoners, the fortified bridge and the defensive works at Southwark provided the town with a series of well-sited fighting platforms capable of hosting a furious defence against any river-borne assault. Given the variety and strength of London's fortifications, and the resolve of its citizens (perhaps also the spiritual favour it enjoyed), it is not surprising that the Vikings suffered such a severe setback.

Having received a bloody nose at London, the Vikings are said to have retired, 'maddened with rage', to their bases at the mouth of the Thames estuary, before later resuming their raiding along the South Coast. Earlier successes at Ipswich and Bamburgh may have allowed a certain amount of overconfidence to creep in, and the devastation they later enacted during their foray that year along the South Coast reflects their frustration and anger at being repulsed. Florence vividly recounts how the Vikings:

> Burnt the vills, laid waste the fields, destroyed as many as possible of both sexes by fire and sword, and carried off great spoil … madly scouring numerous provinces [on horseback], sparing neither women nor children of tender age, but slew all with brutal ferocity.

Aethelred had seen one army destroyed at Maldon in Essex and another recently scattered in Northumbria. The Vikings in turn had been severely mauled by the Londoners. In the circumstances, it is understandable both sides should seek some form of accommodation. Forcing a decisive military encounter with the marauders was both difficult to orchestrate and uncertain of outcome, and may have come a long way down Aethelred's notional list of preferred options. The terrible gamble involved in close combat militated against kings seeking resolution to their problems in such an unpredictable manner. Avoiding battle would likely have been equally important for the Vikings, it being one thing to raid and plunder, quite another to face an English army, led by its king, in full battle array. Even the commanders of the large Viking force at Maldon were described in the poetic narrative as intent – initially at least – on seeking a negotiated settlement (payment of tribute) rather than to fight.

No leader in medieval times willingly committed his men to battle unless confident of a reasonable chance of victory. If the anonymous poet's account can be believed, Byrhtnoth at Maldon appears to have been an exception to the rule. As the historian John Gillingham has observed, the reason why a medieval warlord avoided battle was 'precisely because it could be decisive … decisive for the loser as well as the victor, and no general could be absolutely certain of victory'. Before Brunanburh, Athelstan is said to have hesitated until the last moment before confronting Olaf's and Constantine's coalition; as it was, the losing side suffered five kings and seven jarls slain, with the winning side sustaining notable losses too.

Byrhtnoth lost his life at Maldon, as did Goda at Watchet. Later, the even more dramatic deaths of King Harold at Hastings (1066), and Richard III at Bosworth (1485), are prime examples of the fate that awaited leaders on the losing side. For a warrior king to lead his men into battle meant putting his life on the line. What is more, leaders were routinely targeted by the opposition in set-piece encounters. The surest way for an army to achieve victory was to kill or capture the opposing commander. Even the rumoured death of a leader might panic an army. William the Conqueror fought just a handful of battles, and is said to have avoided them whenever possible because of the high risks involved. Aethelred did the same. A prudent ruler sought other – less risky – means of achieving his ends; battle was only joined as a last resort. No wonder priestly hosts preceded armies into battle on the relatively rare occasions they were fought. By invoking divine support, Christian armies sought to conjure God's intercession in the sincere belief that the outcome rested in His hands; pagan armies did the same, in their case to the Gods of the North.

Other than simply avoiding battle and caving in, the alternative was to negotiate. This is what Aethelred's government decided upon in 994 after the abortive attack on London. The treaty that was drawn up identified Olaf Tryggvason, Jostein and Guthmund as the leaders of the Viking force. There is no mention of Swein Forkbeard. Either the Danish king – having briefly allied himself with the Norse – had fallen out with them, or simply decided to go his own way. Swein is reported as being active in the Irish Sea the following year, harrying the Isle of Man. The disconcertingly named Eric 'the Victorious', the King of Sweden, is thought to have opened hostilities with Denmark at around this time, which could explain Swein's sudden departure.

The treaty drawn up between Aethelred and the Norse leaders formalised what was in effect an elaborate protection racket, but one that at least served to put an end to loss of life and property. Not only was tribute promised – a sum of £14,000 – but its terms enabled the raiders to encamp and overwinter on the coast. Locals were directed to make provisions of food and clothing available to them. Aethelred's government set about the raising of tribute from what may have been the first nationwide tax imposed for this specific purpose. Though an expensive option, it nevertheless meant trade could flow unhindered up and down the Thames between England and the Continent, and that day-to-day inland commerce could be carried out without fear of attack. Aethelred also bought a surety from the Viking leaders that they would police the behaviour of their men, while at the same time detailing them to maintain a guard on the coast against pirates from elsewhere. In this respect, Aethelred was emulating his father, Edgar, who – although revered for his peacekeeping – had nevertheless courted a degree of censure through his fondness for outlandish company, in particular his practice of employing Scandinavian and Frankish mercenaries to bolster England's defence. As far back as Alfred's day, as we have seen, Frisian mercenaries had fought alongside West Saxons against Viking pirates. Mercenaries from abroad had been routinely signed up by successive English kings ever since.

With the onset of winter, part of the Norse fleet set up its camp beside Southampton Water – possibly at Woolston on the east bank of the estuary, close to the open sea. The fortified settlement there is thought to have been founded by Olaf Tryggvason. The name Woolston derives from 'Olaf's tun'. The Domesday Book calls it Olvestune. It was an ideal location from which to police the Solent, and also to guard against being trapped should the English renege on their agreements. Even before the treaty of 994 formalised its existence, the site at Woolston likely provided the Vikings with a secure base within striking distance of the Wessex capital at Winchester.

4.2

Though exceptionally fierce and brutal in his methods, Olaf 'Crowbone' Tryggvason – described by the eleventh-century chronicler Adam of Bremen as 'a pagan wizard' – was noted not just for his military exploits but also for his mystical leanings and juggling and athletic abilities; he was capable, it is said, of keeping three daggers in the air at any one time while dancing along a ship's side over outstretched oars. If later Icelandic tradition is to be believed, he was also a particularly courageous commander. Positioning himself prominently on the quarterdeck of his ship at the height of any battle, he is recounted as wearing a helmet inlaid with gold as well as a bright red coat covering his armour so that might be readily seen by his men. Another account relates how his warriors are said to have recognised him simply by the 'awesome swing of his blood-red sword'. Legend has it he was deeply affected by a religious revelation while encamped with his men in the Scilly Isles, having famously completed a circumnavigation of Britain. More plausibly, he awoke to the political benefits that might accrue, should he – like other Scandinavians before him – embrace the Christian faith.

It is no great surprise therefore that Aethelred was able to procure the Norwegian's loyalty by sponsoring his baptism later the same year (994).

Ealdorman Aethelweard of the western shires and Aelfheah, Bishop of Winchester, acted as emissaries for the king. After hostages were exchanged, Olaf accompanied the two men to Andover – at that time a royal estate in Hampshire. It was here that the baptismal ceremony took place. Aethelred acted as Olaf's godfather for the occasion. The two kings embraced as brothers in Christ once the ritual was completed. Olaf promised to become the English king's loyal ally; he would leave England in peace, never to return again to ravage and plunder. In securing the baptism and alliance of an erstwhile pagan warlord, Aethelred was following in the footsteps of illustrious predecessors – Alfred with Guthrum, Edmund with Olaf Guthfrithsson and Archbishop Wulfstan with Eric Bloodaxe (the latter with fingers tightly crossed behind his back).

Not only did the agreement cement peace between Aethelred's government and Olaf's army, it included a number of more commonplace but nonetheless important provisions for safeguarding future trade between England and Norway. The alliance may also have been designed to undermine trust between the Norwegian leader and his Danish overlord, Swein Forkbeard. Stirring up problems between the two men would help to distract Forkbeard in Scandinavia, where the Dane was already busy dealing with threats from the Swedes. Swein, it would appear, was (correctly) viewed by the English at this time as the main threat to their future security. William of Malmesbury succinctly, if somewhat dramatically, summed up the situation, recounting that, 'The evil Viking threat was not thus put to rest; for they [Aethelred's government] could never provide against their enemies from Denmark, who sprang up afresh, like the heads of the hydra'.

Olaf took his new-found religion seriously, stopping off in the Orkneys and Hebrides to bludgeon the locals into accepting the Christian faith. On his return to Norway, he seized the kingship by defeating his main rival, Hakon, Jarl of Hlathir (Lade). Enthusiastically embracing his evangelical mission, he set about converting remaining pagan Norwegians to Christianity – at the point of a sword if necessary. Terrified refugees are said to have sought asylum in Denmark, where Swein Forkbeard – a man more spiritually attuned to pagan ways, even if formally a Christian – remained open to accepting incomers from the old faith. Tradition has it that Olaf was also responsible for the Christianisation of Iceland, though there is no real hard evidence to support the claim.

Aethelred's ploy of driving a wedge between the kings of Norway and Denmark, while at the same time engaging the remaining Viking force as paid mercenaries, had been well judged. Both Olaf and Swein had departed from England, the former never to return; a sizeable remnant of the once-powerful Viking fleet was firmly in Aethelred's employ. Even better, relations between Olaf and Swein had been undermined and would soon worsen further, before escalating into all-out war. Unfortunately for Aethelred it was the Norwegian king who would be killed in the coming conflict, not Swein.

The decisive battle occurred in the year 999, and was fought between Olaf's Christianised Norwegians and a coalition of Swedes, Danes and renegade Norse at the mouth of the Svold estuary on the Pomeranian coast. Leading the coalition against Olaf were Swein Forkbeard and Eric of Sweden (once enemies, they were now in uneasy alliance). A prominently mounted crucifix is said to have adorned the stem of Olaf's flagship, the *Long Serpent*. Bedecked in iron helmets and coats of ring mail, the Norse king's crewmen held aloft shields bearing holy crosses etched out in red, blue and gold. Then, 'at first peep of day', with breakfast eaten, and Mass heard, the battle horns sounded, and the sea fight began. Roped together to form a solid obstacle, Olaf's outnumbered ships awaited the enemy coalition's frontal assault. As the enemy ships approached, attempts were made to drag opponents into contact using grappling irons. Crews were pelted with arrows, javelins and stones – a fearsome preliminary bombardment, which – if successful – might be followed by boarding and hand-to-hand fighting with sword, spear and axe. Warriors assailed in this way might shelter under shields, forming a 'shield-burh' – a defensive parapet of rippling painted boards – fending off the hail of missiles hurled at them. Sometimes the decks of opposing craft could be cleared by missile fire alone. If not, two or even three ships might attempt to lay themselves alongside a beleaguered vessel. Ships seeking to disengage from such an assault had to have the ropes holding them cut away. Sometimes the complete timber heads of ships were hacked away in an attempt to free them from the grip of enemy grappling irons. Lines from the *Heimskringla* – Snorri Sturluson's chronicle of the kings of Norway – vividly describe such an event:

> Many a Viking's body lay dead on the deck this bloody day,
>   before they cut their sun-dried ropes away,
>   and in quick flight put all their hopes.

It appears Swein and Eric's more numerous fleet soon managed to envelop Olaf's flanks, assaulting each ship in line, cutting them away and pushing in towards Olaf's flagship in the centre. His mercenary allies having fled, and with many of his ships destroyed or cast adrift, the defiant king is said to have fallen in the final desperate hand-to-hand melee on board the *Long Serpent*. Reference to the sea fight appears on a runic stone in Scandinavia, raised in memory of an unnamed comrade who is said to have 'died on the sea to the eastwards when the kings were fighting'. The battle's outcome served to re-establish Swein Forkbeard's military control over Norway, and helped consolidate his rule in the region. Once freed from intermittent domestic strife in Scandinavia, he would once again be able to set his sights on the rich prizes to be won across the North Sea. Even so, the diplomatic and pecuniary arrangements made by Aethelred's government in the 990s – outlawing the Vikings for making use of Norman bases and setting Norseman against Dane – had paid off handsomely in the short term, since, for a few years at least, England enjoyed a hiatus in attacks on its southern and eastern coasts.

4.3

Forkbeard's father, Harald 'Bluetooth' Gormsson, appears to have been a particularly successful king, ruling Denmark as well as parts of Sweden and Norway for thirty years from his base at Jelling in Jutland before his death in 986. In his youth, Bluetooth may have been one of the original leaders of the semi-legendary and fiercely pagan Jomsviking cult. The stronghold of Jomsburg, thought to have been located in the Baltic at the mouth of the Oder, is from where the Jomsvikings got their name. Members comprised a mercenary warrior society, militarily active in summer, but held under tight discipline throughout the winter. Booty gained from raids was, it is claimed, shared out and held in common.

Harald Gormsson's nickname is thought to be a reference to his predilection for having his teeth filed to create grooves; then for the grooves to be picked out with blue dye to make them appear more fiercely prominent. Like warpaint used by American Indians and tattoos and body dye used by the Picts and ancient Britons, such a practice may have been the cultic mark of a Jomsviking warrior. Compelling evidence supporting the idea that coloured tooth grooves were at one time de rigueur was uncovered in a grave site near Weymouth, in Dorset, where major roadworks disclosed a tangled mass of headless skeletons; the severed skulls were piled separately to one side. No artefacts were found in the burial pit, indicating that the victims had been stripped and interred naked. It was established that the fifty-four victims were all male, aged around 20, and further detailed dental research indicated the likelihood of them being Scandinavian. The number of men involved indicates this may possibly have been the crew of one or perhaps two Viking longships. All the victims had been decapitated – not from behind as might be expected, but from the front – indicating a ritual execution. No other trauma wounds were found. These men were not war dead. More likely they were prisoners given the right to die a warrior's death by facing their executioner. More pertinently, the teeth found in the skull of one individual had been filed into grooves, as if emulating a Jomsviking such as Bluetooth.

Baptised into the Christian faith ten years into his reign by the German Emperor Otto II, Harald Bluetooth had overseen the adoption of Christianity as the official religion of Denmark. He had also enlarged his territorial overlordship. Sjaelland and Skane were annexed by him, and the strategically important Norwegian region of Viken, located around Oslo fjord, had been brought under his control. From his base at Jelling he became powerful enough to exert considerable influence over an extensive area, and impressive construction works attributed to him include a kilometre-long bridge crossing the Vejle River at Ravning Enge – a project requiring enormous manpower and a vast quantity of timber. Described as one of the great engineering feats of the Viking age, the sheer scale of the undertaking is indicative of a strong central-ised kingship in Denmark at this time. Also credited to Bluetooth is the reconstruction of an impressive 8-mile-long defensive earthwork known as the Danevirke, which extended across Denmark's southern borders and is thought originally to have been built by the Danish King Godfred at the beginning of the ninth century as a buffer against expansion from Charlemagne's burgeoning empire to the south. The construction of a series of circular forts in Jutland and in nearby islands, speculatively considered to have been garrison posts, may also have been overseen by Bluetooth, but despite all this building work the Danish king struggled to stem the tide of encroaching German migration and suffered military defeat at their hands in 974.

The Germans were not his only enemies. Bluetooth was also twice forced to submit to the fabled Jomsviking prince, Styrbjorn 'the Strong', a Swedish exile; according to myth and legend he was the aggressive Lord of Jomsborg. Tradition has it that Bluetooth, to get even, broke faith with Styrbjorn before the fatal Battle of Fyrisvellir by treacherously withdrawing his fleet at the last moment, leaving the Jomsviking warlord to face his ene-mies alone and outnumbered. Fought in the 980s, near Uppsala, the battle had resulted from Styrbjorn's attempt to wrest control of Sweden from his uncle, Eric the Victorious. This is the same Eric who would later threaten Denmark in the 990s, leading to Swein's hurried departure from England. Faced by the might of the Swedes, and without the support of Harald Bluetooth's fleet, Styrbjorn's forces were utterly destroyed. Combatants are commemorated in a number of surviving rune stones which indicate the momentous nature of the conflict. One reads:

> Áskell placed this stone in memory of Tóki Gormr's son, to him a faithful lord. He did not flee at Uppsala. Valiant men placed in memory of their brother the stone on the hill, steadied by runes. They went closest [fought side by side] to Gormr's Tóki.

Another states:

> Saxi placed this stone in memory of Ásbjörn Tófi's/Tóki's son. He did not flee at Uppsala, but slaughtered as long as he had a weapon.

Tóki Gormr's son, or Gormsson, is thought to have been Harald Bluetooth's brother.

For a time during the 980s Bluetooth managed to regain some of his lost territory in the South by capturing and burning a number of encroaching German settlements – also by allying himself with the Slavs, who had at this time risen up against their German overlords. It is thought most likely the Danish king took a Slavic wife to seal the alliance. But soon after this he was faced by a palace revolt led by his rebellious (still pagan) son and heir, Swein. Forced to flee, the exiled king later died in Poland in 986. Why the revolt took place is not known for sure. Possibly it was due to discontent with Bluetooth's rule following a series of defeats at the hands of the Swedes and Norse – also the threat posed by further German infiltration across Denmark's southern borders. A pagan backlash from within the Danish nobility, led by the king's son, may have been another factor. In truth, nobody knows for sure.

   If the Jomsvikings were an elite military arm of the Danes, whose expansionist activities within Scandinavia had been checked first by Eric the Victorious of Sweden at the Battle of Fyrisvellir (c. 984), and then again by the Norwegian Jarl Hakon at the Battle of Hjorungavagr (c. 986), this might help explain why such a large and dangerously under-employed group of warriors looked westwards to vent their aggression and enrich themselves at England's expense in 991. Loss of prestige resulting from successive defeats at the hands of established Scandinavian leaders, and the enormous costs involved (both in terms of material losses and damaged reputations) might best be remedied by raiding in England – still an enormously rich land, ripe for plundering. A later chronicler described the Scandinavian adventurers as being 'attracted like wolves' to England's shores.

As mentioned previously, there was a marked increase in diplomatic activity in the late 980s between England, Normandy and the papal authorities, suggestive of Aethelred's kingdom experiencing problems with raids launched against the south-east of the country from bases in Normandy; this also implies that the Viking attacks were being launched with Norman connivance. The negotiated peace between Aethelred and Richard, Count of Rouen, brokered in 991, came just months before the large-scale attack which resulted in the Battle of Maldon. Richard's expulsion of the Vikings appears to have had the unfortunate effect of encouraging one or more freebooting fleets to descend on England that year.

Bluetooth had been a close ally of the Normans. Swein and Olaf may also have enjoyed good relations with their Scandinavian cousins in France. For a hefty fee, Richard would doubtless have been happy to provide a ready conduit for their plunder through the thriving commercial centres and slave marts of Rouen and Caen. It was only the threat of English reprisals and a clash with the papacy that forced the discontinuance of the practice – openly at least! To what extent Richard was able, or indeed willing, to police the traffic through the many inlets and harbours along the Norman coast in the following years is open to question. The wily Norman may have continued to provide assistance to his Scandinavian cousins under the cloak of the treaty arrangements agreed with Aethelred.

By the end of the tenth century the Viking dukedom of Normandy had become a discrete and autonomous political province within the loosely knit kingdom of France – its capital, Rouen, was described as a predominantly Danish city, comparing favourably with York and London in commercial importance. Pagan incomers to Normandy had begun to accept Christianity in the early tenth century – a common theme both in France and England at around this period. Their leader Rolf's acceptance of the religion was decisive in enabling him to establish a permanent settlement in the lower Seine Valley in uneasy alliance with successive Frankish kings and nobles. Consequently, his son, William Longsword, was able to forge a permanent political presence. The conversion of Guthrum had achieved similar results in England at an even earlier stage – so too had the conversions of Olaf Guthfrithsson and Eric Bloodaxe. But, unlike in Normandy, sustained pressure from expansionist West Saxon and Mercian kings had prevented the Norse or Danes from gaining a long-term dynastic foothold in England – a failure that would be left to the ambitions of Swein Forkbeard to remedy.

4.4

Richard, Count of Rouen died in 996 and was succeeded by his son Richard II, Duke of Normandy. A year after the count's death, the Vikings still based in England, many contracted as mercenaries in Aethelred's employ, broke faith with him and resumed raiding activities along the South Coast. They travelled from their base on the Isle of Wight down the Devon coast, before ravaging extensively in South Wales and the South West, where the Watchet region was again targeted. Florence recounts many villages being burned and a multitude of men slain. Navigating back around Land's End, the raiding army beached their ships in the Tamar estuary and then marched inland, harrying as far as Lydford in west Devon. The nearby abbey at Tavistock, founded just over twenty years earlier by Aethelred's close relative Ordwulf, was looted and burned, and an immense amount of booty was taken back to the Viking ships. These renewed attacks may have resulted from payment of tribute being neglected or withdrawn – either that or because Viking demands for additional money had fallen on deaf ears. Another possibility is that it was Richard of Rouen's death specifically which triggered resurgence in the raids, and that the Vikings opportunistically took advantage of the count's demise to once again begin offloading their plunder in Normandy. A fresh influx of raiders from Scandinavia, Ireland and from the other Norse colonies in the Irish Sea, as well as adventurers from mainland Cumbria – attracted by the news of the easy pickings to be had now that Aethelred's mercenary force had turned against him – also appear to have launched renewed attacks at around this time.

Since no battles are mentioned as having been fought, it falls within the standard Aethelred paradigm to accept that these devastating raids went largely unopposed. But this was not the case. There is strong circumstantial evidence to suggest a large English army was called out to confront the threat. A contemporary diploma mentions the whole army ('*omnis exercitus*') being raised, and the *Anglo-Saxon Chronicle* for the following year claims that men were often called up at this time to confront the Vikings, though apparently achieving little by way of success.

Rather than make their way back eastwards so late in the year, the renegade Viking forces overwintered in Devon. Then, in the spring of 998, they transported their loot back to their main encampment on the Isle of Wight before once again resuming their rampage deep into Dorset by using the riverine estuary of the Frome at Wareham as a forward base of operations. The next year (999) they launched forays up the Thames. London does not appear to have been directly threatened by them, but much of Kent was ravaged and Rochester may have been besieged for a time. Local forces from Kent challenged them and are said to have joined battle stoutly but fled when support promised by the king failed to materialise. Florence blames treachery and mischance for the failure. The *Anglo-Saxon Chronicle* predictably alludes to a lack of resolution on the part of the English, ominously claiming that 'something always started a retreat'. By 'something' the chronicler – chewing his words somewhat – doubtless meant treachery or cowardice.

From all accounts, the English appear to have been on the back foot, with their leaders at a loss as to how to deal effectively with the crisis. But just how big the crisis really was is open to question. The chronicler of Aethelred's reign may have highlighted and exaggerated its effect because the damage done was mainly directed against Church land and property in the South. Equally threatening events unfolding elsewhere – which also required Aethelred's attention – receive scant mention. Yet just a year later a major military offensive was launched into the North-West by Aethelred, where the threat posed by Cumbrian pirates, their Manx allies and the fierce Gall-Gaels of the Western Isles must have been of an equal, if not more pressing, urgency than the more widely publicised Viking attacks launched from the Solent. Evidence one way or the other is lacking and almost nothing is known of the detailed progress of Aethelred's northern campaign of 1000, and what little there is seeks to downplay its achievements.

Aethelred's biographer, the historian Ryan Lavelle, has suggested that Aethelred's aim might have been to force the hostile kings of the North-West into submission under English control. As we have seen, successive rulers of Strathclyde and Man had been a thorn in the side of the English as far back as Athelstan's day, and were causing trouble during King Edgar's reign. A show of force to assert his overlordship may have been long overdue. True or not, the handling of the Cumbrian campaign attracted negative comments – the judgemental chronicler of Aethelred's reign mentioned apparent breakdowns in liaison between the fleet and army, resulting in supplies of food, tents and clothing failing to reach the fighting men in good time. Florence says high winds, not indifferent staff work, were to blame for preventing the fleet from linking up with the army. Failures such as this are commonplace throughout history. If punitive raiding and harrying were the main objectives of the campaign, the king appears to have achieved them. His land forces are reported as 'laying waste the homesteads of the men of Cumbria, burning and ravaging', while his fleet settled accounts with the Norse pirates on Man.

Adding credence to the assertion that Richard of Rouen's death provided the catalyst for the breakdown in relations between the mercenary fleet in the Solent and Aethelred's government, the renegades set off in the summer of 1000 for Normandy to offload their spoils, including live captives. The departure of the Vikings for the Continent meant that the immediate threat to London and the South-East was lifted – but not for long.

The pact agreed in 991 between Aethelred and the Normans (with papal support) had clearly broken down by the end of the millennium. Another English expedition, this time launched by Aethelred on the Cotentin region of Normandy, could have been a warlike reflection of this. The Cotentin Peninsular, also known as the Cherbourg Peninsular, lay outside direct Norman control – the inhabitants being known as 'free' Vikings, owing no allegiance to the dukes of Normandy. Though it appears the objectives of the raid were not achieved, this seaborne strike against the Norman mainland, in conjunction with the more successful campaign in Cumbria, displays an aggressive and responsive stance on Aethelred's part, and one at odds with the traditional view of the English king's weak governance. It also implies that England was far from helpless, and that it boasted a fleet and armed soldiery sufficient to launch retaliatory strikes, successful or not.

England's military problems soon worsened. A large fleet of Vikings sponsored by Swein Forkbeard returned to England in the spring of 1001. Allied to the earlier resurgence in raids on the South Coast and the problems with the pirates of the Cotentin, this prompted an urgent need for new agreements to be formalised between Aethelred's government and the Normans. Marriage between the English king and Richard's teenage sister Emma symbolically sealed the resulting deal. The same year saw the death of Aethelred's mother, the redoubtable Aelfthryth, and Emma's biographer Harriet O'Brien has speculated that the death of the domineering dowager queen may have been timely for Aethelred in respect to any remarriage. O'Brien also hints at matriarchal rivalry preventing Aethelred's first wife, Aelfgifu, from ever being formally crowned or accepted at court – something that Duke Richard doubtless insisted upon for his sister.

The Battles of Aethelingadene and Pinhoe – 1001

Although Swein is not specifically identified as being at large in England until 1003, he almost certainly led the expedition of 1001 and was present at the opening battle of the campaign fought at Aethelingadene, Queen Aelfthryth's flourishing royal estate in Sussex, in May of that year. The battle site is located on the Hampshire–Sussex border, just to the north of the fortress town of Chichester. Known as 'the Dean of the Athelings', Athelstan – Aethelred's eldest son and heir – and his brother Edmund, later known by the sobriquet 'Ironside', were both raised there by their grandmother. The site may even have been chosen specifically by Forkbeard because of its close connections with the English Royal Family and as a deliberate act of provocation against Aethelred upon the loss of his mother, helping explain why such a spirited defence was put up.

In an attempt to prevent the estate and the surrounding area being devastated, it is said that more Danes were killed than English – this despite the Vikings retaining possession of 'the place of slaughter' – the usual yardstick of victory. Eighty-three Englishmen from Hampshire are recorded as having been slain, including two of the king's high reeves and a bishop's thegn. That relatively few were killed implies either that the battle was a comparatively small-scale affair – the English defenders being largely wiped out – or that the English losses represented a fraction of the overall defending force; that the Vikings were fought to a standstill, too battle weary to pursue their defeated foe. If the first of the two alternatives is correct, the fact the fight is mentioned at all can only have been because of the high-ranking casualties and the prestigious battlefield location. If the second alternative is correct, then assuming a 10 per cent death rate, with twice as many injured, as many as 800 Saxons must have been embattled, with perhaps twice as many Vikings – numbers rivalling the much better-known Battle of Maldon. The overall Viking force in England could well have been larger still, with a detachment of fighting men left behind to guard their ships moored up in Chichester Harbour. This was not the first time a Bishop of Selsey and his retinue of monks had been forced to hurriedly seek safety behind Chichester's strong Roman walls, 8 miles to the north. A regular Viking haunt, Selsey – accessible only at low tide – was at one time the capital of the old Anglo-Saxon kingdom of the South Saxons, and its Benedictine abbey (established *c.* 683) had been founded by St Wilfred.

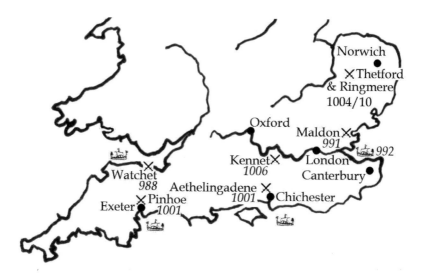

Battles fought during the reign of Aethelred II

Swein's raiding fleet was reinforced sometime later by the defection of several longships under the command of a nobleman named Pallig, a high-ranking mercenary leader in Aethelred's employ. By tradition the defector was related by marriage to the Danish king. During the long days of summer, Swein and Pallig raided up the north bank of the River Teign in Devon, before later travelling back along the coast to the estuary of the Exe at Exmouth, from where they launched a sortie against the stronghold of Exeter. The defenders of the town (its insurmountable Roman walls still intact) are recorded as resolutely withstanding them. Not for the first time the Vikings had bitten off more than they could chew when assault-ing a well-fortified town, and they fell back to their ships, moored up at Exmouth. Some time later, Swein and Pallig are said to have made peace with the locals – but there is no mention of tribute being demanded or paid. It may have been just a temporary truce which enabled the Vikings to forage inland and resupply unmolested.

The raiders are then described as advancing 'in a single journey' (possibly from Exmouth) until they came to Pinhoe, a few miles to the north-east of Exeter. Today, Pinhoe is a bustling suburb dominated by Beacon Hill to the west. The remark 'single journey' was likely made to reinforce the fact that Swein advanced with a degree of rapidity which the English could not match. It was at or near Pinhoe that the English High Reeve Kola and his deputy Eadsige brought the intruders to battle, having first assembled what the Winchester version of the *Anglo-Saxon Chronicle* describes as 'such an army as they could gather' in the time available. Contradicting this somewhat, the Peterborough manuscript describes the English as massing 'an immense army' drawn from the counties of Devon and Somerset.

Fought in the late summer or early autumn of 1001, the battle gets considerable coverage in the annals – more so than the better-known encounter at Maldon ten years earlier. Local tradition places the fighting to the north-west of Pinhoe, on level ground at Poltimore. That the English commanders attacked what may have been a stronger, better-armed force at all is to their credit, although with numerous villages and estates looted and burned, including the important royal estate at Kingsteignton at the head of the Teign Estuary in south Devon, and with Exeter effectively under siege, and commerce up and down the Exe valley disrupted, they probably had little choice. Like most Dark Age battles, a number of scenarios are possible. The earlier mention of a deal being struck between the Vikings and the authorities in Exeter might have enabled the raiders to bring their longships directly upriver and to set up camp inland, before later clashing with the English forces at Poltimore. More cautiously, they may have left their ships under the protection of a strong boat party nearer the mouth of the Exe, and then travelled to the battle site on foot or on horseback. Disregarding the traditional site at Poltimore, the English army could equally well have arrived at the battlefield first, drawing up their forces on the southern slopes of Beacon Hill beside St Michael and All Angels' church (as is sometimes claimed in secondary accounts); an uphill attack was then launched against them by the Vikings.

The two English commanders, Kola and Eadsige, had done the best they could in the limited time available by hurriedly raising a scratch force from the two adjoining counties. Even so, their army was probably smaller than the Danish host. Like at Maldon and Aethelingadene, where both the absolute numbers and the quality of weaponry and equipment favoured the Vikings, the English once again found themselves disadvantaged. Not surprisingly in the circumstances, their resolve faltered almost as soon as battle was joined. Though many are reputed to have been killed, the fact that the two English commanders survived the fight suggests the English managed to break off the action and retreat in reasonably good order. A local legend recounts how a priest slipped through the Danish lines to rally the men of Exeter to come to the English army's assistance, but having returned with reinforcements found the battle was already lost. If not a disaster for the English army, it was for the inhabitants of the immediate area. As Kola and Eadsige's men withdrew, the village of Pinhoe and the other hamlets nearby were ravaged and torched by the raiders.

Successive defeats at Aethelingadene and Pinhoe and the routine trashing of innumerable manors and estates persuaded the king's council to again seek an accommodation with the invaders. The Viking host had by this time retired to their base on the Isle of Wight, but not before ravaging inland throughout southern Hampshire, destroying the manor at Bishop's Waltham along the way. According to the censorious chronicler of Aethelred's reign, the Vikings travelled, 'as was their wont, and none withstood them, nor any fleet by sea dare meet them; nor land force either, however far inland they travelled'.

The following year (1002), Aethelred sent Ealdorman Leosige of Essex, Byrhtnoth's successor, to meet the Viking leaders and arrange for a truce to be agreed. The outcome was for an undertaking on the part of the English to provision the enemy fleet and to pay a tribute of £24,000. Whether the Danish army remained and overwintered in England or dispersed is not known. Some may have remained, settling with other, pre-existing, mercenary garrisons in the South-West and South Midlands.

4.5

Angered by Pallig's defection and emboldened by the arrival of his new queen and the pact agreed with her brother, Aethelred sent out a decree at the behest of his council of leading men that, 'All the Danes who had sprung up in this island, sprouting like weeds amongst the wheat, were to be destroyed by a most just extermination'. The *Anglo-Saxon Chronicle* entry for 1002 recounts that the king ordered all the Danish men who were among the English race to be killed on St Brice's Day, because it was made known to him that they wanted to ensnare his life and the lives of his councillors and to seize his kingdom. How widespread the edict ran and how many Danes were slaughtered as a result is unrecorded. As we have seen, large areas of East Anglia, the East Midlands, and the North had all been settled by Scandinavian *émigrés* during the second half of the ninth century, the incomers having become well established and assimilated. It seems inconceivable the king's directive was aimed at such long-standing communities. All that is known for sure is that on 13 November 1002, many of the Danes living in Oxford, including women and children, were burned alive in St Frideswide's church, having sought sanctuary there from a rampaging Saxon mob. More graphic stories of torture and sexual brutality that circulated later are too salacious to be plausible. Nonetheless, atrocities must have been perpetrated, and the evidence yielded by skeletal remains attributable to the massacre – of frenzied attacks on victims, with slashing, stabbing and crush wounds apparent – supports this assertion.

This massacre is the only historical reference to specific killings occurring. But there must have been others, since the dead of Oxford may have been in large part collateral to the main thrust of the king's draconian initiative. The primary targets of Aethelred's directive were most likely the several hundred or so Danish mercenaries at large in the South-West and along the Thames corridor: relative newcomers comprising men such as Pallig and his followers, who had sided the previous year with the Danish raiders, or were suspected of harbouring treacherous intent against the king.

Having accompanied Swein Forkbeard on his rampage in Devon, Pallig stood rightly accused of betraying Aethelred's trust; this despite the king having made him, according to later chroniclers, 'good gifts in estates, gold and silver'. The mercenary warlord may even have risen under Aethelred's patronage to an elevated rank, a possibility which explains why his defection to Swein appeared so dangerous for the king's security. Lesser land grants had been made to other mercenaries of lower rank. Having contracted to fight on Aethelred's behalf, they too had been well rewarded. Danish settlements may have been established by retired and serving mercenaries in the Severn and Thames valleys, and Pallig may have hailed from one of these communes. Having been allowed to settle in the country, it is little wonder the king was exasperated when many such men sided with the Danish invaders. According to the sometimes unreliable chronicler Roger of Wendover, Aethelred was persuaded to act against the mercenaries by one of his own military commanders, a man called Huna, described as 'undaunted and warlike', who, 'beholding the insolence of the Danes ... came in much distress to the king and made his doleful complaint before him.' The mercenary force in England must have been viewed at this time as a dangerous fifth column, prone to rise up against their paymasters. Understandably, the king and his ministers took steps to neutralise the threat.

To what extent commonplace ethnic tensions also played a part in the killings is difficult to gauge. Disgruntlement arising from mercenary troops being billeted on reluctant villagers would be understandable, but it appears foreign fighters and their families may have set up their own discrete communities, or were settled in mercenary garrisons. It is, of course, quite possible that such places, situated close beside more established settlements became ethnic flashpoints, attracting willing accomplices to enact Aethelred's decree. Speculatively, something along these lines appears to have occurred at Oxford.

Two years after these events, Aethelred offered restitution from St Frideswide's minster at Oxford. But this was not done in the nature of repentance, nor to mitigate the outrage and horror the event aroused, but more prosaically because of the material damage done to the church and for the loss of precious books, manuscripts and artefacts. Escapees from London soon arrived at Swein Forkbeard's court bearing news of the atrocities. Tradition has it that Swein's sister Gunnhild, married to Pallig, was among those killed at Oxford. Caught up in the unfolding tragedy, she is alleged (almost certainly incorrectly) to have been executed on the direct orders of Eadric of Mercia – later Aethelred's right-hand man. Her son is said to have died with her, 'transfixed with four spears'. All of this would be reason enough, were it true, which is doubtful, for Swein to hold a deep-seated personal grudge against Aethelred and Eadric. Nevertheless (the supposed fate of Gunnhild and her son to one side), William of Jumieges, writing seventy years later, considered the rage engendered by Aethelred's decree to have been the root cause of Swein's subsequent attacks on Aethelred's kingdom. Swein had struck firm alliances in Scandinavia by this time, and was therefore free to focus his attention on his rich and vulnerable neighbour to the west. News of the massacres must have served to harden his resolve, and would appear to have resulted in an almost pathological fixation on challenging the English king.

'Winning the Swordmoot'

5.1

The following year (1003) Swein's longships appeared again off Exmouth. Not only was the Dane seeking revenge for the St Brice's Day killings, his failure to take Exeter two years before still rankled. At Queen Emma's behest, Aethelred had appointed a nobleman called Hugh (or Hugo) from her Norman retinue as Ealdorman of Devon. The foreigner predictably became the scapegoat for the town's fall.

Unlike Aelfgifu, Emma was a consecrated queen and her vast dower holdings included Exeter. Swein's determination to ransack the place may therefore have been an angrily pointed response to the treaty agreements reached between the English and Normans; not done simply to avenge the killing of Pallig and the other Danish victims of Aethelred's pogrom. Florence cites carelessness and stupidity on the Norman's part for the town's fall, and hints at treachery. Carelessness is a possibility; treachery is less likely. Only one gate needed to give way, or a single stretch of wall needed to be poorly defended, for disaster to strike. Swein Forkbeard's determined and aggressive leadership likely carried the day, aided by Hugh's indifferent defence. Exeter was then sacked and pillaged with all the accompanying evils of rapine and slaughter. The *Anglo-Saxon Chronicle* states that the raiding army broke in and destroyed the town, taking much spoil. During the attack, or possibly later, they are described as breaking down the town's defensive walls 'from the East Gate to the West Gate'. The devastation they left within can only be imagined. They then returned to their ships, which were soon laden to the gunwales with human and material booty. The unfortunate Hugh's fate is unknown. Perhaps he became a high-profile hostage.

Swein next targeted Wessex. To meet the threat, forces were mustered from Wiltshire and Hampshire under the leadership of Ealdorman Aelfric. This is the same Aelfric previously accused of treachery during the debacle on the Thames in 992. Described as leading 'a very great army' against Swein, a determined stand may have paid dividends. Instead, faced by Swein's great host, he is said to have lost his nerve, 'pulling out his old tricks' and feigning sickness. As soon as the armies embattled, with combat imminent, he is said to have 'pretended to vomit', and claimed he was ill. Later chroniclers observed knowingly that 'when the commander weakens then the whole raiding army is greatly hindered'. The blame for the subsequent failure to confront the enemy is laid squarely on Aelfric's shoulders, though the chronicler's retrospective accusations may have represented as much a veiled attack on Aethelred's military response to the crisis in general, as on Aelfric's leadership in particular.

Just how close together armies in the eleventh century deployed before fighting is of course not known for sure, but cannot have been much closer than 200yds, since this would bring them within longbow range of each other. A Dark Age battlefield must have been a terrifying place. At the start of the American Civil War, the experience of newly recruited men coming face to face with the enemy was likened to 'seeing the elephant for the first time' – a reference to the unexpected shock and horror of combat. The Roman historian Plutarch used a similar analogy when describing an approaching Greek column at the Battle of Plataia in 479 BC, saying, 'Suddenly there came over the entire phalanx the look of some ferocious beast as it wheels and stiffens its bristles.' The terrified Roman General Frigeridus is reputed to have cried off leading his men into battle during the Adrianople campaign (*c.* AD 378) by claiming the sudden onset of gout.

Throughout ancient and early medieval times there are numerous other examples of commanders literally quaking in their boots before battle commenced. Someone such as Aelfric, more politician than soldier, may have hoped to close a last-minute deal with Swein to avoid bloodshed. In like vein, the fourth-century Emperor Valens is said to have remained open to the prospect of a negotiated peace with the Goths at Adrianople right up until the onset of the fighting. Aelfric found himself in a similar situation when faced with Swein's Danish host. But when it became clear his efforts had failed to broker a settlement, Aelfric's discomfiture when faced with the prospect of battle, is understandable. In the face of such an implacable foe his courage must have failed him, and his irresolution led to the dispersal of his army. Nevertheless, the chronicler's use of phrases such as 'up to his old tricks' and 'pretending to vomit' casts the ealdorman in the role of a traitorous villain, rather than merely a man failing to control his nerves under extreme pressure. That he later overcame his qualms would be attested on the field of Assandun in 1016, where he lost his life fighting alongside Edmund Ironside. Despite major upheavals at court in the following years, he also remained – as far as we know – steadfastly loyal to Aethelred. An alternative scenario could be that Aelfric did in fact manage to engineer an agreement or truce. But that once the English army dispersed, Swein (and not for the last time) broke his word and marched on through Wiltshire unopposed, savagely assaulting the West Saxon town of Wilton, among others.

Damaging though the attacks on Exeter and Wilton undoubtedly were, Swein's forces did not at any time threaten Aethelred directly. Nor is there any indication that tribute was demanded or offered as a result of either attack. Rather, the evidence suggests that many of the fortifications in Wessex were hurriedly improved in response to the threat posed, their stone and earthen banks heightened and their ditches deepened. Vulnerable royal mints and monastic treasures were also spirited away to safety out of Swein's reach. The English authorities did not remain quite as stunned and startled as the chroniclers would have us believe, and what steps could be taken to improve security were quickly put in place. Vulnerable locations on the coast or just inland, such as Wareham and Christchurch (Twynham), would have been of particular concern. At Wilton, the moneyers (medieval bankers) had been hurried from the town before Swein struck; they were moved to the nearby Iron Age fortress at Old Sarum. If the Danish king's objective was to raid and harry the English, then he might have been succeeding, but if his aim, as later, was regime change, then he had achieved very little.

The Danish fleet overwintered on the Isle of Wight after the attacks in Wiltshire. The island had become a regular haven for the Vikings, providing them – like Sheppey, Thanet and Grain in the Thames estuary – with a degree of security unmatched by any mainland camp. Swein most likely returned to Denmark. Extended periods away from his homeland were inadvisable with warlike neighbours to the north and east. Yet early the following spring he was once again with his fleet, this time off the Norfolk coast, leading a surprise raid on Norwich.

Hampered from launching attacks from Normandy by the recently renegotiated Anglo-Norman alliance, the sudden switch of target to East Anglia may be seen as a reflection of this. Targeting the East Coast would be more straightforward without recourse to Norman ports. The result was that the English were taken unawares by the timing and ferocity of the attack. Their leaders desperately sought to negotiate, offering tribute to persuade the Vikings to agree a truce. But after several weeks lying to at Norwich, Swein – having grown impatient – once again reneged on his agreement, broke out with his men from their riverside encampment on horseback and attacked Thetford, further inland. In an overnight orgy of looting and destruction, the town was plundered and burned.

On hearing of Swein's breakout, the region's leader, Ulfcytel, ordered an immediate attack on the Viking ships moored in the harbour at Norwich. Later known by the sobriquet 'the Valiant' and described by Florence as East Anglia's ealdorman – Ulfcytel appears to have been an altogether more uncompromising individual than Aelfric, respected by friends and enemies alike for his warlike qualities. The Scandinavian skaldic poet Sighvat refers to Ulfcytel's East Anglians as 'Aelle's kin', and of East Anglia generally as 'Ulfcytel's land'. The former is a reference to the earlier Anglian king of Northumbria, cruelly killed by Ivar the Boneless; the latter, a reference to Ulfcytel's men's Anglo-Danish pedigree. The raiders were well aware of the close ethnic ties shared with the Englishmen with whom they fought, and is one of the reasons why Ulfcytel was held in such high regard by the Vikings as a fierce champion of the land he so resolutely defended. Unfortunately for the East Anglians, Swein had left a strong boat party behind to secure his fleet, and Ulfcytel's attack was beaten off. Had it been successful, the Viking raiding force at Thetford might have been trapped and destroyed. Even so, they were compelled to fight a battle to regain the security of their ships.

The coming together of the opposing forces occurred somewhere to the north-east of Thetford on the road to Norwich, at or near Ringmere – the site of a later battle, sometimes described as a rematch. Such was the fierceness of the fighting, had Ulfcytel's army not been outnumbered, even by their own admission the Danish army would never have managed to escape. It seems that East Anglians were unable to concentrate sufficient numbers against the Vikings. Lack of suitable armour and quality weapons may have also played a part. Chroniclers speak of a great slaughter. Many high-ranking East Anglians must have fallen there. But for the Danes it was a pyrrhic victory at best. Having to fight their way back to their boats, with very little of the loot plundered from Thetford able to be salvaged, many rank-and-file Viking warriors lost their lives too.

Having achieved very little, driven away by the unexpected ferocity of the East Anglian defence, Swein's longships beat out into the North Sea. In doing so, they avoided a devastating famine, which gripped England the following year. Some commentators, including Aethelred's most recent biographer, Ann Williams, have cited this as likely to have been the main reason for their departure – and not the fierce reception meted out by Ulfcytel's warriors. True or not, from the English perspective there was satisfaction in knowing that under Ulfcytel's valiant leadership the raiders had been given a bloody nose, making up to some extent for the earlier defeats in Sussex, Devon and Wiltshire. This would not be the last time Ulfcytel would dig his heels in when faced with overwhelming odds, and he emerges from the shadowy accounts of the period as cast from the same heroic mould as Byrhtnoth and Alfred. Danish veterans of the Battle of Thetford later confessed they had never before in England met such a stubborn and ferocious attack as that made on them by Ulfcytel.

Partly as a result of the rough handling he received in East Anglia, Swein would not reappear in England for the best part of a decade. But other Vikings just as fearsome would emerge in the coming years, and their onslaught would place England on an almost continuous war footing, testing Aethelred's governance and resolve to the limit. Some of their leaders may even have fought with Swein at Thetford, and had most likely lost kinsfolk and close friends in the fighting. Whether present at the Battle of Thetford or not, few warriors in Scandinavia would have remained unaware for long of the potent challenge thrown down by Ulfcytel – among them were men named Tostig, Hemming, Eiglaf, Olaf Haraldsson, Erik of Lade and Thorkill the Tall.

5.2

Eadric of Mercia, known to history as 'Streona', or 'the Acquisitive', was a man on the make. Florence infers that only through cunning and treachery was he able to overcome the handicap of ignoble birth and gain advancement. There seems no doubt he was tough and ruthless, but Eadric did not spring up from the gutter in quite the way Florence would have us believe. Eadric's father, Aethelric, was a nobleman, a thegn from the West Midlands, from the area around Shrewsbury. He is known to have attended Aethelred's court and to have witnessed charters issued by the king from the mid-990s. His son is first identified as witnessing charters in 1002, and is retrospectively linked by Florence with the murder of Gunnhild and her son at Oxford the same year. Eadric's name appears again five years later in 1007, his signature by this time heading the list of thegns, confirming his growing influence at court. Marriage to Aethelred's daughter Eadgyth elevated him to the ealdormanship of Mercia later that year; he controlled an area comprising modern Herefordshire, Worcestershire, Shropshire and parts of Warwickshire.

Eadric's dramatic rise to power coincided with a major upheaval at court in 1006, when Ealdorman Aelfhelm of Northumbria was assassinated, and his sons Wulfheah and Ufegeat were blinded. The reasons for these events occurring are obscure – although in Aelfhelm's case a failure of governance has sometimes been cited as a reason. The Mercian had replaced Aethelred's father-in-law, Thored, as Ealdorman of Northumbria after the fleet debacle in the Thames in 992 and the humiliating military collapse in Northumbria in 993. Being a Mercian, foisted on an unwilling populace, his rule north of the Humber had become fatally undermined and Aethelred used this as a way of ridding himself of a man he had come to fear, for reasons unknown. The *Anglo-Saxon Chronicle* mentions the murders and blindings in a rather terse, matter-of-fact manner, at the same time noting the honourable death the same year of the Archbishop of Canterbury and the elevation to the 'arch-seat' of the ill-fated Bishop Aelfheah, of whom we will hear more later. Florence goes into additional detail, alleging it was the 'crafty and per-fidious' Eadric who bribed the hangman of Shrewsbury (a certain Godwin 'Porthund', meaning Godwin the town dog) to lay an ambush for Aelfhelm while the ealdorman was out hunting in the area. He also adds that the blinding of Aelfhelm's sons was carried out at Cookham in Berkshire in the king's presence.

Countering this, the noted medieval historian Sir Frank Stenton has gone on record as rejecting Eadric's involvement in either murder or blinding, stating that, 'Eadric's notorious treasons in later life made him a person to whom mysterious crimes could safely be attributed, and that the story told by Florence … does not inspire confidence'. He makes a salutary point, one which must be borne in mind when judging future events relating to Eadric. With the State-sponsored killings of Danish mercenaries several years earlier, these purges of the nobility (reminiscent of Hitler's Night of the Long Knives) portray Aethelred in mid-life as a self-assured, cynical and hardened political operator: very much a man of his times. We will never know for sure what crimes or misdemeanours, if any, were laid at the door of Aelfhelm and his sons. But eight years later further killings would be enacted by Aethelred on members of the same extended family, and Aelfhelm's daughter (Aelfgifu of Northampton) would marry Swein

Forkbeard's teenage son Cnut – the future King of England – so it reasonable to assume that the family may (as early as 1006) have posed a threat to Aethelred's regime.

Eadric rose to great prominence in the kingdom in the years between 1009 and 1012, gaining primacy among Aethelred's councillors. Ambition and ruthlessness alone might explain his rise, but other factors were at work too, not least Aethelred's desperate need for strong men of proven military and administrative ability in a period when England was on an almost continuous war footing. That Eadric was a warrior first and foremost (an assertion at odds with the chronicler's portrayal of him as someone who avoided conflict whenever possible) is attested by accounts of him raiding deep into Wales in 1012, as far south-west as St Davids in Pembrokeshire. But it was not only Eadric who gained great office in 1009. Another promoted was Uhtred of Bernicia, who gained the earldom of Northumbria, replacing the murdered Aelfhelm. Three years earlier, Uhtred had inflicted a heavy defeat on the Scottish king, Malcolm II, when the Scots had raided into England from across the border. Newly crowned and flexing his muscles, Malcolm was no lightweight when it came to trading blows. He had seized the kingship of Alba the previous year from his cousin Kenneth III, killing him at the Battle of Monzievaird in Perthshire. Known to medieval chroniclers as 'the Most Victorious', Malcolm would later win undying fame north of the border by defeating the English at the Battle of Carham, on the Tweed, in 1018.

The Scottish attacks in 1006 are recorded in the *Annals of Ulster* as resulting in a heavy defeat for the Scots at the hands of the Northumbrians, an English victory during Aethelred's reign very seldom alluded to, being at odds with the traditional narrative of gloom and doom. Describing Uhtred as a young man of great energy and skilled in warfare, the twelfth-century *De Obsessione Dunelmensis* (a northern tract covering the siege of Durham) claims their hero defeated the Scots by leading the combined strength of Bernicia and York against them. Afterwards the victor is said to have arranged for the severed heads of his captives to be washed by local women before having them impaled on Durham's high walls. The women involved were each given a cow for their troubles. Uhtred's robust defence of the northern borders did not go unrewarded by Aethelred. Occurring at around the same year as Aelfhelm's assassination, the repulse of the Scots at Durham was timely. As a prize, Uhtred gained Northumbria, while Eadric gained Mercia. In this way, Aethelred's new men dismembered Aelfhelm's territories between them.

5.3

The year of Aelfhelm's murder and of the Scottish defeat at Durham, 1006, was fraught with great danger for Aethelred's England. Not only was the North up in arms, but a great Viking ship army, led by the warlord Tostig (thought to have been a relative of Swein Forkbeard's) assaulted the kingdom that year – making landfall at Sandwich in the summer, and raiding throughout Kent and Sussex. Tostig's invasion was serious enough for Aethelred to hurriedly call up the whole strength of Wessex and Mercia. The previous year had been one of famine in England, and Tostig's arrival proved doubly disastrous by exacerbating an already severe food shortage. Not only did the men called up from Wessex and Mercia spend all harvest-time on campaign, but having two opposing armies foraging across Kent and Sussex meant already scarce food resources in the South were further depleted, causing the local people, in the words of the chronicler, 'every kind of harm'.

No battles were fought. Instead, the English forces shadowed Tostig's army, marching and counter-marching, avoiding a head-on confrontation, and launching periodic forays to disrupt the enemy's activities. As winter approached, Aethelred's army dispersed back to their homes. No immediate agreement appears to have been reached with Tostig for tribute to be paid or for his army to be provisioned. Given the antipathy which existed between the king and Swein Forkbeard, Aethelred may have been reluctant to do business with one of the Danish king's proxies. What is more, the food shortages resulting from the previous year's famine, and the current year's disrupted harvest, made any material provision for the Vikings impractical. Instead, the raiders were forced to provide for themselves.

From their bases on the Isle of Wight and the adjacent mainland, Tostig and his men departed from their winter roosts towards midwinter and marched northwards through Hampshire, into Berkshire, to Reading. It appears that a prepared depot – with provisions prudently stashed – lay nearby. These depots – assuming there to have been more than one of them – were, in effect, supply dumps, located around the South at strategic points. Their existence indicates a high degree of forward planning on the part of the Danish high command. But unless protected, or hidden, it seems surprising local English forces would not have sought to destroy them. Berkshire had suffered grievously during Alfred's wars, evidenced by the destruction of Abingdon and its abbey. During Tostig's depredations in 1006–07, the abbeys at Reading and Cholsey were also destroyed. The latter place had been founded by Aethelred in 986 as an act of extirpation for the death of his murdered brother, Edward the Martyr. Doomsayers might have drawn from this that God was not minded to readily wipe the slate clean for that unavenged crime.

Describing Tostig's winter campaign, the razor-tongued chronicler of the times makes a fine play on words, having the firebrand-wielding Vikings defiantly ignite the English warning beacons on their march through Berkshire: a sly dig at Aethelred, emphasising that they travelled inland unopposed before setting Wallingford alight, 'torching it up'. From Wallingford they crossed the Berkshire Downs to Cuckhamsley Knob, a 'moot' or ancient meeting place, daring the locals to fight them there. No challenge materialised. It was not until they reached the River Kennet on the homeward leg that they were confronted by some belated local opposition. But these last-ditch defenders were soon put to flight. The Viking army then marched to Southampton Water, a memorable sight for faint-hearted onlookers tracking their progress from behind Winchester's strong walls.

Aethelred spent the Christmas of 1006–07 with Eadric at Shrewsbury in the Welsh Marches. The chronicler makes a barbed reference to the fact that throughout the period of Tostig's rampage through Berkshire, the king sought safety and comfort north of the Thames. The combination of a Viking ship army at large in the South that year, a Scottish invasion of the North, political upheaval in Northumbria and the ever-present threat of Welsh incursions into the Midlands, may, however, have recommended the Marches as a sensibly central location from which the king could direct affairs of state. While at Shrewsbury, the king and his council decided upon a tax to be levied nationally. It was designed to meet two objectives: firstly to place the country onto a firmer war footing; secondly to bribe Tostig and his men to up and leave. Some commentators have argued that by 1007 it was too late to start rebuilding the country's military infrastructure – but to lay the blame for this on Aethelred is to be retrospectively wise. The plans agreed at Shrewsbury were well formulated and executed. Despite the drain on resources caused by recurrent Viking attacks, England was still among the richest countries in Western Europe. Financial and material means were readily available to set the rebuilding programme in motion, though the money of course had to come from taxation. Part was used to pay the raiding army to leave. The tribute paid was a straightforward bribe to make them go away; there was nothing else to show – no residual mercenary force for Aethelred to call on, nor a treaty signed. In this context, Tostig's invasion can be seen as something of a turning point in English policy, and might best be described as the thin end of the wedge. The country's military capacity had proved to be inadequate to face up to continual onslaughts from powerful foreign adventurers, and at last there was recognition of the fact.

A major militarisation of the country ensued, focused on the building of a sizeable number of warships and the provision of body armour and head protection for the troops. That England was from now on a continuous war-ready footing is attested by the coinage of the period, portraying Aethelred wearing a warrior's helmet, not bare-headed or crowned as would normally have been the case. The directive set by his ministers was for one large ship to be built per 300 hides, with a smaller vessel for every 10 hides. If one man for every 5 'hides', or units of land, was also mustered to crew the ship (in accordance with the traditional Alfredian call-up rate) this would have allowed for a ship's complement of sixty men. Aelfric, the Archbishop of Canterbury (not the scapegoated Wessex ealdorman), bequeathed his best ship, plus sixty helmets and sixty mail shirts to the king – a further indication that sixty men was the standard complement of a warship of Aethelred's day, and therefore larger than in the past, when forty men appears to have been more common. Armour for the ship's crew was also ordered, but this was based on a national levy of one helmet and one byrnie (mail body protection) per 8 hides. Based on a conjectural assessment of around 80,000 hides – which may be too high (since not all regions of England necessarily signed up for the programme) – the overall yield, should it have been realised, would have been approximately 10,000 helmets and byrnies, 250 warships and 8,000 smaller craft.

Ann Williams has suggested in her biography of Aethelred that the provision of armour and helmets might have been the most innovative feature of the directive, claiming the English had up until this time fought largely unprotected. To support her argument she mentions the fact that at the Battle of Maldon the English wielded their spears from behind a 'shield wall', reasonably claiming this might have been because they faced better-armed and better-protected opponents. The Vikings of 991 were warriors by design, not of necessity, so had the advantage. But there are counterarguments. The term 'shield wall', like 'firing line' in the nineteenth century, is a loosely used military term. Harold's men also apparently formed a 'shield wall' at Hastings in 1066, despite being as equally well protected and armed as their Norman opponents. Moreover, the men who manned Aethelred's longships when attacking the 'free Vikings' on the Cotentin Peninsula around the turn of the millennium are described by William of

Jumièges as being well armoured, with mail coats and helmets. Not all of Aethelred's troops were ill equipped. What seems clear is that after 1007 the English fighting men were, by and large, better equipped than before. In respect of 'war gear', battles fought against the Danes in the second decade of the eleventh century were more often fought on an equal footing, as Edmund Ironside's successes against Cnut in 1016 would indicate. It seems that Aethelred's directive of 1007 set in motion a major step-up in military capability – but not necessarily from a zero base.

In spite of the heavy burden placed on them, the regions may have eagerly embraced the militarisation programme. The idea of fighting back, rather than remaining powerless victims, would understandably have been popular among ordinary people, especially for those living on the coast or immediately inland, where the Viking threat was highest, and where the bulk of the shipbuilding effort would be concentrated. By 1009 there were more fighting ships ready to defend the realm than at any other time in the past. No king before Aethelred had ever built as many ships. It is a military achievement rarely referenced, since it is at odds with the dominant discourse of his reign. The new fleet, based at Sandwich, was strong enough to confront and repel any attempt by invaders to strike at England from across the Channel. Not since the great shipbuilding days of Alfred the Great had the country's naval forces been so well prepared to fight off an aggressor. What is more, Aethelred's fighting men were now better armed and armoured than before: a match for their Scandinavian counterparts.

Aethelred's government must have been well aware from reports of traders and travellers of a steady build-up of forces across the North Sea. Swein Forkbeard and his surrogates were known to be planning renewed attacks. The shipbuilding programme can therefore be seen as a hurried attempt to neutralise a known threat, and can be likened to the intensification of efforts to build fighter aircraft in Britain during the 1930s to allay the threat posed by Goering's Luftwaffe. Yet, catastrophically, with the new fleet moored at Sandwich ready for action, many of the ships' crews mutinied. The renegades were led by a certain South Saxon named Wulfnoth, who, having persuaded twenty longships to revolt, set off raiding along the South Coast in much the same manner as any commonplace Viking pirate – causing 'every kind of harm'.

One of those implicated as indirectly sparking the mutiny – having earlier made accusations against Wulfnoth (regarding some undisclosed misdemeanour) – was Eadric's brother Brithtric, the fleet commander.

The sense of the wording in the *Anglo-Saxon Chronicle* is that Brithtric, the brother of Ealdorman Eadric, accused Prince Wulfnoth of some wrongdoing to the king, leading to Wulfnoth's flight; later Brithtric decided to make 'a great reputation for himself' by pursuing the mutineer and attempting to capture him 'dead or alive'. With eighty longships, he set off in pursuit. The fates were conspiring and soon terrible gales blew up. They were storms worse than anyone could remember. Unlike Wulfnoth's ships, Brithtric's were caught by the gales while at sea and were 'battered and thrashed to pieces and cast ashore'. Wulfnoth – having sought shelter in good time, then mercilessly fell on the remnants of Brithtric's battered fleet, destroying any remaining ships by burning them as they lay broken and beached. Brithtric's personal fate goes unrecorded, as does that of Wulfnoth.

It is thought that the king may have been present reviewing the fleet at the time the original accusation was made against Wulfnoth. Though it is impossible, given the lack of information available, to ascertain with any degree of confidence exactly what the nobleman stood accused of, one suggestion is that he was part of a faction working to undermine the influence of Eadric at court. Rather than face the consequences of being accused, he mutinied. Why Brithtric should be indirectly blamed for what occurred is not immediately apparent, but since Eadric (his brother) gets the blame for most of what subsequently goes wrong in Aethelred's reign, such scapegoating might well be best ignored. Wulfnoth was the father of Godwin, who, during the later reign of Cnut, would become the most powerful nobleman in England. This is perhaps why later chroniclers were wary of judging his father too harshly.

The remaining ships still moored at Sandwich (presumably too few to credibly deter invaders) were hurriedly secured and brought back up the Thames to London. This was apparently done on the initiative of their crews rather than on the orders of the king's council. The lamenting chronicler pictures Aethelred at Sandwich, anxiously awaiting news from Brithtric. When he learned of the fate of the fleet, the king is said to have returned home (possibly to London) with an unnamed ealdorman (Eadric, perhaps) and his chief councillors. The chronicler states he 'lightly abandoned' the remaining ships at Sandwich, and that were it not for the initiative shown by his subordinates, the remaining ships might too have been lost. The picture conjured is of a dejected king willing to throw in the towel. It is one of the most damaging passages in respect to Aethelred's governance, portraying the king as weak and overwhelmed by events, and of his council split by factional infighting – carelessly oblivious of the need to secure the remaining ships. But once again we should be wary of taking too much at face value. The chronicler is heavily retrospective and decidedly hostile. Nonetheless, England's windswept coasts were once again wide open to Viking attack.

5.4

As if on cue, another Viking raiding army, led this time by a coterie of fierce Scandinavian warlords, probably operating independently of any Scandinavian king, arrived at Thanet in August of the same year (1009). Prominent among them (both in a command sense and in stature) was Thorkill the Tall, described as 'the leader of a gang of thugs from the Baltic', the son of the Danish Jarl of Zealand, Strut-Harald. Florence describes how:

> Turkill, a Danish jarl, came over to England with his fleet [and that] afterwards in the month of August another countless fleet of Danes, under the command of Hemming and Eiglaf, came over to the isle of Thanet, and without delay joined the other fleet.

Little or nothing is known for certain of Thorkill's earlier career. Though mentioned in the sagas as having fought alongside his brother Sigvaldi (the leader of the notorious Jomsborg Vikings) at the Battle of Svold, the historian Alistair Campbell (no doubt correctly) describes such early accounts as 'shadowy and uncertain'. Though just one of a number of Viking leaders who arrived in England that year, Thorkill's prominence in the chronicles and later histories reflects the close ties he retained with England from then onwards, more than his initial standing among the invaders.

Hemming and Eiglaf remain no more than names, although the former could possibly – like Sigvaldi – have been Thorkill's brother. According to Campbell, Eiglaf might have been the same man who later became an earl during the reign of Cnut. But such claims are far from certain. If Thorkill's background is shadowy, Hemming's and Eiglaf's are even more so. Thorkill's brother Sigvaldi is thought to have been killed in England during one of Swein Forkbeard's attacks on the country earlier in the decade. Claims that Thorkill's motive for attacking England was to wreak revenge on the English for his brother's death may relate to this event. Even so, the lure of treasure in the form of tribute and loot would have been reason enough for a hardened opportunist like Thorkill to abandon his Baltic base on the River Oder in 1009 and lead his warlike band to England, without any added vengeful incentive.

The mercenary gang Thorkill was part of hailed from far and wide, not just comprising Danes, but also Swedes, Norwegians and other Baltic raiders. Separate saga evidence places the future saint and King of Norway, Olaf Haraldsson, as being among Thorkill's companions. In the *Heimskringla*, Snorri Sturluson has this to say:

> Then Olaf [Haraldsson] sailed to Denmark. There he met Thorkill the Tall, the brother of jarl Sigvaldi, and Thorkill joined him, because he was at that time all ready to set out on a warlike campaign. So they sailed south along the coast of Jutland, and at a place called Suthrvik they won a battle over many Viking ships.

Olaf Haraldsson's early career is no less hazy than Thorkill's. Like his tall companion he would go on to play a major role in unfolding events in England. Born in 995, or thereabouts, Olaf must have been just 14 years of age in 1009. Nevertheless, Campbell has described him as someone who had followed a career of desultory violence and robbery around the coasts of the Baltic and the North Sea up until this time. Confirming this, the *Heimskringla* boasts that Olaf had already fought a number of battles before arriving in England. The first three occurred in Scandinavia; a fourth, at a place called Suthrvik, probably Sondervig in Jutland. A fifth battle in the sequence took place off the north coast of Holland, and a sixth is recorded as an attack on London Bridge. The latter probably relates to a fight in 1013 or 1014, so is most probably misplaced chronologically. The Battle of Hringmara-heidr, fought in Ulfkell's land in May 1010 (Ringmere, near Thetford, fought in Ulfcytel's land), is listed as number seven in the sequence. Olaf would have been just 15.

Having made landfall at Sandwich, the Vikings marched on Canterbury, where the terrified citizens agreed a peace by making them a payment of £3,000 to go away. Florence describes how, having been paid off, 'The Danes went back to their ships, and directed their course to the Isle of Wight, whence they made frequent descents for pillage on the sea coasts of Sussex and [Hampshire] the province of Southampton'. To meet the threat, Aethelred raised another large army, just as he had done three years earlier in similar circumstances. This time it was raised on a national basis and apparently collected from all parts of England, although regions such as Wessex, East Anglia and Mercia must have borne the brunt of the burden. Whether the same kind of shadowing tactics were employed as in 1006 against Tostig is not clear. The Vikings apparently ravaged unchecked in Sussex, Hampshire and Berkshire from their base on the Isle of Wight, burning 'numerous vills' throughout the autumn. But this may have been before the English army had been fully mustered.

Aethelred deployed his forces at strategic points along the coast, and on one occasion managed to interpose an army between the Vikings and their ships. Intent on a showdown – having made up his mind on this occasion 'to conquer or die' – the king was persuaded against such a drastic course by his advisors. Florence relates how Eadric used all his endeavours, 'by wiles and crafty speeches', to prevent a battle and to allow the enemy to depart unchallenged. The *Anglo-Saxon Chronicle* ruefully adds that 'everybody was ready to attack them, but it was Ealdorman Eadric who hindered it, as it always was'. There is no explanation given as to why this should have been the case, just that the 'perfidious' Mercian allowed the enemy to regain their ships unhindered. Florence even goes so far as to make an accusation of treachery.

Like Aelfric before him, Eadric is targeted by the chroniclers as the scapegoat for the ills afflicting the nation at this time. But since we are not in possession of all the facts as regards the size of the armies or the terms of the agreement, it would be wrong to rush to judgement. Yet, with hindsight, Aethelred may have wished he had acted more aggressively, since whatever was agreed was soon reneged on by the marauders.

At the height of the Viking depredations, the king's council, in desperation, initiated a programme of penitential prayer and fasting. The nation's priests led their flocks barefoot to church, carrying relics and invoking Christ. It made no difference – the military crisis deepened. The religious counterattack was led by Archbishop Wulfstan, known by his nickname 'Lupus' – the wolf. Contemporaries claimed that when he spoke it was as if his listeners were hearing the very word of God himself. Ann Williams has suggested that if Eadric was the evil genius of Aethelred's reign, the role of good angel should be assigned to Archbishop Wulfstan. Addressing the growing Viking menace with a barrage of prayer, the churchman saw the attacks as a scourge visited on his people by a wrathful God, and sought to use the fear invoked by their terror to bring people closer to salvation.

While ardent believers invoked God's intercession, Eadric, more practically, led the call for tribute to once again be paid. The chroniclers castigate him for this, claiming the English were ready to fight back, but that any military response was thwarted by the ealdorman. Despite the loss of a sizeable number of ships during the recent disastrous mutiny, Aethelred's defence programme must have yielded some tangible increase in the nation's fighting capability, so squaring this with what appears to have been a triumph for contrasting religious and pecuniary intervention strategies is something of a puzzle. Wulfstan, as we have seen, had his own apocalyptic reasons for talking up the threat. Eadric too is accused of having an agenda – seeking to gain financially from the raising of the tribute tax (Danegeld). An illustration of this is provided by the case of Aethelric, Bishop of Sherborne. Short of funds, he was obliged to sell an estate in Dorset to pay the tax. Eadric apparently snapped up the property at a knock-down price, and sometime later sold it on at a fat profit. Transactions such as this may have gained the unpopular ealdorman his nickname Streona – the Acquisitive.

As a result of Eadric's intervention, and the promise of tribute, the Viking fleet set off from the South Coast for the Thames sometime after Martinmas (the Feast of St Martin, 11 November), and set up their winter camp at Sheppey, from where they launched raiding sorties into Essex and Kent. If they had promised they would leave England altogether, the king and his ministers were to be disappointed. Only London's strong defences prevented the town from being stormed, and several furious attempts were made by the marauders to do so. After Christmas, the heathen army marched inland to Oxford, via the Chilterns. The fortress town was burned – possibly a belated response to the earlier massacre. By avoiding an English blocking army outside London, the raiding army then crossed the Thames at Staines and returned to its base on the south bank. In the spring of 1010 the Danes are recorded as being securely moored in Kent, mending their ships in preparation for a major onslaught into East Anglia (Ulfcytel's land). The military highpoint of this would be another great battle fought, as before in 1004, near Thetford.

Echoing the ubiquitous vengeance theme, Ann Williams has speculated that the battle fought there (known as the Battle of Ringmere) may have been conducted in the nature of a rematch of the Battle of Thetford – a sort of long-overdue settling of accounts. As previously mentioned, Thorkill's high-profile Jomsviking brother, Sigvaldi, may have been killed while campaigning with Swein Forkbeard soon after the turn of the millennium. Other Vikings (and Englishmen too) may have had their own scores to settle. Cause enough, if true, to make (for Thorkill at least) the rematch personal. Having landed at Ipswich, the Vikings are said to have 'sought out' Ulfcytel's land specifically. Long-held grudges needed closure.

The Battle of Ringmere – 5 May 1010

Ringmere, located just to the north-east of Thetford, is where Thorkill's army is recorded as destroying Ulfcytel's coalition of forces from the eastern counties on 5 May 1010. Fighting far inland from their base (which was maybe at Harwich), the Danes 'piled up a heavy heap of slain', and Ringmere Heath is said to have been 'reddened with blood'. There are echoes of the Maldon campaign nineteen years earlier: Ipswich was targeted prior to both battles, and then an Anglo-Saxon army was hurriedly assembled, agreeing to fight a stronger Viking host on equal ground – in this case at an apparently prearranged battle site, most likely the same one that hosted Swein and Ulfcytel's bloody encounter in 1004. Tostig's unfulfilled challenge at Cuckhamsley Knob in the winter of 1006–07 ticks the same boxes. But unlike at Cuckhamsley, where the English failed to show up, Ulfcytel, with the men of East Anglia, Cambridgeshire, and perhaps Hertfordshire and Bedfordshire, was there, ready and waiting. Located on level heathland, the 'moot' place at Ringmere was in easy travelling distance for fighting men from far and wide.

Florence describes the battle as 'severely fought', the Cambridgeshire contingent of Ulfcytel's army standing firm when combat was joined. The men of East Anglia were, on the other hand, immediately broken by the ignominious flight of a war-band led by the exotically named Anglo-Danish turncoat Thurcytel Mare's Head. Previously a Dane in Ulfcytel's service, Mare's Head's actions unmanned the easterners. The *Anglo-Saxon Chronicle* as usual implies treachery, which, if it were true, would rank the renegade with other equally memorably named turncoats, such as Sir Faithful Fortescue, famous for dramatically switching sides at the last minute at Edgehill in 1642. But the placement of blame on Thurcytel draws a suspicious parallel with earlier allegations, where ethnicity was implied as a factor – the main example being that of the three northern Danelaw thegns: Fraena, Frithugist and Godwine. Those men, like Thurcytel, had their names blackened when accused of 'setting the example of flight' in 993.

Whatever the truth of the matter, the Cambridgeshire men, unlike the East Anglians, remained unfazed by Thurcytel's desertion and fought on. They are said to have held their ground for a long while, until at last being overcome and compelled to retire. Whether this was done in good order or as a rout is not mentioned. The latter seems most likely, since many English noblemen were killed at Ringmere, including the king's son-in-law, Aethelstan. Olaf Haraldsson's saga makes no mention of how the battle was fought or of Thurcytel's treachery, merely lauding him as 'winning the swordmoot' there. Thord Kolbeinsson's *Lay of Eirik* describes how its hero, Erik of Lade, another participant of the battle, was at the forefront of the fray, 'thinning out' the English ranks, and 'reddening Ringmere'.

After the battle, the Danes took horses from their beaten enemy and ravaged the Fenlands for the next few months, burning down Thetford and Cambridge. Unlike London and Exeter, such places had not maintained adequate fortifications. The victorious Danes then travelled westwards, ravaging Oxfordshire and Buckinghamshire, and along the River Ouse to Bedford and Tempsford. Sometime before the feast of St Andrew (30 November), they torched the market town of Northampton, before travelling south into Wessex and looting the greater part of Wiltshire. Cannings Marsh (Old or All Cannings in Wiltshire) is mentioned specifically as being targeted by the marauders. At midwinter the Vikings fell back, unopposed, to their ships on the Thames.

The raiding itinerary undertaken by the Vikings in the late autumn and early winter of 1010 appears unusually complex and wide-ranging. There may have been two or more raiding armies at large in the country: one or more operating north of the Thames; another, or others, in the South. Given that several high-status leaders are known to have been in England at the time, two or more armies operating semi-independently seems not at all unlikely, and might explain why the English failed so abjectly to contain them. Supporting this contention, the *Anglo-Saxon Chronicle*, in its usual exasperated and mocking fashion, criticises the English response to the Danish incursions, stating that when the enemy was ravaging the eastern counties, the king's army was in the West, and when the southern counties were attacked, the English army was in the North.

Unlike in Alfred's day, the Viking threat in the first decade of eleventh century was a more mobile and unpredictable one. With no intention of settling down, and without the encumbrance of wives and children, the Viking raiders – freelance operators such as Tostig, Thorkill and Olaf Haraldsson – were much more difficult to pin down and subdue than men such as Guthrum or Haesten. Whereas a high proportion of Alfred's and Edward the Elder's victories were the result of overrunning or laying siege to established Viking encampments, Aethelred was faced by Viking armies which operated directly from where they moored their ships, usually somewhere inaccessible such as the Isle of Wight, Thanet or Sheppey. Examples where Alfred and his successors pinned their enemies down, such as at Chippenham in 878, Benfleet in 893 and at Buttington the same year, were not repeatable in Aethelred's day. At Tempsford in 918 Edward the Elder destroyed the Vikings' forward base on the Ouse, allowing him to make inroads into the eastern Danelaw. But, unlike Edward, Aethelred was not at war with the Danelaw, and was therefore denied such a strategy. Little wonder he grew increasingly desperate.

Just before Thorkill's attacks on Northampton and Wiltshire, the king hastily convened a council of war. All his councillors were required to attend. The only item on the agenda was how to stop the Vikings. But the plans that were drawn up were never executed. By this stage – in the wake of Ringmere – none of the English leaders were willing to put their lives on the line. It appears that individual shires, when attacked, failed to assist each other, 'each [leader] fleeing as best as he could'. Though faced with an unprecedented challenge, it is both a damning indictment of the king's inability to orchestrate a united response and of the morale of the nation's leaders at this time of crisis.

5.5

The following year (1011) messages were sent out to the Viking leaders suing for peace, with the promise of a hefty tribute. The response mirrors the approach made to Tostig several years earlier. The *Anglo-Saxon Chronicle* lists the counties devastated during the raids of the preceding year:

> East Anglia; Essex; Middlesex; Oxfordshire; Cambridgeshire; Hertford-shire; Buckinghamshire; Bedfordshire; half of Huntingdonshire; much of Northamptonshire; parts of Kent and Sussex, especially the area around Hastings; Surrey; Berkshire; Hampshire; much of Wiltshire.

Since the attacks were focused on East Anglia, the South-East Midlands and the South, including areas we would today call the Home Counties, the Viking raids appear to have left most of the northern Danelaw and the western regions of England, with the notable exception of Wiltshire, unscathed. The chroniclers bewail the fact the English could not be mar-shalled to fight, and that payment of tribute could not be made in time to prevent bands of marauders from travelling about everywhere, raiding and 'roping up' the wretched people. In the autumn of 1011, upping the ante, the Viking forces raided into Kent and dug a great trench around Canter-bury. They then laid siege to the city, blockading it for nearly three weeks before launching a successful assault. The fighting at Canterbury is listed by Snorri as 'battle number eight' in the series of battles fought by Olaf Haraldsson. Simeon of Durham paints a lurid picture of the events, describing how the Vikings broke into the town and went on the rampage, killing many and seizing Archbishop Aelfheah, among others. Simeon states:

> On the twentieth day of the siege [29 September 1011] part of the city was burnt, the enemy entered, and took the town. Some were killed with the sword, some perished in the flames, many were thrown headlong from the walls, and some died, being suspended by the privy members. Matrons dragged by the hair through the streets of the city, at last were thrown in to the flames and perished. Infants torn from their mother's breast were carried on pikes, or crushed to pieces by a wagon driven over them. Meanwhile Archbishop Aelfheah was taken, bound, imprisoned, and tormented in various ways. Christ's church [the cathedral] was pillaged and burned, and all the monks and laity, men, women and children were decimated; nine out of every ten being slain, and the tenth kept alive. This decimation extended to the total amount of four monks and eight hundred laymen.

Taking the archbishop captive held the promise of a hefty ransom. Other important hostages included Godwin, Bishop of Rochester; Leofrunna, an abbess from Thanet; and Alfred the king's reeve, as well as many other common people, who were enslaved.

The price demanded for the archbishop's freedom was £3,000, but the stubborn churchman, allegedly, refused to allow himself to be bartered, despite being imprisoned in fetters for seven months. As if enacting judgement on the Danes, Florence details an outbreak of plague or typhus, described as 'an excruciating disorder of the bowels' afflicting the garrison at Canterbury. Upwards of 2,000 of the raiders are said to have been struck down by the outbreak – 'as if by God's wrath'. Though this is likely an exaggeration, the attack mirrors the experience of soldiers through the centuries encamped in foreign parts. The 250 or so skeletons unearthed at Repton attest to a similar fate befalling the Danish garrison there during the winter of 873–74. In more modern times the experience of servicemen in the Crimea comes to mind.

Eighteen years earlier, Archbishop Aelfheah had taken part in the baptism of the equally fierce Olaf Tryggvason. It is unlikely therefore that he would have been discomfited to find himself once again in the close company of warlike pagans. He was a pious and brave man who may have welcomed martyrdom and the certainty of being received into Heaven as one of God's chosen. But he cannot have welcomed the manner of his death. He was dragged before a committee of drunken Danes, then bludgeoned with stones, bones and the heads of oxen, until a Viking named Thrum, converted the previous day into the Christian faith, took pity on him and clove his head in two with an axe. Thorkill is stated to have been angered at the indiscipline of his men, and from then on sought to break away from their company. Yet neither the taking of prominent hostages, nor the violation, death and enslavement of the populace of Canterbury is recorded as disturbing Thorkill's conscience. The giant Dane and most of his colleagues remained of a heathen mindset, worshipping the spear-wielding Odin, Thor with his mighty hammer and Frey with his potent phallus. It seems unlikely therefore that the Jomsviking warlord would lose much sleep over the death of the archbishop, though that is what we are led to believe. The following day, 20 April 1012, the archbishop's battered corpse was transported from Greenwich to London, later to be buried with much ceremony at St Paul's.

Eadric of Mercia and other English leaders had arrived in London in the spring of 1012, before Easter time, and had raised an amount variously stated as £8,000 or £48,000 (the latter seems more likely) to end the Danish depredations. The tribute equated to approximately £3,000 per county (taking the higher monetary figure, and fifteen counties as the divisor). To raise the money, King Aethelred was forced to institute a new and oppressive annual land tax. No doubt the collection and payment procedures left plenty of scope for corrupt practice. If true to his nickname, we can only speculate as to what extent Eadric Streona benefited. Archbishop Aelfheah was still alive at this stage, and it seems likely – if Florence is correct – that he was killed before the tribute was paid, though there is no firm evidence to support this. Thorkill's outraged reaction to the killing adds credence to the notion, however; conjecturally, his anger was stoked not by the cruel treatment meted out to the churchman, but by the possibility that the offer of tribute might be withdrawn following the prelate's brutal and unwarranted killing. He need not have worried. The threat of further violence persuaded the English to hand over the money. Once paid, the bulk of the hostile raiding army left for Scandinavia, dispersing 'far and wide'.

Though not specifically named in the near-contemporary sources, Thorkill appears to have stayed behind in England with the forty-five longships (almost 2,000 men) at his disposal, and to have come to a separate understanding with the English king, promising to protect England from further raids if supplied with winter provisions and granted secure moorings. Perhaps Jomsborg was no longer safe for this tall Dane? His falling out with former colleagues after the death of Archbishop Aelfheah may have been more deep-seated than the sources indicate.

Thorkill may also have broken faith with Swein Forkbeard in making the deal with Aethelred. Swein possibly exerted a loose overlordship over the various bands of adventurers such as Tostig and Thorkill – though there is nothing definite to suggest this to have been the case. Nevertheless, Thorkill's arrangements with the English king were provocative, and against Danish best interests – fuelling Forkbeard's resolve to neutralise the threat, and at the same time to bring Aethelred to book for long-standing grudges held. Some historians have even speculated that Forkbeard might have been present when Archbishop Aelfheah was martyred. They base this on a brief account in the *Annales Cambriae* which claims Swein was shipwrecked off the British coast at some point in 1012. It is a claim which also ties in with another one made by the Canterbury chronicler Osbern, who recounts how the archbishop's killers came to grief in a storm shortly after setting sail from England. Osbern's story of 160 ships being wrecked at sea and a further 65 being swept to some distant shore, where their crews were slaughtered, is likely an exaggeration, if not a religiously inspired fiction; nevertheless, the coincidence of the two accounts is suggestive. Given the size of the tribute paid, it would not be incredible that Swein should have wished to be on hand to secure his share of the prize.

Thorkill's decision to hire out his men's martial services to the English must have promised a better return than Swein could match, or than could be achieved by operating alone, on a freelance basis. To the modern mind this bears all the hallmarks of a blatant protection scam. But, given the military shortcomings of the English, it must have seemed a necessary evil. From Aethelred's perspective (the archbishop's death to one side) the developments were positive overall. The bulk of the Viking fleet had by this time sailed away and was either destroyed at sea or dispersed back to Scandinavia as widely as it had been collected. Money raised from taxation was now being channelled into paying Thorkill for the services of a ready-made fleet. At the time it may have seemed Aethelred's England had bought the necessary breathing space to recover. England was still a wealthy state, with a burgeoning population estimated at around 1.5 million. Now, for the first time in many years, it was free from depredating Viking forces – but for a short while only!

6

Swein Forkbeard's Invasion of 1013

6.1

The chickens came home to roost in the summer of 1013 when Swein Fork-beard launched his invasion of England. Colourful figureheads shaped as mythical or monstrous creatures are said to have gazed expectantly landwards from the prows of his 'dragon ships' as they made first landfall at Sandwich in Kent. Some were carved as angry bulls with necks erect; others, as gaping serpents. Vanes at the ships' mastheads fluttered in the form of fabled birds and fire-breathing dragons. The Danish king remained at Sandwich for several days. Each tide brought in fresh reinforcements. No resistance came from Thorkill's mercenary fleet, now in the pay of the English king, or from the remnants of the old English fleet, if it still existed in a useable form at this time. Imposing an effective screen or blockade against invasion was near impossible in any event and the Viking roost at Sandwich (a defensible headland) had been used by raiders with impunity many times in the past. The greatest danger to Swein's ships would come while they were moored up, open to a sudden attack from the sea – but none materialised.

Sandwich in the Dark Ages appears to have been a magnet for Viking invaders from the Continent. The short crossing time across the Channel minimised the risks involved. Located at the apex of an anvil-shaped promontory, jutting out towards the Isle of Thanet, and sheltered between the North and South Forelands on Kent's east coast, the Sandwich area was geographically well sited for first landfall. Once the Vikings had travelled across the narrow Straits of Dover, the nearby Isle of Thanet, more wooded then than now, and separated from mainland Kent by the Wantsum

1. The River Trent between Newark and Nottingham – the route inland for Ivar's forces when attacking Mercia in 867.

2. The monument at Athelney in Somerset, the site of Alfred's refuge in 878 prior to the battle of Ethandun.

3. Lynmouth harbour. In the distance the clifftop ramparts of Wind Hill at Countisbury, where the West Saxons were driven by Ubba's Vikings in 878 before the Battle of Cynwit.

4. The probable battle site of Ethandun, looking toward the high ground of Salisbury Plain from Edington priory church.

5. The White Horse near Edington in Wiltshire, close to the battle site of Ethandun – 878.

6. Kingly Vale in Sussex, the alleged site of a battle fought between the men of Chichester and the Vikings in 893.

7. The strong Roman walls at Chichester – one of Alfred's coastal burhs.

8. The West Wall of the burh of Wareham in Dorset.

9. St Michael's & All Angels' church on Beacon Hill at Pinhoe, near Exeter – thought to have been built on the scene of fighting in 1001 between the Danes and the men of Devon and Somerset.

10. Beacon Hill near Pinhoe – one of several possible sites for the battle fought in 1001.

11. Remains of Iron Age fortress, known as Kenwalch's Castle, at Penselwood – the probable scene of fighting between Edmund Ironside and Cnut in the spring of 1016.

12. The Rattlebone Inn sign at Sherston – close to the site of the battle fought at midsummer in 1016.

13. The Saxon church of St Martin in the Walls, Wareham – destroyed by Cnut in 1015, and reconsecrated by him in 1020.

14. Bosham church in West Sussex – Harold Godwinson prayed there before setting out on his ill-fated journey to Normandy in 1065.

15. Viking longship at sunset. (*Courtesy of and copyright of Mark Milham*)

16. The Burrow Mump near Athelney, a defended outlier.

The replica Viking longship at Pegwell Bay, Sandwich, Kent.

Channel, afforded a naturally moated and defensible haven for an extended stay. Canterbury (*Durovernum Cantiacorum*), more than once a target for the raiders, lay just 20 miles inland along the then-navigable River Stour. The Wantsum Channel remained an important and commonly used route for traders and raiders – avoiding the perils of Kent's North Foreland – right up until the twelfth and thirteenth centuries, when heavy silting occurred. By the sixteenth century it had dried up completely, Thanet becoming no longer really an island, though it was still named as such.

In an effort to contain earlier piratical forays across the channel, the Romans had built imposing forts at Richborough (*Rutupiae*) and Reculver (*Regulbium*), located at either end of the Wantsum Channel. Roads linked the two coastal forts with another at Canterbury. During later centuries the forts lay unmanned. Vulnerable then, the area remained so right up until Aethelred's time and beyond. Inhabitants are said to have sought the heavily wooded areas inland as sanctuary from Viking pirates who regularly infested the island. At Chesmunds, in central Thanet, there are still traces of defensive entrenchments. Also, several underground caves have been discovered which appear to have been deepened and enlarged by locals hiding out from raiders. Named by the Danes as 'the camp on the sands', Sandwich had earlier been chosen as a convenient landing place for Claudius' legions in AD 43, and later in AD 449 by the fabled Saxon leaders Hengist and Horsa, who had sought out Britain 'in the landing place named Ebba's Creek', or Ebbsfleet, located at the southern entrance to the Wantsum Channel.

Swein's arrival was not just a preliminary to raiding. It was a whole-sale bid for the conquest of England. An ancillary objective may have been to eliminate the threat posed by the recent military arrangements agreed between Aethelred and Thorkill, and to punish the latter for siding with the English. Aethelred had sponsored unrest in Scandinavia in the past – his backing of Olaf Tryggvason in 994 being a prime example. Olaf Haraldsson, the most recent pretender to the kingdom of Norway, was likely still in England with Thorkill, along with Hemming and Eiglaf, though firm evidence one way or the other is lacking. Some historians believe he left England when the tribute was paid. But even if Olaf was not there in person, his recent collaboration with Thorkill posed a threat to Swein. Olaf was a dangerous rival – though still young, around 18 years of age. The combination of Aethelred, Thorkill and Olaf acting against him would have given the Danish king cause for alarm. What is more, if the medieval historian William of Malmesbury is to be believed, Swein still had scores to settle with Aethelred dating back over a decade, from the time of the St Brice's Day massacre.

Not all of what William of Malmesbury claims can be taken at face value. William also states, unconvincingly, that Thorkill remained on good terms with Swein, despite the latter being in Aethelred's employ. According to William, Thorkill actively encouraged Swein to invade England, telling him:

> The land was rich and fertile [which Swein already knew], but that the king [Aethelred] was a driveller ... wholly given up to wine and women.

This character assassination of Aethelred has helped spawn the myth of the king being weak and feckless. By likening him to a decadent Roman emperor of old, wallowing in greed and debauchery, a damagingly inaccurate gloss is placed over the later part of his reign. As previously mentioned, moralising chroniclers of William's ilk took the simplistic view that anyone in power who suffered ill luck or a series of defeats must have been marked by God as deserving it in some way. Wickedness and corruption attracted God's wrath. Less judgementally and more accurately – given the almost unchallenged rampage of Thorkill and his allies – Henry of Huntingdon poetically likened England to 'a bed of trembling reeds' – powerless in the face of Swein's aggression.

Was Thorkill playing both ends against the middle? It seems unlikely, but of course cannot be completely ruled out. Even without the encouragement of a man such as Thorkill – who Swein Forkbeard had no reason to trust – it must have appeared a favourable time for him to launch his invasion. With two sons of an age able to accept delegated responsibility, he could leave the eldest, Harald, in Denmark and bring the younger, more aggressive and ambitious Cnut to assist him in England. Relations with his neighbours in Scandinavia were unusually friendly. His son-in-law, Erik of Lade, controlled large parts of Norway, while his stepson, another Olaf, ruled in Sweden. A number of the notorious, predatory Jomsvikings, who might otherwise have threatened Denmark in his absence, were in England with Thorkill. Others had already enriched themselves at Aethelred's expense and were now set up in their own homelands. Another potential enemy, Henry II of Germany, was at the time more focused on prising the imperial crown from a reluctant pope than with affairs unfolding in north-west Europe. The fact that Swein's landfall at Sandwich went unopposed and that he navigated up the coast to Northumbria without being intercepted or pursued cannot be construed as collaboration on Thorkill's part. Treachery might explain why Thorkill's fleet remained ineffectively moored up in the Thames during the invasion, but it seems more likely the suddenness and scale of the event simply wrong-footed both him and Aethelred; this despite a build-up of ships, men and materials across the North Sea, which cannot have gone unnoticed by English merchants and other travellers.

Swein is said to have pressed men from all over Denmark to man his invasion fleet, as well as sending out messengers across Scandinavia to attract warriors to his side with the promise of loot. Historians and archaeologists at one time believed a series of great circular forts unearthed in Denmark represented garrison camps. With timber-faced earthen ramparts, the structures were designed to be impregnable, and like later Norman castles may have been built as centres of power to control and overawe the surrounding population. All five fortresses had similar designs, being perfectly circular, with four gates and a courtyard divided into four areas. Dendrochronology (timber dating) indicates that most were built around the year 980, at least a decade earlier than the first large-scale Viking attacks on England, so were not built specifically to house Swein's troops. Strategically located at Fyrkat and Aggersborg, in Jutland, Nonnebakken on the island of Fyn, Trelleborg on Zealand, and another two in Scania, in present-day Sweden, they once contained houses set out in blocks – the largest at Aggersborg contained forty-eight of these. But whether they were used as barracks in the lead-up to the invasion of 1013 is not known.

Swein had raided in the south of England numerous times before. He had received a bloody nose in Norfolk in 1004 for his trouble. It is telling, therefore, that his first objective after arrival at Sandwich should have been to sail northward to the Humber, rather than to the Isle of Wight or to Norwich. The *Anglo-Saxon Chronicle* relates how Swein 'very quickly' bypassed East Anglia and travelled into the mouth of the Humber before heading inland via the Trent to Gainsborough. That he did so provides an insight into the Dane's strategic thinking. By avoiding Thorkill's fleet in the Thames and resisting the urge to raid into East Anglia – risking battle with Ulfcytel – he could quickly establish a base in Lincolnshire on the Trent; Thorkill and Ulfcytel would be taken out of the equation. Swein is thought to have formed covert alliances with key men in Northumbria and the Five Boroughs prior to his invasion, a tactic historians suggest he might have earlier employed in East Anglia in the early 990s – but with less success. Focusing the first stage of his campaign in the north of England, where he had likely already laid the groundwork prior to his arrival, Swein could hope to secure both active and passive support from the Anglo-Danish nobility without recourse to bloodshed. The *Anglo-Saxon Chronicle* confirms this, stating that Earl Uhtred and all the Northumbrians, along with all the people of Lindsey and the Five Boroughs, and soon after that the whole military establishment in the shires to the north of Watling Street – the old Danelaw border – submitted to him and provided him with hostages.

As well as Uhtred, two other prominent English noblemen also threw in their lot with Swein. Their names were Morcar and Sigeferth, described as the chief thegns of the 'seven boroughs': the usual three, plus York and Torksey. To gain Morcar and Sigeferth's support, Swein promised his son Cnut's hand in marriage to their cousin Aelfgifu of Northampton, a noble-woman famed for her beauty, the daughter of Aelfhelm, who was killed on Aethelred's orders in 1006. The marriage arrangements cannot have been made on the spur of the moment, but must have been diplomatically agreed in advance. The notion that Swein and Cnut had long-standing ties with members of the nobility in the northern Danelaw therefore gains credence. Aelfgifu's marriage into the Danish royal house must have seemed like fitting revenge for the young woman – taking account of her father's murder and her brothers' blindings on Aethelred's orders. The alliance sealed between the Danish king and Aelfgifu's powerful Anglo-Danish kinsmen helps explain the ease with which Swein occupied the Danelaw, though erosion of trust in Aethelred's administration must also have been a crucial factor. Through such means, Swein secured his base of operations.

The choice of a base at Gainsborough, on the Trent, rather than at York is telling. Instead of locating himself in Northumbria, as had Viking aspirants such as Olaf Guthfrithsson and Eric Bloodaxe in the past, Swein's choice of a more central locale – closer to the population centres of the Five Boroughs – betrays his broader intent. While the likes of Olaf and Eric sought dominion over the North, Swein's ambitions encompassed the whole of England.

The English were caught up in 'a perfect storm' of events. Swein's ships (the number of which are unknown) had sailed northward unopposed to make landfall in Lincolnshire. Thorkill's fleet had remained bottled up in the Thames. Valiant Ulfcytel's fierce warriors were bypassed in East Anglia. On arrival in the North, Uhtred 'the Bold', the bulwark of Northumbria, had submitted without putting up a fight and provided the Danes with hostages. No intervention was made by Eadric and his Mercians. The king had remained powerless in London. His martial sons, Athelstan and Edmund (both fighting men in their mid to late twenties) had remained firmly in the background – shadowy figures, loitering in the wings, awaiting their opportunity to take the stage. If true, it is an astonishing collapse, and one orchestrated without bloodshed.

With half of England already won over through intermarriage, diplomacy and the threat of violence, Swein could concentrate his attention on bringing the South to heel, this time by force of arms. In the event, no battles are recorded as being fought upon crossing Watling Street, indicative of the speed and ruthlessness of the Danish offensive. The relevant passage from Simeon of Durham's account of the campaign reads like a Dark Age equivalent of Hitler's *Blitzkrieg* terror tactics in Russia in 1941, describing the devastation wrought when his mounted warriors descended on the southern shires, burning down towns and indiscriminately slaughtering many of the inhabitants:

> Taking with him auxiliaries chosen from them who had surrendered to him, he [Swein] made an expedition to the southern Mercians; and crossing Watling Street, issued his orders that they should devastate the land, burn the towns, plunder the churches, put to death (regardless of pity) all of the male sex who might fall into their hands, preserve the females for the gratification of their lust, and perpetrate all the evil they could.

Having secured provisions and horses for his warriors while in Northumbria, Swein's army could count on travelling 20 miles a day in good weather. But not so the baggage wagons, which trailed behind under close escort. The route taken may have mirrored Olaf Guthfrithsson's invasion of 940, striking south via Lincoln, down Roman roads now followed by the modern A15 to Peterborough, then heading inland through the Nene valley towards Northampton. Circumstantial evidence for this is contained in documents claiming compensation from the Crown for damage inflicted by Swein's men on property owned by Croyland Abbey along this route. Croyland's abbot beat a hasty retreat to London before their arrival, sensibly fearing the worst.

Swein's army would have crossed the River Welland at Bourne (Brunnr), on the edge of the Lincolnshire Fens – a location claimed by some to be the site of the lost battlefield of Brunanburh, where Athelstan repelled Olaf Guthfrithsson's coalition in 937. Swein's men met no such resistance seventy-six years later. Nor were they challenged further inland when skirting the Bruneswald forest (now Bromswold), on the Northamptonshire–Huntingdonshire border – an area also tentatively linked with the Battle of Brunanburh. Wrong-footed by Swein's northern-focused attack, Aethelred's strategy appears to have been to retain a tight hold on London with Thorkill's support, relying on local forces to bring the invader to battle. But with Uhtred of Northumbria having defected, and Ulfcytel in East Anglia marginalised, it proved a forlorn hope. Unlike in 937 and 940, when Aethelred's ancestors had rallied the men of Wessex and Mercia, then marched against Olaf Guthfrithsson, the English king decided instead to play a waiting game. Quite why he chose this option and did not take to the field with his sons Athelstan and Edmund is impossible to say. He may have been right to be cautious. Swein's forces were on a roll. Stopping them in their tracks would have been difficult, perhaps impossible. Nevertheless, this failure to defend his people, the primary obligation of any Dark Age king, served to further alienate him from the English nobility – and it would appear from some members of his own family too.

That Oxford, the site of the only recorded massacre linked to St Brice's Day, was chosen as Swein's first target in Mercia adds credence to William of Malmesbury's claim that revenge was driving the Danish king. Swein increased his tally of hostages there and captured the town sooner than he expected. Oxford had been sacked by Thorkill just a few years earlier, so it is hardly surprising that so little resistance materialised from the cowed garrison. After crossing the Thames, Swein hastened southwards to Winchester, where the citizens immediately submitted to him, 'terrified at his excessive cruelty'. Swein's ability to claim as many hostages as he liked and of

The Saxon tower at
Wimborne – all that remains
of the earlier buildings torched
by Swein Forkbeard's forces
in 1013.

his own choosing indi-
cates the completeness
of the military collapse
in Wessex. It must have
been at around this time
that the monastic centre
at Wimborne in Dorset
was destroyed and the
grave of Aethelred I
despoiled – an act of vandalism which may have
given Swein some vicari-
ous satisfaction, although
the death of Aethelred
II might have pleased
him more. Little now remains of the original monastic site at Wimborne,
though the current minster, remodelled and rebuilt by the Normans in
the twelfth century, occupies the same location. A brass plaque with a likeness of Aethelred I marks the spot where his grave once lay. Otherwise,
just a single small stone turret in the west wall of the north transept harks
back to those times. Believed to be of Saxon origin, it must have survived
the conflagration which engulfed the surrounding timber structures when
Swein's men torched the place. If there were Saxon or mercenary garrisons
further south, ready to repel attacks from the sea, then they either sat tight
or dispersed without a fight. London, however, would be a much tougher
nut to crack.

Swein had quickly gained a decisive military advantage over the
English king by using his Scandinavian pedigree to attract support
in the North: securing York, recruiting among the Northumbrian
Anglo-Danish community and taking hostages, and then launching a
determined attack southwards through the Midlands into Wessex and
Mercia. Despite the existence of Thorkill's mercenaries and Aethelred's
remilitarisation efforts, it would appear that England, just prior to Swein's
invasion, remained ill equipped to meet the challenge, and the overriding

impression is of a country on the verge of anarchy, with powerful regional lords vying to expand their control at the expense of their neighbours. For this reason, many may have seen Swein Forkbeard as a preferable ruler to Aethelred – in some instances even as a liberator. Successive onslaughts launched by Tostig, Thorkill and Olaf Haraldsson had done more than simply drain the English coffers, they had fatally damaged the people's trust in Aethelred and his advisors to protect them. The conduct of the nobility in the North and in the Five Boroughs demonstrates the truth of this. Worn down by years of continuous warfare, with the country run by a progressively discredited administration, the factionalised English warrior classes were simply outmanoeuvred and out-generalled by a Viking warlord at the peak of his powers.

6.2

As Swein's forces rampaged southwards, his son Cnut (variously spelt as Knute, Knutr or Canute) remained in Lincolnshire with the boat party. Thought to have been born around 990, the prince would have been in his early twenties in 1013. M.K. Lawson, Cnut's biographer, gives two possible dates for his birth – 990 or 1000. If the latter is true, this would have made him just 13 at the time of his father's invasion, and just 15 when he launched his own invasion two years later. Not that youth need be a barrier to success. The famous Ostrogothic leader Theodoric (d. 526), who ruled Italy after the fall of the western Roman Empire, commenced his warlike campaigning at the age of 18. As we have seen, Olaf Haraldsson was likely just 15 years of age when fighting side by side with Thorkill at Ringmere in 1010. Many of the Viking warriors in England with Swein would have been of a similar age, or have been barely out of their teens.

Cnut was trained for warfare at an early age, and there is a tradition (of somewhat doubtful provenance) that he was fostered by the Jomsvikings under Thorkill's tutelage. On his maternal side, the prince was of Polish descent, and several of his grandparents may have been Slavic, since his grandfather Harald Bluetooth married an Eastern European princess. Cnut had been left behind in Lincolnshire by his father to shoulder the heavy responsibilities of ensuring the fleet's security. His arranged marriage into the nobility of the northern Danelaw helped facilitate the overseeing of his father's newly acquired northern territories. It was no mean undertaking, since in geographic extent and population they exceeded his Danish homeland. At the same time, he was detailed to keep a weather eye on the local Anglo-Danish nobility – many of whose allegiance and loyalty remained untested. It may not have been Cnut's first visit to England. Ottar the Black's *Knutsdrapa* poem recounts how the young Dane had accompanied his father on an earlier campaign, describing how Cnut was but a boy when he first set homes ablaze. Assuming the poem to have historical merit, the raid in question was most probably the one launched against the East Anglians in 1004.

Being left in command at Lincoln indicates that Swein placed absolute trust in his son to maintain control in the North. Cnut's brother Harald had been left at home. The fact that Cnut's relative youth is stressed again and again in Ottar's skaldic verses – he claims that no king younger than he had before cast off from his land to fight abroad, 'with red shield raging along the shore-line' – implies he was the younger of the two brothers, despite appearing to contemporaries as being mature beyond his years.

By contrast, Athelstan and Edmund (Aethelred's eldest surviving sons from his first marriage, with Aelfgifu) were both older than Cnut, and appear to have played no part in the defence of the kingdom at this time – at least none that has left any record. Athelstan was almost 30 in 1013 – Edmund, a few years younger. Among Athelstan's personal possessions (listed in his will) were no fewer than eleven swords, one of which had belonged to the legendary Offa, King of Mercia. Also among his belongings were a string of thoroughbred horses, two shields and a drinking horn. The image created is of an outgoing prince, cast in the same mould as his glorious martial ancestors.

A claim that Cnut promoted his father's invasion and was left in control of Northumbria while his father invaded the South begs the question what was Athelstan doing in 1013? Did he have any influence over his father? Did he attempt to assert himself militarily at any time during the crisis? If not, why not? Despite his father's marriage to Emma and the fact she had borne Aethelred two young sons (Edward and Alfred), Athelstan remained the king's nominated heir, with more to lose than most should Swein triumph. In a short biographical sketch of Athelstan contained in the *Oxford Dictionary of National Biography* the historian Simon Keynes asserts that Athelstan must at some stage have become 'a significant political force in the kingdom'. Keynes also considers it likely that the prince may have frowned on the growing influence of Eadric at court, and may even have become his political enemy.

Both Athelstan and his younger brother Edmund appear to have developed close ties with men from the Five Boroughs of the East Midlands.

Athelstan lent Morcar, Aelfgifu of Northampton's cousin, a coat of mail. He also made bequests of land and military equipment in his will to Morcar's brother Sigeferth. Both men would later be held accountable by Eadric (on Aethelred's behalf) for collaborating with Swein. As previously mentioned, their cousin Aelfgifu had married Cnut. Where then did this leave Athelstan and Edmund? Though unanswerable, the question (when added to the many claims of intrigue and double-dealing) raises the possibility of a Royal Family and court ruptured by rivalry and self-interest. Aethelred's coronation pledge to defend the realm, and ensure, 'God's church and [that] all the Christian people hold true peace', must have appeared to contemporaries as well and truly broken.

6.3

Swein's first setback was on the Thames (where many of his men were drowned crossing the river). This was followed by the failure of his Danish storming parties to breach London's strong defences. The saga evidence contained in Snorri Sturluson's *Heimskringla* relating to Olaf Haraldsson's battles, indicates that he and his men (now in the employ of the English) were instrumental in overcoming an attempt by Swein's men to force London Bridge. The bridge at that time is thought to have been a large, fortified, wooden structure, linking the town with its defensive bastion at Southwark, on the south bank of the river. As we have seen, the sequencing of the *Heimskringla* must be treated with caution, and the events described might equally well be assigned to those occurring the following year – or even earlier, when Olaf first arrived in England with Thorkill.

Snorri describes the stronghold at Southwark as a great work, around which were dug large ditches. The fortress itself was made of stone, timber and turf. Within it were stationed a company of English defenders. Some may have been armed with crossbows, a weapon thought to have been introduced in small numbers from the Continent at around this time. After several failed attempts, Swein's forces succeeded in driving the defenders back from their stronghold onto or across the bridge. With London's first line of defence breached, and the bridge at their mercy, Olaf Haraldsson's ships were called on to undermine the structure to prevent the Danes from forcing their way across. So broad that two wagons could pass each other, the bridge was protected by raised barricades, towers, and wooden parapets. Each of these obstacles needed to be secured by Swein's men before the structure could safely be crossed. During the siege of Paris, more than 100 years earlier, fire ships had been successfully used against a similar wooden structure. Instead, the young Norwegian prince laid his longships – now transformed into fighting platforms – alongside the bridge. Some were immediately damaged by large stones and iron-tipped wooden beams being cast down upon them. But despite these dangers, Olaf's crews managed to lay cables around the rotting wooden piles supporting the structure. They then rowed as hard as possible, fatally dislodging the stanchions, bringing down the bridge and many of Swein's men. The skaldic poets had a song to mark the occasion:

> London Bridge is broken down,
> Gold is won and bright renown.
> Shields resounding,
> War-horns sounding,
> Hild is shouting in the din!
> Arrows singing,
> Mail-coats ringing –
> Odin makes our Olaf win!

Despite Olaf's brave intervention and Swein's withdrawal, many English-men within the town remained nervous of the consequences of continued resistance. News arriving that Aethelmaer – one of the king's own kins-man – had led a delegation which surrendered the south-western shires to Swein (Cornwall, Devon, Dorset, Somerset and also perhaps the shires of south-west Mercia) and proclaimed the Dane 'full king', dampened their spirits still further. When it was announced that Queen Emma was leav-ing for Normandy, messengers from London were hurriedly sent to Bath, where Swein had set up his camp, confirming the Londoners were willing to consider surrendering on terms.

Establishing himself at Bath had not been an arbitrary choice for the Danish king. Being on a major Roman road (the Fosse Way), the location afforded him a direct route back to his ships moored up along the Trent at Gainsborough. What is more, Swein may have taken some satisfaction from being hailed as 'full king' in the town where Aethelred's father, Edgar, had been formally consecrated almost a half a century earlier. The Dane (now the rival King of England) was travelling back towards Lincolnshire when the messengers from London arrived. Presumably he had left a garrison at Bath, as well as at other important places in the South and South-West – places such as the strategic bridging points at Wallingford and Oxford. Elsewhere, the taking of hostages was thought sufficient to secure the loyalty of those who had submitted to him. Now that London appeared likely to fall, additional hostages from the Londoners, plus troops to garrison the place, would be required. What Swein urgently needed now was money to pay for their upkeep. It was money he did not have, but was determined to demand from the English.

If Aethelred was under any allusions he could sit things out, he was rudely disabused when many of the great and the good of the land (including the influential Archbishop Wulfstan) made it clear he no longer held their trust. Exactly what occurred in the late autumn of 1013 is not known for sure, and the sequence of events as related by the chronicler has been challenged by historians. Aethelred's own security and that of his wife and younger children were, doubtless, his first priority, and arrangements were made quite early on to extricate the queen and her two sons to Greenwich under the protection of Thorkill's lieutenants. Soon after this, Emma took a ship to Normandy to join her brother Richard, accompanied on the journey by Bishop Aelfsige, Croyland's runaway abbot.

Because Emma travelled to Normandy in this first instance without her two sons, it has been surmised her journey was made with the intention to raise support for her beleaguered husband. But when this support failed to materialise, Edward and Alfred (aged around 10 and 8 respectively) were both sent for; they later travelled to Normandy under the protection of Aelfhun, the Bishop of London.

By this time, Aethelred too had left London for Greenwich. If not already in the town, Swein's garrison forces were stationed nearby. Hostages had been sent to him, and the Dane had proudly proclaimed himself King of Denmark, Norway and England. It was far too dangerous for Aethelred to remain at large. At Christmas the deposed English king parted from his fleet in the Solent, and spent a period of religious observance, 'the season', on the Isle of Wight before taking a ship for Normandy to join his wife and brother-in-law, Duke Richard. It is unlikely he expected ever to return. Had he not done so, then we might know him better today as Aethelred 'the Exile', rather than as 'the Unready'. Who else travelled with Aethelred? It seems not his eldest son and heir, Athelstan; nor his son Edmund – nor indeed Thorkill, who stayed with his fleet in the Solent before reoccupying his base at Greenwich. Both Thorkill and Swein separately ravaged the English coasts to subsist during the desperate winter of 1013–14. For the average Englishman on the receiving end, scant distinction would have been made between them. Nevertheless, Aethelred would later authorise a payment of £21,000 to be made to Thorkill for keeping faith with him.

Saga evidence suggests the Norwegian pretender Olaf Haraldsson also remained loosely allied to Aethelred. But whether he accompanied the king to Normandy or remained with Thorkill, or was active elsewhere at this time is unclear. He is reputed to have fought on the Norman side against Count Odo of Chartres sometime in 1013, and is credited by the skalds with ravaging Brittany and capturing the fortress of Dol. So it seems likely he may have departed for the Continent sometime earlier than Aethelred. Eadric's whereabouts during the king's exile are also unknown. There is no evidence he accompanied the Royal Family to Normandy. But neither is there any evidence he submitted to Swein. Had he done so, the chroniclers would have been quick to accuse him. In any event, Swein's familial alliance with Morcar and Sigeferth – almost certainly enemies of the beleaguered Mercian – would have made any early compact with the Danish invader far too dangerous for him. In the circumstances, there seems little reason to doubt he remained loyal to his father-in-law – a man who had raised him from relative obscurity to become the most powerful and influential of the country's ministers. Indeed, of Aethelred's three known sons-in-law (Eadric, Ulfcytel and Uhtred) it appears most likely Eadric, the national scapegoat, alone remained actively faithful to the Royal Family at this time of crisis.

Descriptions of Swein Forkbeard as 'full king' indicate that most if not all of the country had submitted to him by this time. He held the important ports and regional capitals, such as Canterbury, London, Winchester and York, all of which may have been garrisoned. Swein may even have agreed a separate non-interventionist pact with Richard, Duke of Normandy prior to his invasion. If so, this might have served to strain relationships between the duke and Aethelred, making the latter's stay in Normandy more uncomfortable than might otherwise have been the case. Had Swein been a younger man, Aethelred's position would have been hopeless. As it was, the conquering king died unexpectedly (almost certainly of natural causes) at Candlemas, 2 February 1014, at Gainsborough. Swein was aged in his mid-50s, and the event was described as 'a happy one' in the *Anglo-Saxon Chronicle*. But not so happy for those who had sided with him: men such as Uhtred, Morcar and Sigeferth. Suddenly the future must have appeared ominously uncertain for them. But now, too far down the road to switch sides, and with Cnut immediately elected king by the Danish host at Gainsborough, it was politic to fall in line behind the young Danish prince – for the time being at least.

An eleventh-century obituary of Swein would have identified the dead king as among the most energetic and enterprising of all the Vikings: a man who had eventually brought England to its knees, gaining the kingship through a potent mix of terror, diplomacy and guile – at all times very much Aethelred's nemesis. Briefly King of England and Denmark, Swein was buried with some ceremony at York in February 1014, before being hurriedly brought back to Denmark to avoid his corpse being despoiled by the English. He was then interred beside his father in the church of the Holy Trinity at Roskilde. Denmark had at one time been lost to him, was later re-won, and neighbouring regions in Scandinavia, including the area around Oslo fjord, had been subjugated by him as part of a tight-knit, but volatile, Nordic Empire. Skalds praised him as 'a brave warrior who often gave the raven bloated flesh, and left the imprint of a sword's edge on opposing warrior's limbs'. Named as active against England in 994, 1003, 1004 and 1013, it is, even so, quite likely his raids dated from as early as 991, and that from then onwards he represented an ever-present threat to the English, directly or indirectly. Tostig may have acted for him in 1006 – Thorkill too in 1009–10 – though neither case is proven.

6.4

The Peterborough version of the *Anglo Saxon Chronicle* states that the fleet elected Cnut as king upon the death of his father. Another version – the *Canterbury Bilingual Epitome* – claims he gained a broader approval right across the Danelaw. Having sided with Swein, it appears the northern nobility, plus the nobility of East Anglia, stood by the young Dane. This was not the case further south, where all the councillors – 'both ordained and lay' – advised that King Aethelred should be sent for from Normandy. That the southern shires, some of them garrisoned by Danish soldiers, should be willing to have Aethelred back after so recently submitting to Swein (and giving hostages) is noteworthy, and reinforces the notion that the divide between the Anglo-Saxon South and the Anglo-Danish North – so prominent in the days of Olaf Guthfrithsson and Eric Bloodaxe – remained an on-going issue.

This was not a spontaneous eruption of support for so recently discredited a king. Other than Cnut – an unproven youth, whose power base, such as it was, lay in the Five Boroughs – Aethelred was really the only viable choice open to the southern nobility. Even so, the offer to have him back came on the heavy condition that he should govern them more justly than

he did before, a veiled reference to both the king's recent military failures and the corrupt practices of his favourites at court. Complaints against
his previous administration included high taxation (a necessary adjunct
to maintaining a large mercenary fleet), extortion and the enslavement of
free men. The charge of extortion may have been directed at acquisitive
men such as Eadric, but exactly what was meant by enslavement of free
men is unclear, though the charge must have had some substance, since
Archbishop Wulfstan indirectly alluded to it in a sermon preached on the
king's return.

Negotiations that followed, though not covert in the modern sense,
were nevertheless likely to have been initiated in the nature of a guarded
exchange. Aethelred promised to pardon those who had submitted to
Swein and who now willingly resubmitted to him. Once agreement was
reached, Prince Edward, Aethelred's eldest son from his union with Emma,
carried the king's response back to England in the form of a proclamation
designed to be read aloud at the shire courts and to be widely circulated.
The fact that the 10- or 11-year-old Edward acted as his father's emissary implies that Athelstan – the king's nominated heir – was not with
his father in Normandy. Why this should be the case is unclear – indeed
neither Athelstan nor Edmund figure in accounts of Aethelred's return.
The wording of Aethelred's proclamation was that:

> He would be a gracious lord to them [the English], and would improve such
> of the things which they all hated, and each of those things that were done or
> declared against him should be forgiven, on condition that they all resolutely
> and without treachery turned to him.

The pact reached between the exiled king and his councillors is the first
of its kind that we know about. Although the detailed terms are lost, it
is clear the king was promising to remedy ills which had become widespread during the previous decade as the price of his return. The king's
words seek to make common ground with his people, both in abhorring
the military failures leading to the country being overrun by Swein's
forces, and by promising to put things right if everyone worked together
and made an end to faction fighting. The agreement has been seen as
marking an early milestone on the road to Magna Carta (1215) – the
Great Charter – drafted during the equally troubled reign of King John.
Both agreements were designed to limit or temper a monarch's powers
and protect the privileges of his people. Wulfstan, the moral voice of the

English at this time, was the likely architect in 1014, though his sermon preached that year, known as 'the sermon of the wolf', diplomatically turned the blame for the nation's ills on the English people, rather than blame the king directly.

As a result, friendship was pledged on both sides and the councillors declared that every Danish king would be outlawed from England forever. This may not just have been a reference to Cnut, whose father they had so recently submitted to. The English also may have had in mind Aethelred's coterie of unpopular mercenary warlords, men such as Thorkill and Olaf Haraldsson. The former in particular was loathed by the church authorities. Given that he had been so heavily implicated in the murder of Archbishop Aelfheah at Greenwich just a few years earlier, it is hardly surprising. More practically, both he and Olaf Haraldsson may now have been viewed as a very considerable and unnecessary drain on the country's resources.

Cnut can have been under few allusions as to how perilous his position had become. His father Swein had ruled England for less than three months. Though hostages had been taken and vital points garrisoned, there had been little time to consolidate a hold on the country. Equally ambiguous was his position with regard to Denmark, where his brother Harald had been left as a caretaker ruler. Even more worrying were ominous mutterings among the Danish rank and file, which may have smacked of defeatism. Some later accounts speak of Swein enjoying an edifying death, and even impressing upon his son the need to follow and support the Christian faith. Whether Swein ever wholeheartedly embraced Christianity is unclear, and Cnut may not have become a Christian until after gaining the throne of England.

In the aftermath of Swein's death, wild rumours of divine retribution were rife. A vivid blemish disfiguring the dead king's forehead had apparently raised the spectre of revenge being wreaked from beyond the grave. Some claimed Swein had been visited in a dream by the avenging spirit of Edmund the Martyr, who was killed by Ivar the Boneless more than a century before. Edmund's spectral lance was said to have fatally pierced the king's brow. A martial Saxon ancestor had taken a ghostly revenge on the Scandinavian invader. Florence, picking up on this theme, would later claim that Swein alone saw St Edmund coming armed against him. Florence's *History of the Kings of England* recounts how Swein had unwisely demanded tribute from Bury St Edmunds, where the 'uncorrupted corpse' of the saint lay – bringing on the dead king's wrath.

Aethelred's return to England occurred in the spring. Cnut had remained in winter quarters with his raiding army in Gainsborough until Easter. Only then did he muster his forces and secure horses for the new campaigning season. Rather than Aethelred being unready, it was the Danes and their northern allies who were caught unprepared. The relevant passage from the *Anglo-Saxon Chronicle* reads:

> After the death of Swein, Cnut sat with his army in Gainsborough until Easter; and it was agreed between him and the people of Lindsey, that they should supply him with horses, and afterwards go out together and plunder. But King Aethelred with his full force came to Lindsey before they were ready; and they [Aethelred's army] plundered and burned, and slew all the men that they could reach.

A detailed reconstruction of the military campaign of 1014 is impossible to establish, but it seems clear Aethelred had the financial clout to raise forces to assist his return. Olaf Haraldsson and his Norwegians rallied to his banner, for a price. A skaldic verse applauds the fact:

> Land-shielder, you aided
> Aethelred homeward
> Brought him back
> To his birthright

Moreover, Duke Richard now felt it more politic (with Forkbeard's death) to assist his sister and brother-in-law, and provided ships and men for the expedition. Most importantly, Thorkill's powerful fleet was moored up at Greenwich and was still in the English king's employ, and had there been any thought of his switching allegiance after Aethelred's departure, Swein's death had put this possibility to rest for the time being. If Aethelred had promised the English he would expel Thorkill and Olaf, now was not the time.

Most likely the south and south-east coasts of England were targeted for this medieval D-Day. Winchester and Canterbury, both places having been garrisoned by troops loyal to Swein and likely still in situ, would have been among the first places to have been assaulted and recovered. London would also have been a priority target, and the story of Olaf's earlier defence of the town against Swein's forces in 1013 could almost equally well apply to 1014, with Olaf's ships breaking down the bridge to isolate a conjectural Danish garrison at Southwark, rather than preventing a Danish attack on the town. The recapture of London must have taken place in parallel with events unfolding elsewhere, including the retaking of Wallingford, an important bridging point on the upper Thames. The burh at Wallingford consisted of a fortified embankment (vallum) on three sides, with the Thames protecting the fourth. Outside the embankment was a moat filled with water from a diverted stream flowing from the west. Remnants of the burh's earthworks can still be seen today – bearing witness to the impressive scale of its defences. But despite such strong defences, garrisons such as this cannot have held out for long. The Danes at Wallingford, as at other places, must have surrendered or retreated back into Lincolnshire.

Ulfcytel's allegiance throughout the great crisis of Aethelred's reign is clouded in doubt. Arguably, hatred of Thorkill may have led to him to switch his support to Swein at a relatively early stage – but there is no firm evidence for this. The *Heimskringla* mentions a battle being fought in East Anglia during Aethelred's reoccupation but confuses it with the Battle of Ringmere, fought in 1010. Whether Ulfcytel ever broke faith with Aethelred and was reconciled with him on his return is unclear. Later, upon Thorkill's defection to Cnut, he once again chose to fight alongside Aethelred's son Edmund Ironside, so at some point must have switched back his allegiance, if indeed he ever changed sides at all.

Had Uhtred and his Northumbrians held firm, all might have been well. But they did not. Cnut's and Uhtred's forces – when combined – were a match for Aethelred. But without Uhtred's support, Cnut was doubly vulnerable. The Northumbrian's defection to Aethelred swung the balance of power in the North decisively back in favour of the English king. Uhtred's support for Swein may have been lukewarm from the beginning. The northerner was apparently of impeccable Anglo-Saxon pedigree, and his homeland of Bernicia, situated north of the Tees, had never been conquered or settled by Danish incomers. Like Eadric and Ulfcytel, he was Aethelred's son-in-law. For all of these reasons, he quickly severed ties with Cnut upon Swein's death and his father-in-law's return.

Coincidental with Aethelred's fight back in England was the Irish king Brian Buru's offensive against the Vikings of Orkney and their Dublin–Norse allies. The Vikings were defeated on 23 April 1014 at the great Battle of Clontarf; any assistance Cnut might have sought from Scandinavian allies in the North and West was immediately curtailed. Whether the shockwaves from the defeat were felt in Northumbria is not clear, though to contemporaries it must have appeared the catastrophe in

Ireland and Swein's death in Lincolnshire augured a major downturn for Viking ambitions in the West. Perhaps it was this that influenced Uhtred's decision to switch sides.

Aethelred is said to have fallen with his 'full force' upon Cnut and his allies in Lindsey – punitively ravaging and burning the province. In the face of Aethelred's unexpected advance, and concerned he might be cut off from the open sea by an enemy now all around him, the Danish prince hurriedly gave the order for the withdrawal of his longships from the Trent to the Humber. The need for haste stranded many of them. Only a small number of his ships are said to have been able to make the journey back to Denmark, via Sandwich. Later accounts, attempting to patch over the ignominy of the rout, claim he left some behind deliberately to retain a foothold in England, but despite medieval spin, it seems clear he was caught wholly unprepared by Aethelred's rapid advance. This and the additional impact of Uhtred's last-minute change of sides sealed his fate. Tragically, it also served to seal the fate of the hostages taken by his father. Aethelred's return and the willingness of their parents to part faith with Cnut had placed the young men's lives in jeopardy. Some may have barely reached adolescence, the more adventurous happily embracing the novelty of shipboard life. Murder, blinding and castration of rivals were commonly undertaken by medieval kings, but were brutal exigencies generally reserved for adult offenders. In a cruel age, such methods were doubtless seen as necessary for running the affairs of State, and dealing harshly with the hostages would have served to confirm Cnut's strength of resolve. Even so, their youth should have told in their favour. If the Viking prince demurred, we will never know. The chroniclers simply state that when Cnut berthed at Sandwich, he put his father's hostages ashore 'minus their hands and ears and noses'. Even in an age hardened to cruelty, the way Cnut treated his father's young hostages was seen as unnecessarily brutal.

Cnut's precipitate flight left his erstwhile supporters in the East Midlands and in the North in the lurch. The chronicler concludes with the words, 'So were the wretched people deluded by him'; they were left undefended to face Aethelred's fury. Other accounts speak of the 'poor people of Lindsey' being 'betrayed' by him. By disembarking with his fleet for Denmark, stopping only to put ashore his ghastly trophies, he is portrayed as indifferent to the fate of those left behind, who were dealt with by Aethelred's lieutenants. This version of events demonizes Cnut for his heartlessness, while at the same time placing an almost equally cruel gloss over Aethelred's accomplishments in winning back control in Lindsey. The nobility of the northern Danelaw had sided with the Danish invaders in 1013 (on other occasions too) and had become a dangerous conduit for further attacks on the kingdom. In the context of early medieval conflict, Aethelred was well within his rights to punish his people in this way. How else could he prevent a repeat occurrence? Usually cast militarily as 'an accident waiting to happen', Aethelred became the first of only two English kings to win back his kingdom through force of arms – the other being Edward IV in the fifteenth century. It was an achievement which belies his reputation for ineptness, and one which Icelandic poets recognised, but which English chroniclers and historians decided to heavily edit.

How comprehensive Aethelred's military reoccupation was is not completely clear. The *Heimskringla* suggests that pockets of Danish resistance – called the 'Companies of Thingmen' – remained at large after Cnut's withdrawal, Snorri describes them as continuing to hold out around the country for some time. Bypassed by the king's forces when heading north, these outposts may have contained men who had fought for Aethelred in the past, but who had then thrown their lot in with Swein when Aethelred fled to Normandy. Ulfcytel's war-bands, in predatory fashion, are said to have fallen on two such units, one at London and another at an unlocated garrison town to the North, called Slesswick. At both places the garrisons were massacred. Whether Ulfcytel was fighting for or against Aethelred is unclear. Political and familial affinities had become fractured by Swein's brief takeover. Among those killed apparently was Hemming, Thorkill's brother. If true, the antagonism between Thorkill and Ulfcytel – festering since the Battle of Ringmere in 1010 – ratcheted up another notch.

'After Great Toils and (Difficulties'

7.1

Despite the unexpected death of Aethelred's son and heir, Athelstan, on 25 June 1014, and severe storms in the autumn, which inundated coastal areas and 'further inland than ever before', 1014 proved to be a successful year for the English king. Cnut had been sent packing and Aethelred's authority had been reasserted throughout the kingdom by employing a judicious mix of diplomacy and punitive force. The downside was the payment of £21,000 to Thorkill's fleet at Greenwich. Even so, contemporaries could be forgiven for considering that the worst might be behind them – but they would be wrong.

Upon Athelstan's death, his brother Edmund Ironside became their father's prospective heir. He was the third of six sons by the king's first wife, being born after Athelstan and Ecgberht (d. 1005), and being followed by Eadred (d. 1012?), Eadwig and Edgar (d. 1008?). Only two of these were still alive – Edmund and Eadwig. His two sons by his second wife, Emma – Edward and Alfred – were both minors in 1014. Athelstan and Edmund had been close companions. How close Edmund and Eadwig were is not known. When Athelstan died, Edmund was present at his brother's bedside. Important bequests were made to Edmund in Athelstan's will. Other bequests had also been made (as we have seen) to a number of Athelstan's close friends, including Sigeferth – one of the two prominent thegns from the northern Danelaw – a man compromised for submitting too readily to Swein Forkbeard in 1013. Both Morcar and Sigeferth were still at large as late as the spring of 1015, having somehow avoided Aethelred's retribution. Sigeferth's cousin, Aelfgifu of Northampton, had fled to Denmark at the same time as her husband Cnut, or did so shortly afterwards. Some historians have even suggested it was she who had arranged for Swein Forkbeard's remains to be hurriedly disinterred from York Minster, and spirited away to Denmark to prevent them from being despoiled by Aethelred's advancing army.

As a consequence of Morcar and Sigeferth being so heavily implicated as collaborators, and now more firmly linked to the Royal House of Denmark by their cousin's marriage, Aethelred settled accounts by having them arrested while attending a great council meeting at Oxford. Their subsequent executions – described as 'dishonourable' in the *Anglo-Saxon Chronicle* – are said to have been carried out by Eadric's henchmen after the men had been cornered in the ealdorman's chamber; they were, it is said, lured there by the Mercian.

Other noblemen from across the length and breadth of the country had also submitted to the Danish king in 1013, including one of Aethelred's own close relatives, Aethelmaer. But only Morcar and Sigeferth (so far as we know) were targeted for retribution in this way, leading to claims that Eadric may have had the men killed to bolster his own position at court. But like all the stories involving Eadric, such allegations must be treated with caution. On the basis that the northern thegns had supported Swein against Aethelred, the executions at Oxford were justified. What is more, the accused were probably seized by Eadric's guards and brought to book without the need for any great subtlety. Eadric, as executioner, may have been doing no more than looking out for his father-in-law's best interests.

After their deaths, Sigeferth's and Morcar's lands were immediately confiscated by the Crown, and Sigeferth's widow, Ealdgyth, was forcibly removed and brought to the abbey at Malmesbury and kept under close house arrest. Ealdgyth was Aelfgifu of Northampton's cousin, the niece of Ealdorman Aelfhelm – Aelfgifu's father – the nobleman executed on Aethelred's orders in 1006. Aelfhelm's demise and the blinding of his two sons had coincided with the rise to power of Aethelred's sons-in-law, Eadric and Uhtred. Like her cousin Aelfgifu, Ealdgyth (her husband having been so recently executed) also now had good reason to bear a grudge against the king. Whether she had personally welcomed Swein Forkbeard when he took control of the Danelaw, and had been gladdened by her cousin's marriage into the Danish Royal Family is not known – but seems likely. Being the bereaved wife of Sigeferth and a noblewoman of some considerable local status, Ealdgyth would have enjoyed a popular following in the Five Boroughs. Given her standing there, along with the enmity she harboured towards Aethelred's regime, and additionally her close familial ties with Cnut's queen, she must have posed a political threat to Aethelred as a potential focus for disaffected pro-Danish factions in the Danelaw. It is for this reason that the king had her seized and removed to Malmesbury, and it is in this context that Edmund Ironside's immediate intervention and marriage to her assumes such importance.

The fortress site of Malmesbury is claimed to be the oldest continually inhabited town in England, having originated as a Neolithic stronghold. It was described by the seventeenth-century Parliamentarian general Sir William Waller as the best naturally defended inland location he had ever come across. It is unsurprising therefore that it had been chosen by Alfred as one of the burhs of the Burghal Hidage, nor that Athelstan later made it his capital, nor that Aethelred should place Ealdgyth there in the late summer of 1015 for safekeeping. He was not to know that his ambitious son Edmund would marry her there and prise her from his grasp. Florence describes how:

> During her captivity, Edmund the atheling [Prince] came there [to Malmesbury] and married her against his father's will; between the feast of the Assumption [15 August] and the feast of the Nativity of St Mary [8 September] he went to the people of the Five Burgh's, invaded the possessions [lands] of Sigeferth and Morcar, and brought the inhabitants thereof under his own dominion.

Whether Edmund had been married previously and had had children is not known, but seems likely. As related by Florence, and confirmed in the *Anglo-Saxon Chronicle*, the prince rode back with his bride to the Five Boroughs, staking claim by force and right of marriage to Morcar's and Sigeferth's confiscated lands. By doing so, Edmund was flouting his father's authority in dramatic fashion. Forfeiting traitor's lands and then bestowing them on men of his own choosing was an important way by which the king could hope to exert control in the northern Danelaw. Having a rebellious son snatch the territories from him and make off with a traitor's widow was tantamount to an act of war. By ambitiously setting himself up as a Lord of the Danelaw (with echoes of Aethelwold, Olaf Guthfrithsson and Eric Bloodaxe before him), Edmund had thrown down the gauntlet, making it clear he would brook no opposition in staking a claim to a slice of the kingdom – something he perhaps saw as an advance on his birthright.

It is easy for historians to over-romanticise someone such as Edmund Ironside, his emblematic nickname conjuring the idea of someone larger than life, of Churchillian resilience, charismatic and capable of taking hard knocks. But little is known of the real Edmund at any stage until 1015. Even his age is uncertain, although he was probably in his mid to late twenties during this great crisis of his father's reign. The only glimpse of the type of man he might have been is a reference to him in 1006, when, in his teens, he took possession of estates in Somerset from their monastic owners, who, it is said, 'dared not refuse him'. He was clearly a strong-willed and uncompromising character. Now, in the wake of Swein Forkbeard's invasion and his father's comeback, Edmund may have been making an early, opportunistic bid for power by setting himself up as an overlord of the Five Boroughs – an act which posed a very real threat to his father's regime.

Edmund's northern pedigree, gained from his mother, may have helped secure tacit acceptance of his action from men who might otherwise have opposed him, such as Uhtred in Northumbria. But his heavy-handed land-grab and enforced rule could well have been seen by others as unwelcome – the prince being viewed as a dangerous troublemaker. The *Anglo-Saxon Chronicle* uses phrases such as 'invaded the Five Boroughs' and 'brought men under his dominion', which would tend to support such a premise. In the recent past, the nobility of the northern Danelaw had submitted and then suffered under Swein and Cnut, and had then faced retribution from Aethelred. With Edmund setting himself up as a virtual king, they must now have harboured mixed feelings as to what the future might hold. Nevertheless, firm evidence one way or the other is lacking.

Underlying these events was doubtless the question of the succession. After Athelstan's death, Edmund may have feared his father would side with his increasingly influential wife, Emma, (supported by Eadric and others) in championing her son Edward (later known as 'the Confessor') to succeed him. Aethelred was by now quite elderly, and may have been unwell, so the question of the succession was bound to loom large in the thoughts of the important powerbrokers of the land. The king's anger at being wrong-footed by Edmund in the Danelaw was perhaps further stoked by the corrosive Queen Emma, who saw her own dynastic ambitions threatened by Edmund's behaviour. In a violent power struggle, her two young sons (Edward and Alfred) would be at risk from the turbulent prince.

Aethelred, through illness or dependence, may have been unable, or loath, to assert his own wishes at this time. Emma, a teenager when Aethelred first married her, was now a formidable and uncompromising woman.

How close she was to Aethelred's elder sons is unknown, but neither she nor her two children by the king were named as beneficiaries of Athelstan's will, so it could be that the two strands of the family existed separately, and remained estranged. Whether Queen Emma actively opposed the arrangements made to confirm Aethelred's sons from his first marriage from taking precedence in the succession is not known. Privately, she may have worked to promote the case for her own son Edward over Edmund, mirroring her late mother-in-law's motivations more than thirty years earlier, at the time of Edward the Martyr's murder at Corfe. Supporting these assertions, a later history of Edward the Confessor's reign asserts that all the leading men of England took an oath to uphold Edward's claim to kingship as early as the time of Emma's confinement. Another history says Edward was anointed and consecrated as a future king while still a boy. Most likely both these tales were later, Norman validation constructs.

Nevertheless, it was Edward whom Aethelred had sent to England with his ministers when negotiating the terms of his return. None of the king's sons from his first marriage were tasked with the mission, despite the king's heir, Athelstan, still being alive at the time. It was the issue of the succession above all others which served to position the nobility in opposing camps in the hiatus between Cnut's departure in the late spring/early summer of 1014 and his return the following year. The historian Simon Keynes has compellingly portrayed Edmund as being 'forced' by Athelstan's untimely death to take a stand against his ailing father's regime, now controlled by Eadric. Exploiting an opportunity to increase his territorial holdings upon his brother's death, Edmund hoped to carve out for himself an autonomous power base in the Danelaw. Even though Aethelred had already formalised the succession in a charter drawn up in Edmund's favour, the prince may have feared that his father, under pressure from Emma and her supporters, might yet recognise his stepbrother Edward over him.

Influential men such as Eadric, in the thrall of the queen, stood to gain from the succession of a teenager like Edward – an unworldly youth, easy to influence and gain control over. What is more, it is probable that Eadric was on uneasy terms with Edmund – an antipathy exacerbated by recent events at Oxford. There are parallels with the latter years of Alfred the Great's rule, when tensions had arisen between the king and his eldest son, Edward the Elder, caused by his son's impatience to take over the reins of power. Alfred, in statesmanlike fashion, had resolved the problem by setting his son up in overall control of Kent – the equivalent of a regent or sub-king. Aethelred might, sensibly, have done something similar for Edmund. As it was, Edmund took it upon himself. Tellingly, none of Edward the Elder's male offspring were named after their grandfather. Nor so were Edmund's. Edward's cousin Aethelwold – Aethelred I's surviving son – may have been closer to his uncle than Edward was to his father. As a result, the future rebel felt cheated of his birthright after Alfred's death, leading to a breach with Edward. Only his death at the Battle of the Holme prevented a more protracted internecine conflict. Had Eadric done battle with Edmund on behalf of Emma's sons in 1015, the wheel might have come full circle.

The chroniclers of Aethelred's reign skim over these underlying tensions in the Royal Family. Despite being in open rebellion against his father, Edmund is portrayed as energetically asserting his rights, while Aethelred's 'first minister', Eadric, is unswervingly cast as the evil catalyst of all the country's ills, characterised as a scheming arch traitor and a villainous assassin, intent on promoting his own agenda. Eadric's treachery and Edmund's noble standing are consistent themes in all of the primary sources of the period and of most accounts that have followed, so cannot be wholly disregarded, though it is tempting to do so. The king as ever (though suffering ill-health) is characterised as a dithering and enfeebled onlooker. Emma, interestingly, is nowhere mentioned.

7.2

The king's ever-worsening health coincided in the autumn with the sudden and unexpected return of Cnut off the Kent coast at the head of a large invasion force, comprising 200 ships. The Viking fleet travelled unopposed along the South Coast to the Frome estuary at Poole from where raiding parties were launched inland into the Wessex heartland – Dorset, Wiltshire and Somerset. The impressive spectacle of Cnut's departure from Denmark and arrival in England is highlighted in the *Encomium Emmae Reginae*, an otherwise unreliable political tract in praise of Queen Emma written in the 1040s. The encomiast describes how Cnut bade farewell to his mother and his brother Harald, and returned to 'the winding coast' where his fleet awaited him. In colourful terms, the encomiast states that anyone spying the fleet from afar might have gained the impression that the ships were 'made in the substance of flame rather than of wood'. As the sun beat down upon them (and also on a brilliant sea), the ships glinted: the reflection of sunlight off swords and armour, and also from shields suspended over the ships' sides. Gold is said to have shone on the prows – silver from the bows. Somewhat implausibly, the ships are said to have been manned by heavily armoured 'men of metal', of whom none were slaves or freed from slavery, nor low-born or aged. All are said to have been noblemen, strong and mature, fit enough for any type of fighting – all fleet of foot, so that they 'scorned the speed of horsemen'.

Cnut is said to have tried to persuade his brother Harald to accompany him on the invasion, promising to split any gains made down the middle. Harald's age and status is unclear from the sources, though, as previously asserted, it seems probable he was the elder of Swein's two sons. Being in Denmark at the time of his father's death may have facilitated Harald's seizure of the kingship. However, early Scandinavian coins – inscribed 'Cnut, King of the Danes', minted at Lincoln no later than 1015 – indicate that Cnut might have taken issue with this. Emma's encomiast portrays Harald as reluctant to get involved with Cnut's plans or to agree to any deal to divide the spoils. Nevertheless, by allowing the use of the extensive Danish barracks and numerous harbours for his brother's invasion preparations implies a close collaboration between the two men. Warriors from far and wide are said to have bolstered Cnut's invasion fleet, and the build-up of troops, ships, supplies and weaponry must have been considerable.

Cnut's concentration of forces in Denmark would have posed too great a risk for Harald to countenance if they did not share a common ambition. All things considered, it seems most likely that Harald supported the venture and that the two brothers worked closely together on the planning and preparations. Despite the encomiast's description of Cnut waving farewell to his brother, the two siblings may even have travelled together to England, later fighting side by side in several battles.

Cnut's decision to invade England must have been made quite early in the year 1015, since the build-up preparations would have been immense. What is more, his own forces would not have been strong enough without the assistance of other interested Scandinavian parties. Sweden and Norway enjoyed good relations with Denmark at this time. In particular, Cnut would have been anxious to gain the support of the Norwegian Jarl Erik of Lade, a loyal ally, and a veteran of many earlier campaigns. Though no longer a young man, Erik was someone the Danish prince could count on implicitly. He was the son of Hakon Sigurdson, Jarl of Hlathir, or Lade – today part of the Norwegian province of Trondheim. He was also Cnut's brother-in-law. The jarls of Lade were famed warriors. Erik had engaged in piratical raids on England in the company of Forkbeard and others in the past and may have been among those who attacked London in 994. Olaf Tryggvason's seizure of the overkingship of Norway shortly after this had forced both Erik and his brother Sven into exile in Denmark. After the death of Tryggvason at the Battle of Svold in 999, the brothers returned to Norway, acknowledging Swein Forkbeard as their overlord. Scandinavian sources maintain Erik fought at Ringmere alongside Thorkill in 1010. If true, this adds credence to the earlier assertion that Thorkill, like Erik, was acting as the Danish king's surrogate, and must therefore have enjoyed good relations with Swein at that time, before Thorkill's later pact with Aethelred soured relations between the two men.

The young Danish prince could not have chosen a better time to invade. Aethelred lay sick at Cosham in Hampshire, unable to intervene, and Edmund, as we have seen, was in open revolt. Accompanied by strong bodyguards, and backed up by small armies, Edmund and Eadric met somewhere in the South Midlands, almost certainly as a consequence of Cnut's return. The relevant passage in the *Anglo-Saxon Chronicle* is among its most opaque, and needs to be read with a degree of caution. It states:

> Ealdorman Eadric collected an army there, and Edmund did the same in the north. When they came together, the ealdorman designed to betray Edmund, but he could not; whereupon they separated without an engagement, and sheered off from their enemies.

Breaking this down, we can conclude that Eadric gathered an army from Mercia (his power base), and Edmund did likewise; in his case from the lands he had gained lordship over in the northern Danelaw. The phrase 'when they came together' indicates that they were at this stage intent on combining forces against Cnut, and not as might otherwise be construed to fight each other. The *Anglo-Saxon Chronicle* directly links the meeting of the two men with the threat posed by Cnut in southern England and the inconvenient fact of the king's illness. If enmity between the two men could be quickly mended, Cnut might yet face a challenge in the South. Eadric may have proposed they put the past behind them and pool their resources for the common good – an initiative enacted on his own volition or as an intermediary for Aethelred. Edmund may for his part have wished to make amends for his recent rebellion in the face of a common foe. Another agenda item for Eadric and Edmund may have been the question of territorial claims in the wake of Edmund's marriage to Ealdgyth. Because the prince's new possessions abutted Eadric's own, this may have been cause for friction between them. We really just do not know.

With respect to the chronicler's claim that Eadric intended to betray Edmund, we also have almost no information. Assuming the long litany of accusations made against the Mercian to be exaggerated – which seems reasonable – and also taking account of the chronicler's invariable glossing over of Edmund's motives, all we can safely say is that the two men met but failed to reach any agreement. Later accounts make additional claims. Florence describes Edmund as raising 'a great army' against the Vikings, but that Eadric, 'full of treachery and guile', hindered him by laying 'all manner of snares' in the hope of bringing about the prince's death. Henry of Huntingdon goes so far as to speak of a proposed battle against the Danes in Wessex being 'abandoned' because of Eadric's treachery. William of Malmesbury states that Cnut, having laid Wessex waste 'with fire and slaughter', was opposed by Edmund, but that the prince was thwarted by Eadric, who forced him to withdraw his forces. All echo, with embellishments, the retrospectively prescient Anglo-Saxon chronicler's account, pointing the finger at Eadric while absolving Edmund of any blame. In reality, the protagonists may each have considered the other as posing a greater immediate threat than Cnut.

It should be remembered that Viking attacks on the South Coast were nothing new. Cnut was an unproven youth who had recently been chased ignominiously from the kingdom, and was seen by many as just another opportunistic Viking warrior lord seeking to gain treasure at England's expense – a man not far removed from Thorkill, Olaf Haraldsson or others of their ilk – if anything somewhat weaker. Everything we know about this period is written with a heavily retrospective slant. Neither Edmund nor Eadric can have anticipated just how much of a danger to the kingdom Cnut might yet become – and may even have considered him as a potential ally, one against the other. If so, Eadric, the more insecure of the two, was quicker to act. His father-in-law's failing health and Edmund's likely assumption of power must have appeared, with merit, to have placed the Mercian's life at risk. For this reason he sought an uneasy alliance with the Danes, throwing in his lot with Cnut.

All accounts agree that forty longships and their crews defected from the English to Cnut at the end of 1015, and that Eadric was the main instigator. Containing approximately 2,000 fighting men, forty longships was a considerable reinforcement for the Danes. But since the number of longships roughly equates to the size of Thorkill's fleet, the defection of the ships and their mercenary crews might more simply be explained by Thorkill changing sides. Stories that Thorkill travelled to Denmark prior to 1015 to mend his relationship with Cnut after Swein's death, and that he impressed upon the young Dane the desirability of an immediate attack on England, may or may not be true. Nevertheless, the mercenary captain's first priority would have been to ensure he positioned himself on the stronger of the two sides. Ever the opportunist, it seems probable he made an early compact with Cnut. On this basis, it is hard to fathom why Eadric should have been required to act as a 'go-between' – even though he was now in alliance with the Danes. Only if Thorkill remained loyal to Aethelred (which appears unlikely) can the accusation that Eadric lured the ships away from the English be accepted at something like face value. The presumption would then be that the forty shiploads of men were either taken from Thorkill against his wishes (again unlikely), or that they comprised the Mercian's own ship levy from the Midlands.

William of Malmesbury claims Eadric meant to switch sides all along, and 'deserted' the king's service, taking with him forty longships. He also asserts that the nobility of Wessex did the same:

> Eadric, thinking it unnecessary longer to dissemble, but that he might now openly throw off the mask, deserted to Cnut with forty ships; and all West Saxony likewise followed his example, both delivering up hostages and giving up their arms.

Quite why Eadric is singled out and named can only be explained by reference yet again to the unrelenting bias of the chronicler of Aethelred's reign. Of course, to think in terms of the existence of long-standing national allegiances at this time is dangerous. Words such as desertion have a more modern resonance. The lands of western Europe were still medieval constructs. Once a local king could no longer provide the necessary security for his people, or the promise of treasure, all bets were off. Even in good times, factionalism was impossible to eradicate. By this late stage of Aethelred's reign, faction fighting appears to have broken out in England in spades, initiated in no small measure by his headstrong son Edmund. The likelihood of both Eadric and Thorkill switching allegiance to Cnut, among others, can be directly linked to Aethelred's failing health and ruptured court. In Eadric's case, the failure to settle relations with Edmund would have been a crucial element in making his decision to side with the Danish prince. In Thorkill's case, his switch of allegiance may also have been triggered as a response to the attacks made by Ulfcytel on Danish outposts – the mysterious Companies of Thingmen. If Thorkill's brother Hemming was a casualty of one of these attacks, then revenge on

Thorkill's part might have been a motive for changing sides. What is more, although relations between Thorkill and Cnut had been strained, the two men had perhaps been close in a familial sense in the past. Thorkill's relationship with Aethelred, on the other hand, was conducted on a strictly 'business only' basis.

7.3

After overwintering on the southern coast of England – probably on the Isle of Wight – Cnut raided deep into the heart of the Midlands after the turn of the year. The *Anglo-Saxon Chronicle* recounts how he attacked England with his raiding army, and that Ealdorman Eadric accompanied him. Thorkill and Erik of Lade are not mentioned specifically. The giant Dane may have remained in the Thames, blockading London. Erik may still have been in Norway, preparatory to setting sail to support his young Danish ally. Reckoned at 160 ships, including transports for horses and equipment, and assuming his ships to have been substantially similar in size to those from earlier times, Cnut's strike force might have numbered as many as 4,000 men – though around half this number is more probable.

After rampaging through Wessex, where the nobility had apparently submitted to him the year before, Cnut crossed the Thames into Mercia at Cricklade, and then raided estates in southern Warwickshire. Florence claims Cnut's force comprised both Danes and West Saxons. The Wessex nobility had earlier been forced to submit and provide Cnut with hostages. Though doubtless pressed into fighting against their fellow Englishmen, many may have harboured residual or renewed enmity towards Aethelred for his failure to protect them the year before.

Cnut's raiding army is said to have 'burned and killed all that they came to'. With little opposition to face, and determined to lose no time in overrunning the country, this midwinter foray parallels Tostig's earlier close season campaign in 1006. The role Eadric played (though given headline coverage) remains uncertain. Because of the unrelenting bias of the chroniclers, damning statements made against him must be treated with some scepticism. Now, in an alliance with the Danish invaders, he is said to have lent his direct support to Cnut's ravaging of Warwickshire – a shire abutting his own territories in Mercia. Administered by Ealdorman Leofwine, a man still presumably loyal to Aethelred, Warwickshire would have been a good target for Cnut to vent his aggression. All the sources name Eadric as being part of the raiding party, so without firm evidence to the contrary we must accept this to have been the case. Biding his time, rather than firmly siding one way or another, may have seemed a better option for Eadric so early on in the game. Self-preservation was uppermost in his mind. He was still a powerful regional overlord in his own right. Reaching an understanding with the young and aggressive Danish invader had been a pragmatic response on his behalf, done to protect his territorial interests in the short term. He was not alone in doing so, as the reluctant intransigence of the Wessex nobility attests.

The sudden emergence of this large coalition of forces in the Midlands in midwinter must have served as a long-overdue wake-up call for Aethelred, who up until then may have been too ill to provide even a modicum of leadership. There are no details in the narratives of the time as to the nature of Aethelred's illness, but he was now aged around 50 (a reasonably advanced age by early medieval standards). He had ruled England for the best part of thirty-seven turbulent years, and physical and mental breakdown cannot be ruled out. The defection to Cnut of much of the Wessex nobility, plus Eadric's abandonment of him, may have made the task he faced seem hopeless. Nevertheless, at some stage the king made the 70-mile journey from Cosham to London, if only to gain the safety of its strong walls. Queen Emma's whereabouts at this time are not known. She may once again have left England for the security of her Norman homeland, taking with her the two young princes, Edward and Alfred.

In the circumstances, there was little (apart from damaged pride) to prevent a reconciliation between the ailing Aethelred and his wayward son, Edmund. Edmund may have made the first move. Having recently failed in his bid to confront Cnut's Viking army in Wessex, and now threatened by a strong coalition of forces ravaging the Midlands, Edmund needed the king's authority to raise the nation. Perhaps it was with a sense of relief that the ailing king passed the baton of responsibility for the defence of the realm to his son. Edmund had most likely already begun raising forces in Mercia to confront the Viking threat. William of Malmesbury states unequivocally that the Mercians were 'repeatedly assembled'. But Edmund's attempts at recruiting failed without the king being present to add legitimacy to the undertaking. Also, many of the Mercians called up insisted that the garrison of London should turn out before they themselves would muster. When neither the king nor the garrison materialised, they disbanded.

The closest Edmund came to raising a viable force is dated to early January 1016, 'after the festival of Epiphany', the 6th of that month. On this occasion the king formally sanctioned the concentration of forces.

Each man called up, and fit enough to fight, had to attend the muster or face a penalty. Aethelred's presence added weight to the proceedings. Men from the garrison of London were also present. The army stood ready to ride out against the Vikings operating in Warwickshire. But, warned of some threat to his safety, Aethelred is said to have abandoned the gathering and hurriedly ridden back under heavy escort to London. The army once again disbanded.

The *Anglo-Saxon Chronicle* states, ominously, that 'someone who should have been a help to the king wished to betray him'. The traitor or traitors are not identified specifically, but Florence makes the claim that some of the auxiliary units raised by Edmund were untrustworthy. It might have been these were Danish mercenaries hired by Edmund – men who later switched sides and joined Cnut. The mysterious Companies of Thingmen come to mind. The national scapegoat, Eadric, cannot have been involved otherwise either Florence or the vociferously anti-Eadric chronicler would have said so. If not Danish mercenaries, the king may even have been in fear of some faction from within his own son's Anglo-Danish retinue. The chronicler's vague allusion to 'someone close to the king' may even have been a veiled reference to Edmund himself – not implausible given the recent bad blood between the two men. On the other hand, and more credibly, it may be that Aethelred was suffering a spate of recurring anxiety or paranoia linked to his recent illness. William of Malmesbury saw this as a continuation of an avoidance strategy on the king's part, claiming Aethelred was 'long accustomed to commit his safety to fortifications and not to attack the enemy'. The king's sudden departure stripped the gathering of its legitimacy. Once again the fighting men dispersed. Setbacks such as this persuaded Edmund to seek help from further afield.

While Cnut's forces continued to ravage the West Midlands, Edmund travelled northwards to Northumbria, where (relying on his northern pedigree on his mother's side) he might hope to attract support. After successfully rallying the men of the North and joining forces with Uhtred, Northumbria's earl, he led raids into Staffordshire, Shropshire and Cheshire. Ostensibly, this was done to punish the men from those shires for refusing to join his earlier musters. But more pointedly it may have been done to damage Eadric's credibility, and to disrupt the Mercian's own recruiting. The lands mentioned as being ravaged constituted tracts of Eadric's heartland, and the specific mention of Shrewsbury as being targeted is telling. The raids must have represented more than just the normal sparring between rival warlords. Florence uses the term 'laying waste' when describing their impact. In response, Eadric persuaded Cnut to target Edmund's and Uhtred's estates in the northern Danelaw and Northumbria – presumably as a means of drawing them away from his own territory. Only later nationalistic chroniclers saw this as treacherous or underhand. Contemporaries would have viewed it more pragmatically.

The *Anglo-Saxon Chronicle* details the direction taken by Cnut at the head of his mounted infantry, stating:

> He [Cnut] went out through Buckinghamshire into Bedfordshire, from there to Huntingdonshire, and so into Northamptonshire, along the fen to Stamford, and then into Lincolnshire; then from there to Nottinghamshire, and so into Northumbria towards York.

From this, the raiding route taken appears to have followed the modern A1 from Huntingdon to Grantham via Stamford; then on to Newark-on-Trent in Nottinghamshire via Ancaster. The Roman fortress town of Ancaster in Lincolnshire lay at the junction of two major Roman roads – Ermine Street and King Street. By travelling inland from Ancaster to Newark, rather than continuing up Ermine Street to Lincoln, Cnut's forces might have linked up with the Danish fleet at Gainsborough, on the Trent.

The campaign of 1016 in the north of England.

This invasion of the northern Danelaw and Northumbria turned the tables on Edmund and Uhtred, and the latter immediately abandoned his ravaging in Cheshire and hastened back to York. Edmund is recorded as hurriedly riding back to gain the security of London at the side of his father, though he may first have fallen back into Wales, where there is tenuous evidence he sought to foster alliances among the Welsh. Having overrun much of the northern Danelaw largely unopposed, Cnut then had to fight to gain a secure bridgehead into Yorkshire. According to Ottar the Black's *Knutsdrapa*, the Dane fought a battle at 'broad' Hemingbrough (Hemming's burh), near Selby, where he is said to have 'laid waste the English west of the Ouse'. If true, the battle fought there may have been one of the more decisive actions of the 1016 campaign. The Northumbrian earl, hurrying back from Cheshire must have arrived too late to influence the outcome of the battle, though he may have later rallied men to defend his homeland of Bernicia by disputing a crossing of the Tees against the advancing Danish forces.

The direct route to York for Cnut's mounted forces would have been from Gainsborough to Doncaster, then on to York via Castleford and Tadcaster. Maybe his mounted men took this route, while the fleet travelled from Gainsborough down the Trent to the Humber, then concentrated near Ousefleet before striking north up the River Ouse towards Selby, bringing on the fight at Hemingbrough. The flat and extensive floodplain of the Ouse (part of the Humberhead Levels) provides few defensive options today, but in those far-off times Hemingbrough may have been the site of a fortress, a riverine stronghold, possibly one of several established by Swein Forkbeard.

With his men scattered, Uhtred concluded at some point that the game was up. Isolated militarily and politically, he sent messengers to Cnut to indicate he was willing to submit. Continued resistance must have appeared pointless. Once again, as in 1013, the Northumbrian nobles offered up hostages. But Cnut was in no mood for a rapprochement, especially not with men he vehemently distrusted, nor with the wider society of Northumbrians, who had let him down so badly in 1013. For this reason Uhtred was immediately executed, along with forty of his followers. The killing was enacted by a certain Thurbrand 'the Hold', a Deiran who is said to have held a long-standing grudge against Uhtred, his Bernician rival. The repercussions of the murder would be felt in the North for generations. Not only were forty of Uhtred's entourage (presumably powerful and important noblemen in their own right) murdered with him, leaving

the North bereft of local leaders who might oppose Cnut, but the assassination of the earl would also become the subject of a celebrated vendetta,
leading to the massacre of Thurbrand's descendants by Uhtred's great-
grandson, Earl Waltheof in 1073. Thurbrand may have hoped to seize the
earldom of Northumbria as a reward for carrying out the brutal purge.
If so, he was to be disappointed. Cnut replaced Uhtred at York with his
brother-in-law and loyal ally, Erik of Lade. Once again a fierce Norwegian
warlord ruled over Northumbria.

Although contemporary historical accounts agree that Uhtred was
immediately murdered on Cnut's orders, a later northern source, Simeon
of Durham, claims Uhtred's removal occurred two years later, after
the English defeat at Carham in 1018. Cnut had motive enough to kill
Uhtred straight off, but it is argued he may have deferred his revenge for
past transgressions, retaining the earl's services at Bamburgh for a further
two years. If Simeon is correct, Cnut's anger at having been so decisively
defeated by the Scots in 1018 may have been the cause of Uhtred's execution then, rather than 2 years earlier. Because the *Anglo-Saxon Chronicle*
entries for Aethelred II's reign were written after the event, it is argued
that the record for 1016 may have become contaminated with another
event occurring later but known by the chronicler. Cnut's other purges
all took place much later, which adds credence to the claim. However,
under the entry for 1072, Simeon appears to contradict himself, claiming,
like others, that Uhtred was treacherously slain when Cnut first attacked
Northumbria in 1016, after having taken an oath and given hostages.
It appears Simeon most probably got his dates muddled.

Having successfully gained control of Northumbria, Cnut rode back
south for a showdown with Aethelred. The Norse longships and crews
belonging to Erik of Lade most likely remained behind in the Trent. York
and other important places in Northumbria would need to be held by men
loyal to Cnut. The Danish prince's own ships travelled back down the East
Coast, while mounted men made their way across country and arrived in
the South at Southampton, where the Dane rejoined the fleet sometime in
April. If their route was to the west, then Cnut – having already overrun
large tracts of the East Midlands and Northumbria – was likely recruiting in the West Midlands and linking up once again with Eadric's forces
in advance of confronting King Aethelred. But a confrontation between
Cnut and Aethelred was destined never to materialise. The exhausted king
passed away on St Georges Day, 23 April, 1016 – in the lamenting words of
the chronicler –'after great toil and difficulties in his life'. Illness and worry

may have done for him. Rather than being unready for death, he may have welcomed it.

Though sometimes lacking in wisdom and at times placing his trust too readily in unscrupulous favourites (a common failing among English kings), Aethelred had ruled with varying levels of success for the best part of four decades – much longer than most modern-day leaders. Viking assaults to one side, throughout his long reign Aethelred was at the helm of a growing and prosperous kingdom. More law codes were produced by him than by any other early English king, and it was said of him that the army feared him 'no less than God' – evidence at odds with the stereotype of him being ineffective and weak. On occasion he had allied himself with erstwhile enemies, such as Olaf Tryggvason, Pallig, Thorkill and Olaf Haraldsson. Both Olafs had stood by him, as Thorkill had done, until Aethelred's health and England's prospects declined. Pallig and his associates were harshly punished when they transgressed.

Aethelred stands accused by some modern historians of failing to retain the loyalty of the English nobility, including for a time his own son. Yet men such as Eadric and Aelfric, both vilified as untrustworthy, stood by him as long as they dared, and there are good indications that Edmund was pursuing his own agenda in the latter years. Many of the problems the king faced were inherited from his father's, Edgar's, time, including an atrophying military infrastructure. Pauline Stafford has rightly asserted that it was Edgar's premature death – he was aged around 30 – which helped ensure the reputation of his reign as 'peaceable'. Had he lived to a ripe old age, he would have faced the same problems as his son, with, arguably, similar violent outcomes. Unlike his father, Aethelred was confronted by powerful and ambitious neighbours with large armies and fleets at their disposal – the threat they posed was even more potent than Olaf Guthfrithsson's coalition in Athelstan's time – more comparable in scale, if not in nature, with Ivar's 'great army' of 865. Moreover, internal tensions apparent during Edgar's reign remained on-going issues. England was only recently a joined-up entity, a patchwork of nationhood. Although Archbishop Wulfstan's admonishment of Aethelred's governance in 1014 suggests that the king's leadership had come under question prior to his exile, Aethelred briefly atoned during the campaign of 1014. A bloody aftermath, failing health and a growing fear of assassination had then forced him to take more of a back seat before his death – these latter months of his life unfortunately serving to reinforce a stereotype of him as being a hapless and lacklustre ruler. In doing so, it attracted the scorn of later historians such as Sir Charles Oman, who considered Aethelred's dying to have been 'the only good service' he could do for England. Although London retained a strong and loyal garrison, the only effective opposition to Cnut and his allies in the field could now come from Edmund.

'Flet Engle ...
(Ded is Edmund'

8.1

Edmund's struggle against Cnut in 1016 is described in exceptional detail in the *Anglo-Saxon Chronicle*, and his undoubted leadership qualities are properly lauded. This is in stark contrast to the reportage of his father's campaign of reconquest two years earlier. But because Aethelred's achievements are understated, it does not follow that Edmund's are necessarily overstated. Once openly declared as King of England while in London, an empowered Edmund proved adept at marshalling armies and maintaining pressure on the occupying forces. Though short-lived, his resolute hounding of the Danes during his momentous year of battles in 1016 stands out in stark contrast to his father's long, militarily patchy and politically troubled thirty-seven-year rule. Whereas Aethelred's occasional successes are disparaged, Edmund's short career – like the passage of a briefly flickering but quickly falling star on a Dark Age night – is at once remarkable and memorable.

Having been made king in London – with Aethelred's body newly interred at St Paul's – Edmund departed the city with an armed retinue just in time to avoid being trapped by Cnut's blockading forces. The *Anglo-Saxon Chronicle* establishes the timeline, stating it was during 'the Rogation days' (the week including the 7–9 May) that the Danish ships arrived in the Thames and made landfall at Greenwich. Florence's account specifically identifies Cnut as being present – the *Anglo-Saxon Chronicle* does not. Florence also adds that Cnut and Edmund were both chosen to succeed Aethelred at around the same time – the former at Winchester, the latter at London:

Campaign of 1016 in the south of England.

The bishops, abbots, ealdormen, and all the nobles of England assembled [at
Winchester], and unanimously chose Cnut to be their lord and king; and
having come to him at Southampton, and renounced and repudiated all the
descendants of king Aethelred [specifically Edmund], made peace with and
swore fealty to him … but the citizens of London and some of the nobles
who were then at London unanimously chose Edmund to be king. Exalted
to the kingly throne, he boldly and without delay marched into West Saxony
[Wessex], and being gladly welcomed by the whole population, he quickly
reduced it under his dominion.

It seems apparent that Edmund lost no time in immediately setting off to
secure Wessex and its capital at Winchester, and must within a relatively
short period of time have established himself there, despite the nobility of
the region having so recently submitted to Cnut and accepted the Dane as
their king, and given hostages. Cnut, meanwhile, had somewhat paradoxi-
cally hurried away from the South with his fleet to lay siege to London.
No mention is made of Thorkill's whereabouts or involvement in these
proceedings, though it seems likely the two Danish warlords were reconciled by this time, having agreed to co-operate and to pool their resources.
With Aethelred dead, Thorkill (ever the realist) now counted on Cnut to
pay his wages.

Once settled in the Thames and encamped on the Isle of Sheppey, Cnut
set in motion preparations for laying siege to London by having a great
ditch, described as a 'circumvallation', dug. The waterway created once

the ditch flooded, located on the south bank of the Thames, would allow Viking longships to be hauled around to the west of London Bridge, and in this way both the eastern and western riverine approaches to the city might be sealed. The Viking plan was then to construct ramparts outside the landward walls of London in an attempt to prevent the townsmen from getting in or out. Slave labour must have been used to carry out the work, which represented a stupendous undertaking. An echo of these events is related in Ottar the Black's *Knutsdrapa*, which speaks of Cnut's forces assaulting the fortress at London and of his success 'in the shallows of the Thames', manhandling his longships through the newly dug canal.

Meanwhile, once loosely established in Wessex, Edmund set about the difficult task of raising an army, an undertaking which may have proved initially quite difficult. Although Florence speaks of the men of Wessex making a spontaneous submission to the newly arrived English king, and that they gladly welcomed him, it is just as likely Edmund's arrival was met with fear and foreboding. His heavy-handed stance as a teenager when confronting the Church authorities in the West Country, and his later seizure of estates in the Five Boroughs, indicates that his ride into Wessex, accompanied by a heavily armed retinue of bodyguards and henchmen, afforded the nobility of the region, when pressed, little option but to submit to him. His nickname 'Ironside' – to give hard knocks – meant hard knocks to both English and Danes alike. Having already recently submitted to Cnut, and been forced to hand over hostages, it seems unlikely (given the Dane's track record with adolescent males) that the nobility at Winchester, or anywhere else for that matter, would have willingly repudiated their oaths and submitted to Edmund, unless their very lives depended on it. The locals may have felt caught between a rock and a hard place – to use a modern idiom. Little wonder the armies clashing in the Wessex countryside in the late spring of 1016 both contained West Saxon contingents. Some families may even have had relatives fighting on both sides to hedge their bets.

By the early summer of 1016, with the siege of London having stalled, Cnut headed westwards once again. The young Dane appears to have been intent on bringing Edmund to battle. Florence describes how:

> They [Cnut's forces] marched into West Saxony with such speed that King Edmund Ironside had no time to muster an army. Nevertheless, with the troops which in this short space of time he had got together, he boldly marched into Dorsetshire against them, trusting to God for help, and attacking them at a place called Peonn near Gillingham, routed them and put them to flight.

By speedily reinvading Wessex – temporarily abandoning the siege of London, and leaving a portion of the army to guard the ships in the Thames – Cnut, intent on allowing Edmund little time to press gang the men of Wessex, prevented the English king from mustering sufficient men to confront him decisively. Their first clash, which occurred on high ground at Penselwood, near the royal manor of Gillingham, in Dorset, may have been more in the nature of thrust and parry than a full-blooded battle. Despite claims that Edmund took the initiative as the attacker, the likelihood is that he was too weak in numbers to have done so. More likely it was he who fell back onto the high ground at Penselwood, on the southern edge of Selwood Forest, taking up a defensive position on Penn Hill beside the present-day St Michael's church. A mile or so further to the north lay Kenwalch's Castle, an Iron Age hill fort converted by the Romans into a stronghold. Only overgrown ramparts and a ditch now remain, half-hidden in deep woodland. Much of the subsequent fighting may have taken place here, since the ditch and vallum at the castle would have proved a good defensive layback for the English king if driven from Penn Hill.

The battle site of Penselwood had a strong martial pedigree. In the year 658, the Saxon King Cenwalth defeated the Britons there. Almost 200 years later, Alfred rallied the men of Somerset, Wiltshire and Hampshire nearby, before decisively defeating Guthrum at the Battle of Ethandun in 878. In the porch, on either side of the door of St Michael's church at Penselwood, the carved heads of two kings implacably stare out at each other. Dating from Norman times, they are thought to depict Alfred and Guthrum; but in the circumstances might equally well represent Edmund and Cnut. If an earlier wooden church ever existed, it was likely burned by the Vikings during Swein Forkbeard's offensive of 1001. It too might have been dedicated to St Michael, a saint often associated with high places.

Cenwalth and Alfred would have discerned little difference in the weaponry on display at Penselwood in 1016. The small armies involved still relied on javelins and axes as missile weapons, and fought hand-to-hand with swords and thrusting spears in much the same way as had their ancestors. One notable variation with earlier armies may have been the English adoption of the Danish two-handed axe – a fearsome weapon, which would later, in the reign of Edward the Confessor, become as common as the sword among the English warrior class. Another difference may have been that, unlike earlier Dark Age armies, where mail armour was only afforded by the nobility, Aethelred's militarisation programme of the previous decade may have resulted in it being available to many more

The curious door arch at St Michael's church, Penselwood – showing two fabulous beasts and two ominous king's heads.

Clean-shaven king's head at St Michael's, Penselwood.

Bearded king's head at St Michael's, Penselwood.

English; their heads would also be protected, by conical iron helmets with projecting iron bars, called nasals, designed to prevent the wearer's nose from being hacked off by a downward sword strike. Usually associated with the Normans, such helmets are thought to have been introduced by this time into England, along with kite-shaped shields, though to what degree is not known. The kite design was adopted to provide mailed cavalrymen in Europe with greater torso protection than the traditional round buckler, and the new style is believed to have rapidly found favour among both English and Danish heavy mounted infantry. In contrast to the well-accoutred soldiery present, others in Edmund's army remained less well-equipped, some even fighting un-armoured, as of old. Seeking shelter behind their heavily protected colleagues during the initial missile offensive, they would have awaited their chance to rush forward and launch javelins and throwing axes.

No details of the fight at Penselwood survive. Despite Florence's jingoistic claim that Edmund routed the Danes, the clash – more credibly initiated by Cnut – appears to have resulted in a Danish victory of sorts, but one which left the Danes exhausted, buying Edmund sufficient time to break off the action and fall back to the north-west, skirting the Somerset levels, towards Bath. Edmund was operating on 'interior lines' – a strategy considered advantageous when faced by an unpredictable and stronger opponent, enabling him to fend off attacks and regroup deeper into Wessex when threatened. It was a tactic that had worked for Alfred in the 890s when faced by Viking armies on the Thames and in Sussex; earlier too when based at Athelney, squeezed by Guthrum and Ubba. Cnut's strategy may have been to pin Edmund in Dorset or Wiltshire with a mounted force, while striking westwards with Thorkill's fleet, targeting the western shires. If successful, the Vikings would (like Swein earlier) gain control of the main Roman road – the Fosse Way – running south to Exeter and north to Lincoln. Cnut's strike against Bath and the Severn Valley might explain why Edmund hurriedly fell back into Avon to counter the threat. As we have seen, Viking warlords were adept at exploiting tactical opportunities like this – the ninth-century pincer attack mounted by Guthrum and Ubba against Alfred in 878 being a prime example. Bath must have been high on Cnut's list of places to secure, and Edmund would doubtless have been well aware of this.

The Battle of Sherston – Midsummer 1016

As a result of these manoeuvres, a second battle was fought at Sherston, near Bath, after midsummer, where Edmund is said to have come close to overwhelming the Danes in a hard-fought engagement. The traditional site of the Battle of Sherston is known locally as 'the Gaston', placing the fighting on the south-eastern slopes of Sherston Hill. The Fosse Way lies nearby. Also close by was the River Avon, which wound its way across an extensive flood plain towards the sea at Avonmouth. It may have been here that Thorkill's fleet had arrived some time before, providing support for Cnut's mounted army.

At Sherston, as at Penselwood, Roman ramparts and ditches attest to a long-standing military pedigree. Pennymead at Sherston (the prefix Pen in both Pennymead and Penselwood meaning hill or height) marked an ancient strongpoint, long known to Saxon, Roman and Celt. Who gained the high ground in 1016 is not known. Nor is it completely clear who commanded the Danish forces. The *Encomium Emmae Reginae* states that Thorkill – stressing Cnut's youth and inexperience, and in an attempt to demonstrate his loyalty – insisted that he alone should bear the risk of leading the army into battle. At odds with this version, Ottar the Black's *Knutsdrapa* credits Cnut, its hero, as the army's leader at Sherston, the relevant verse, concatenating events occurring earlier in the year in Northumbria, saying that it was the young son of Swein who 'made the Angles yield by toppling them at the Tees', and who then 'broke the crow's fast' at Sherston.

Being something of a polyglot force, the composition of the Danish army is worthy of note. The evidence, such as it is, suggests it comprised a mix of Danes, Mercians, Norse and West Saxons. The Mercians may have been led by Eadric, who is strongly associated with the fight (for all the wrong reasons). Florence, in accusatory manner, names him along with Almar and Algar as men who should – 'by right of nationality or allegiance' – have fought with Edmund. The chronicler then goes on to describe Cnut's English allies from Mercia and Wessex as constituting 'a countless host'. But given the overall size of the armies involved at this period, these specific English elements cannot have numbered more than a few hundred men apiece.

The English king is said to have had with him fighting men from at least three Wessex counties – 'Dorsetshire, Devonshire, and Wiltshire', plus his own heavily armed retinue of mounted infantry. The English king had many more fighting men on hand at Sherston than at Penselwood, where he had been caught unprepared by Cnut's rapid advance. It appears that support, previously held back or denied him, had now begun to materialise in the south and west of the country. He may even have attracted a mercenary following of sorts, with a number of Scandinavians and Welshmen fighting in the ranks of his army. Florence recounts how the English king 'arranged the positions and divisions of his forces [and] placed the best men in the foremost ranks'. According to the same chronicler, it was Edmund who 'boldly resolved to attack Cnut', claiming that the Englishman invariably throughout the campaign took the fight to the Danes. This glorification of Edmund, like Asser's hero-worship of Alfred, is at the root of the king's unwarranted reputation for being a somewhat gung-ho commander. The *Anglo-Saxon Chronicle* more often uses words such as 'resolute' and 'strong' – more in keeping with his nickname Ironside – to describe the king's military prowess, while Florence uses the words 'bold' and 'hasty'. Dramatically embellishing Edmund's reputation as an inspiring general, he also (somewhat implausibly) envisages him as addressing each man in his army by name, and in Churchillian fashion exhorting and entreating them to remember that they were about to fight for their country, their children, their wives and their homes. Edmund is then said to have ordered the trumpets to sound and the army to advance upon the enemy.

His front line is described as comprising his most experienced and well-armed men – the Optimates. At their head, the English king is said to have bravely exerted himself to the utmost, providing for every emergency. By setting an inspiring example, fighting in the foremost rank, the chronicler claims he more than fulfilled the duties of a brave soldier and an able general.

The battle extended over an incredible two days of fighting, the first of which was so severely fought 'that at sunset both armies were unable to continue … for very weariness'; Florence boasts a great victory might have been won on the second day had it not been for 'the faithless' Eadric's novel ruse of holding aloft a severed head, claiming it to be that of the English king. The ealdorman is alleged to have cried out, 'Oh ye men of Dorsetshire, Devonshire and Wiltshire, flee quickly; ye have lost your leader'. The stunned and momentarily demoralised English, who by this stage of the battle may have succeeded in driving Cnut's men back in some disorder, are said to have been temporarily halted in their tracks, allowing the Dane's exhausted and shaken units to regroup. Edmund is then said to have leapt onto a mound, taking off his helmet so he could be plainly seen by all, before hurling a javelin at Eadric. Glancing off the traitor's shield, the dart impaled two men beside him. If Florence is to be believed (and he probably should not be) the fighting on the second day – like the first – continued unabated until dusk, at which time the two armies separated, exhausted. Later, during the night, Cnut's army stole away, leaving silently so as not to alert the English. They then returned to their siege lines on the Thames. Perhaps a small rearguard kept the campfires burning on the opposite bank of the Avon throughout the night.

Florence's claim that the Battle of Sherston raged unabated for two days is doubtless an exaggeration. Dark Age battles were fierce and brutal, but given the physical exertion involved, cannot have been overly long once it came to hand strokes. The Battle of Hastings, a larger and much harder-fought affair than Sherston, lasted less than a day. Even at Brunanburh, the great battle of the tenth century, the fighting was done and over with by nightfall. Not until the nineteenth century, with combatants numbering in the hundreds of thousands, did battles routinely extend for longer than a day. At Sherston the sides were numbered in the high hundreds or low thousands. Since neither side broke in rout, the death toll is unlikely to have been sizeable, despite claims made in the *Anglo-Saxon Chronicle* of a great slaughter falling on either side. Rather than a costly, inconclusive draw (as is usually assumed), the Battle of Sherston would appear to have been a marginal English victory. It seems clear that Edmund retained possession of the battlefield – 'the place of slaughter' – the usual yardstick of victory. Cnut, on the other hand, was forced to retrace his steps back east. In doing so, he lost control of the western shires and allowed the victorious English king to pursue a recruiting campaign more widely than might otherwise have been the case. After Sherston, Edmund's posture changed from defender to attacker.

At this stage of the campaign Edmund had the edge over Cnut. Since the death of his father, and now a king in his own right with a growing military backing, he could offer valuable inducements for men to follow him. A traditional verse indicates how this might have been done before the Battle of Sherston:

> Fight well Rattlebone,
> Thou shalt have Sherstone.
> What shall I with Sherstone doe,
> Without I have all that belongs thereto?
> Thou shalt have Wyck & Willesly.
> Easton towne and Pinkeney.

The rhyme recounts how Edmund bought the legendary Rattlebone's loyalty by promising him the manor of Sherston and other hamlets nearby. Inside the church at Sherston there is a wooden chest in which the mythical Rattlebone's armour is reputed to have been stored. The chest bears the initials 'R.B.', almost certainly the source of the curious name. The legend goes on to recount how Rattlebone was wounded at the battle, his abdomen ripped open by a Danish sword or axe. Undeterred, he fought on, covering the wound with his shield or a piece of slate from a nearby quarry, until victory was assured.

Another shadowy participant at the battle, according to Cnut's biographer M.K. Lawson was Edmund's brother Athelstan – someone more generally accepted as having died in 1014, two years earlier, in bed rather than on a battlefield. Lawson bases his assertion on the fact that the date of Athelstan's death and the battle coincide – both occurring on 25 June – along with a somewhat muddled version of accounts penned by the German chronicler Thietmar of Merseburg. But if Athelstan died at Sherston, it seems likely English chroniclers would have picked up on the fact. Notable casualties of other battles generally are named, so it seems incredible that a report of Athelstan's demise would be neglected.

The unusual Anglo-Saxon chest with the suggestive R.B. initials at Sherston Church.

8.2

Emerging from the Battle of Sherston the stronger of the two, Edmund pursued Cnut back to his siege works around London. Keeping to the north of the Thames, his men debouched from clayey wooded slopes near Tottenham, driving the Danes back to their ships, relieving the pressure on the garrison. The English king must have spent some time in the town, though none of the chroniclers mention the fact. Two days later he crossed the Thames at Brentford. Cnut's forces had by this time rallied and another battle was fought on the south bank, where Edmund was once again victorious. Nevertheless, it proved impossible for the English to capitalise on their victory. For reasons that are obscure, a large number of Edmund's men – 'travelling ahead of the army, and intent on looting' – were apparently drowned 'through their own carelessness'. This unfortunate event cannot have taken place before the battle at Brentford; if it had, Edmund would have been too weakened to press home his attack. It must have occurred afterwards, during the pursuit phase. Having outstripped their main body in their haste to plunder the Danish camp and slaughter the stragglers, the pursuers were presumably overwhelmed by an unexpectedly high flood tide. Not being Londoners, the danger of being caught unawares by the tide in the immediate area of the canal dug by the Vikings would not have been known to them. Partly because of the loss of life incurred, Edmund was forced to retreat back into Wessex to recruit another army, this time even larger than before – leaving Cnut able to reconsolidate and resume the siege.

Ottar the Black's *Knutsdrapa* predictably claims its hero to have got the better of Edmund; the verse in question also mentions a fight against the Frisians, presumably Edmund's mercenary allies. It praises Cnut, describing him as a 'shield-beater', claiming he flattened the fortifications and homesteads of the English at Brentford. Since so many of Edmund's men appear to have fallen victim of the tide, there may well be some truth in it. English scribes were no less prone to falsehoods in the name of propaganda than their Scandinavian equivalents. True or not, the Danes resumed their siege of London, and according to Florence assaulted it 'on every side – but through God's mercy were wholly unsuccessful'. Boosted by Edmund's earlier (apparent) success, and (presumably) the promise of his return, the garrison commanders at London were not minded to negotiate or to capitulate, and continued to put up a fierce resistance. Who these commanders were is not known, but Ottar the Black conjures an image of Emma of Normandy as a 'war-maiden', exulting each morning upon seeing the river 'dyed red'; he describes Cnut as a 'ravenous Dane-king' battering the English armour. A number of other medieval pundits also place Emma in London at some point during the siege, at one stage even negotiating directly with Cnut, promising to betray Edmund if she got the chance. Thietmar of Merseburg thought that Cnut accepted a £15,000 bribe to allow Emma safe conduct to Normandy, but this has too much of a storyteller's ring about it to be credible. It seems clear that her children, Edward and Alfred, had earlier made it safely back to the security of their uncle's court at Rouen. In all likelihood, Emma had done so too, probably accompanying them, so was not at any time present during the siege.

Their attempts to storm London's defences having failed, the Vikings – based at Sheerness on the Isle of Sheppey – now set off on a major raid, travelling up the Essex coast to the estuary of the Orwell River and launching attacks into Mercia. Cnut's scurriers killed and burned wherever they went in their usual manner, rounding up cattle which were then herded south, while their longships – loaded to the gunnels with provisions – sailed back down the coast to the Medway. William of Malmesbury describes how the richest of the spoils were conveyed to transports assembled there for carriage back to Denmark. Though many of Cnut's men must have returned to the Medway by ship, mounted raiding parties continued to harass the countryside without let-up.

Michael Swanton, the translator and editor of the 2000 edition of the *Anglo-Saxon Chronicle*, points out in his notes that this sortie into Mercia would have necessitated a round trip of some 400 or 500 miles. Dark Age armies are known to have been able to cover relatively long distances with impunity. Even so, this represents a staggering sweep for the Danish forces to have made, especially so soon after their defeat by Edmund at Brentford and their setback at London. William of Malmesbury's account differs somewhat from the *Anglo-Saxon Chronicle*, making no mention of the route taken by the raiders, stating instead that Cnut's forces – having been repulsed when laying siege to London ('both on the land and the river side'), and with Edmund 'relaxing a little' and getting his affairs in order – 'wreaked their anger on adjacent Mercia – laying waste the towns and villages with plunder, fire and slaughter'.

The idea of Edmund relaxing is novel, though being at the time the rightful King of England he would doubtless have had other, numerous, and some more mundane, tasks to oversee, not least the raising of a new army. Since there is so little information to go on, explaining Edmund's inaction or attempting to reconstruct Cnut's movements is near impossible, but what William's account does highlight is that Cnut's detour into Mercia may not have been quite so stupendous a diversion as that envisaged by Swanton. The phrase 'wreaking revenge on adjacent Mercia' might equally well apply to attacks being made on nearby Hertfordshire or Buckinghamshire – and since Cnut's investment of London encompassed both the north and south banks of the Thames, such raids might equally well have been launched by a mix of mounted infantry and seaborne assault. It is also possible that more than one raiding army may have been operating in England at the time, with Cnut, Thorkill and Erik of Lade all launching independent strikes, some into East Anglia, others into shires abutting London. Ottar the Black's *Knutsdrapa* indicates this might have been the case: it mentions Cnut fighting at around this time in Norwich – 'bloodying the English mail coats'. Ravaging on such a scale conforms to the classic model of behaviour typical of warring parties in medieval times. If Cnut was determinedly set on harrying the lands of his enemies – men such as Ulfcytel, who may have been actively opposing the siege at London; Eadric too, whose support he may have lost by this time – then the launching of a series of raids would have made military sense. Rather than merely gathering supplies for a long winter on the Isle of Sheppey, the young Danish king and his allies were asserting their warlike intent by engaging in a series of wide-sweeping chevauchées.

8.3

The time taken by Cnut's harrying was not wasted on Edmund. He raised yet another army. With this he launched a repeat attack on Cnut's returning forces by again crossing the Thames at Brentford, and falling on their works. The Vikings fell back to their base on Sheppey, unwilling to make a stand. Stragglers are said to have been mercilessly killed in a running fight at Otford, near Sevenoaks. The ford at Aylesford, the lowest crossing point on the Medway, may also have been disputed. It was here that Edmund was joined by Eadric, who appears to have either already changed sides, or did so then – 'turning' to join the king there. The distinguished historian Sir Frank Stenton concluded in his history of Anglo-Saxon England that the English victory gained at Otford was significant enough to persuade Eadric to change sides. But if Florence is to be believed, the Mercian's change of heart may have occurred as early as the aftermath of Sherston.

Whenever it occurred, the jaundiced Anglo-Saxon chronicler retrospectively makes clear his misgivings about the reconciliation of the two men, bewailing that Edmund was unwise to allow the perfidious ealdorman back into his confidence. Accepting for the sake of argument the standard Eadric paradigm, the coming together at Aylesford can be variously interpreted. Either the Mercian cynically turned his coat after the battle at Otford, convinced Cnut's momentum was foundering; or, unsure which side would prevail, he attempted to keep a foot in both camps. Less credibly, but consistent with later accusations, he may have joined up with Edmund for the sole purpose of undermining him. It could be, however, that none of these are correct. Instead, Eadric may have looked to build bridges between the protagonists – acting as a willing go-between for the rival kings to broker a deal. Blunt political realism may have motivated him then, as it had done earlier when – forced by fast-moving events – he had sided with Cnut against Edmund and Uhtred.

By coming to some agreement with the Danes, the English king and his nobles might yet retain the lion's share of any territorial split. Edmund was, after all, the 'home-grown' heir to the throne of England, descended directly from a long line of powerful West Saxon and English kings. Eadric was still a powerful regional lord. The Viking challenge faced was not markedly dissimilar to that faced by Athelstan and Edmund when challenged by Olaf Guthfrithsson, or Eadred when opposed by Eric Bloodaxe, or, for that matter, by Aethelred against successive powerful Scandinavian warlords in the first decade of the millennium. The payment of tribute and the ceding of territory (even if only temporary) were strategies that had worked in the past and could work again. Diplomacy in the Dark Ages was the extension of war by other means – not the other way round. Nobody was better at playing this game than Eadric. Having driven the Danish invaders back in some disarray to their island fortress at Sheppey, and having once again disrupted the siege of London, it may have appeared a good time to negotiate. Nevertheless, Edmund's willingness to commence a dialogue with Eadric attracts the rueful comments of the chroniclers, who claim any let-up in campaigning to have been ill-advised (*unraed geared*). The usual smear stories are recounted, and Eadric is blamed for dissuading Edmund from attacking Cnut's base on the Isle of Sheppey. Eadric's urgings to one side, Edmund needed little coaxing to conclude that an attack on the heavily defended Danish base was impractical. The rapid currents of the Medway would have made any seagoing sortie against the island stronghold dangerous in the extreme. But whether Edmund was ever seriously minded to open negotiations with Cnut on Eadric's insistence is impossible to know. If he did, nothing came of it.

Almost all the sources agree that after their defeat at Otford the Danes regrouped and then travelled again into Essex, and from there further inland as far as Mercia, to pillage. Unlike the first raid, where the Orwell estuary is named as their point of ingress, no details of the raiding route are provided on this second occasion. Edmund, upon hearing that Cnut was again actively harrying inland, is said to have raised a great army from all parts of England (for the fifth time, according to the *Anglo-Saxon Chronicle*). William of Malmesbury's account differs somewhat, making no mention of a Mercian raid, claiming instead that Edmund was compelled into action in response to calls for assistance from the East Anglians who had come under heavy attack. On learning of the Vikings' whereabouts, Edmund is said to have vigorously pursued them and to have overtaken them on their return march to their ships at a hill in Essex called Assandun. Linking up with Ulfcytel's forces and interposing his strengthened army between Cnut and his ships, the king was able to decisively bring the Dane to battle.

None of the accounts specify the exact route taken by Cnut's raiding army, nor Edmund's pursuing forces, in the days or weeks leading up to Assandun. Cnut's first attack on Mercia is better detailed, specifying that the raiders 'turned away from London' and travelled up the East Coast to the Orwell estuary in Suffolk; then raided into Mercia before returning to the Medway. References to the second raid are less concise. Florence states:

> When the king [Edmund] had gone back into Wessex, Cnut led his forces into Essex, and again went into Mercia to pillage ... burnt numerous vills and laid waste the fields [and] returned with spoil to their ships. Edmund Ironside, king of the English, pursued them with the army he had collected from all parts of England, and came up with them on their march at the hill called Assandun.

The phrase 'and again went into Mercia' appears to imply that this second raid was very much a repeat of the first. On both occasions Harwich might have been a secure coastal base of operations for his longships – it is the northernmost coastal town in Essex, lying beside the estuaries of the Orwell and the Stour. In early medieval times Harwich (*Here-wic*, meaning army base in Old English) was renowned as the only safe anchorage between the Thames and the Humber. Lying far enough away from London to eliminate the threat of a surprise English attack, and quite probably an already established haven for Viking raiders, its geographic attributes would have provided Cnut with the security he needed while travelling inland. Similar but progressively less strong cases could also be made for the Blackwater and Crouch estuaries further to the south.

The generic term Mercia, used by the chroniclers to locate Cnut's raids, might encompass a large number of shires. At one time even London was described as a 'Mercian' port. Using the Orwell as ingress on the first raid, the closest target shires for Cnut's forces (if not in Essex or Suffolk) would have been Bedfordshire, Cambridgeshire, Hertfordshire, and Huntingdonshire. William of Malmesbury described Cnut as wreaking his anger on adjacent Mercia on the first occasion, after having been being repulsed at London. 'Adjacent' would appear to earmark Buckinghamshire, Hertfordshire and Middlesex, and also perhaps southern Cambridgeshire – indicating that if Cnut's ships were moored at Harwich he must have travelled overland in a south-westerly direction from the coast.

Assuming the Danes to have once again targeted southern Cambridgeshire or north Hertfordshire, the English forces would have marched up Ermine Street or the Icknield Way to intercept them. Once aware of the threat, Cnut ordered a return to base, but may have left it too late. In a well-timed and well-executed approach Edmund overtook them on their march, preventing their escape. Simeon of Durham's account in particular is une-quivocal in speaking of a pursuit, and of the Danes seeking to escape, while also making it clear that the battle was fought on Cnut's return leg, in the process of withdrawing to his ships. It appears therefore that Edmund had succeeded in interposing his army between Cnut and his base, by doing so forcing a decisive battle. Consistent with such a scenario, Ashdon – a good place name fit with Assandun – on the Essex–Cambridgeshire border, and on a direct route (via Roman roads) from Cambridge back to the East Coast at Harwich, would have been a logical place for the two armies to have clashed. If this is true, Cnut was still 60 miles from his base when intercepted – at Edmund's mercy. If, on the other hand, the armies came together at the more traditional site of the battle – at Ashingdon, further to the south-east, beside the Crouch estuary – Cnut might more likely have avoided battle and escaped outright.

The Battle of Assandun – St Luke's Day 1016

Accounts of the campaign and Battle of Assandun agree that Edmund's army was collected from far and wide. A small, hurriedly gathered force had fought with him at Penselwood in the spring, whereas a larger army is evident at Sherston in the summer. Two distinct levies, assembled to lift the siege of London, made up the third and fourth instances of armies being raised by him in the late summer and early autumn. Assandun marked the fifth time. Recent successes meant he was able to attract substantially greater numbers than before – especially as now he had also joined up with Ulf-cytel's East Anglians. But with respect to the whole English nation being assembled five times – as is claimed in the *Anglo-Saxon Chronicle* – the army which Edmund raised before Assandun was almost certainly the first and last time such a thing was achieved by the Englishman – if in fact it was ever achieved at all. Grandiose claims of 'raising a national army' more likely applaud the widespread reach of Edmund's appeal rather than the absolute size or geographic reach of his recruiting. Aethelred more often raised the nation's armed forces than Edmund, but never gets such plaudits. Neverthe-less, due to the snowballing nature of the campaign of 1016, Edmund's string of successes almost certainly encouraged men who might otherwise have held back from supporting him to now come forward. Edmund's brother Eadwig, of whom so little is known, may have been among them.

The men of East Anglia, on whose territory the battle would be fought, were marshalled by both Ulfcytel and Aethelweard, the latter the son of East Anglia's senior ealdorman, Aethelwine. Ulfcytel had the experience, prestige and reputation to attract widespread support in the eastern shires. He and Thorkill were rivals of long standing, certainly since the blood-bath at Ringmere in 1010. Thorkill may still have been nursing a grudge in respect to the death of his brother Hemming in 1014, and the pair might have clashed swords since, in the weeks and months leading up to Edmund's arrival in East Anglia. Indeed, the East Anglian contingent must have comprised by far the largest part of Edmund's army at the battle. The force from Wessex and the shires around London, which accompanied the king into East Anglia, may have been substantially smaller – though numbers are impossible to gauge.

The Wessex contingent was led by the earlier much maligned Ealdorman Aelfric of Hampshire, whose place Eadric had usurped as English 'scape-goat-in-chief'. This is the same Aelfric who had once been accused of feigning sickness in the face of Swein Forkbeard's army in 1003, and of 'scurrying away' when tasked with leading a naval force against the Danes eleven years earlier, in 992. The nation's current scapegoat, Eadric, is said to have brought with him the men of the Magonsaete – warriors from the 'marcher' regions of Herefordshire and Shropshire. Like the men of Wessex, they were a long way from home – perhaps uncomfortably so. Evidence from the list of high-ranking casualties suggests Edmund's army also included men from the Five Boroughs, since Lindsey's ealdorman, Godwine, was among those who fell at the battle. Though Godwine was quite a common name, it is thought that this may be the same man who – when faced by Swein Forkbeard's and Olaf Tryggvason's armies twenty-five years earlier in Northumbria – had 'set the example of flight', along with the two other northern thegns, Fraena and Frithugist. If so – older now – he was to give a better account of himself. Because Lindsey may well have been under Danish control in the autumn of 1016, it has been suggested that Godwine may have died fighting on the Danish side. But the casualty list from the battle in the *Anglo-Saxon Chronicle* reads very much like a list of notable English dead from Edmund's ranks, so it is probably safe to assume he was Edmund's man. Godwine and his retinue may even have accompanied the English king from the very beginning of the campaign, and may have fought at Penselwood, Sherston and Brentford.

The king's marriage into the nobility of the Five Boroughs had had the effect of locking in committed support. His affinity in the region cannot simply have melted away by the eve of Assandun. Other warriors in the English army hailed from even further afield. An epic poem entitled the 'song of the men of the host' describes how blows from Danish swords fell on Welsh armour at Assandun. Edmund may have fallen back into Wales when Uhtred tracked back northward to counter Cnut's invasion of Northumbria earlier in the year. An alliance made there may have secured Welsh support – some Welshmen may have fought at Sherston and elsewhere. The twelfth-century poet Gaimar recounts how King Edmund took the sister of a Welsh king as a consort – the promise of marriage sealing the deal to provide Edmund with fighting men. Edmund may also have recruited Frisian mercenaries as well as other men of Danish origin settled in the West Country. The Severn valley was thought to have been heavily settled by ex-Viking warriors (as a buffer against the Welsh). The ill-fated Pallig is a good example. Ethnicity counted for little when land or money was promised.

Churchmen were also present in the vanguard of Edmund's army. They included Eadnoth, Bishop of Dorchester, and Wulfsige, abbot of the Benedictine monastery at Ramsey in Cambridgeshire. They rode at the head of their monkish retinues (all from Ramsey), bravely bearing saintly relics into battle. The *Ramsey Chronicle* confirms that they had gathered at the battlefield in accord with the custom in England, 'to aid the fighting – not with arms, but with prayers and orations'.

Precise numbers engaged at Assandun are of course not known, but if Edmund managed to attract the widespread support assumed, and Cnut had the bulk of his mobile army to hand, the armies must have num-

bered several thousand men on either side. The English may even have
outnumbered the Danes, though there is really no reliable evidence for this
one way or the other.

The term 'Danish', in respect to Cnut's army, may be something of a
misnomer. 'Scandinavian' might better describe it, with its sprinkling of
pressed or renegade Anglo-Saxons from Wessex and elsewhere. A memorial stone erected in Norway by Arnsteinn in memory of his son Biorr
who 'was killed in the guard when Knutr attacked England' attests to a
Norse contingent at the battle. Swedes were also present. A rune stone
from Uppland in Sweden records that Alle took Knutr's Danegeld while
in England. The *Anglo-Saxon Chronicle* provides no clues as to the composition of the Viking army, but Emma's encomiast claims that Thorkill's
mercenaries played a prominent part, while later saga evidence also places
Erik of Lade at the fight.

At the heart of both armies were men wearing iron helmets with nasal
guards, with either short or long corselets (*hauberks*) of mail worn over
thick leather tunics. If the mail corselet stretched below the knees, as was
becoming the fashion, the skirts would be tied to the legs to ease move-

The English 'shield wall' at Hastings in 1066 from the Bayeux tapestry – both Edmund's
and Cnut's armies might have been similarly armoured and equipped at Assandun; note the
diminutive archer depicted.

ment when fighting dismounted. The lower half of a warrior like this can be seen on a fragment of masonry from the old minster at Winchester, which depicts a scene from Sigmund's saga. Based almost certainly on one of Cnut's housecarls, the soldier carries a sword, strapped to his waist, and wears a corselet of mail, trousered by being fixed by ties just below the knee. The Bayeux Tapestry depicts both Anglo-Saxons and Normans protected in much the same way in 1066.

Before battle commenced, Edmund is described by Florence as resolutely forming up his shield wall, and then supporting it with bodies in reserve, three deep. The English king's great dragon banner marked the centre of his battle line. In the distance, the Danish king's white banner could be seen fluttering in the breeze, similarly positioned. Before dismounting to fight, Edmund is recounted as riding along the serried lines of his troops, warning and beseeching them that:

> They be mindful of their former valour and victory, and defend themselves and their kingdom from the rapacity of the Danes, for their contest was with those whom they had before conquered.

Great battles attract legendary anecdotes, sometimes of a supernatural nature. The 'angel' of Mons in 1914 is a good example; the three suns rising on the morning of the Battle of Mortimer's Cross during the Wars of the Roses in the fifteenth century is another. Before the fight at Assandun, the heavily armoured men of Cnut's bodyguard are said to have witnessed the spectacle of a black raven appear from the folds of Cnut's plain white flag. With feet firmly anchored, it flapped its wings impatiently, and its beak opened, emitting a hoarse croak of anticipation, heard above the noise of the embattling army. The story comes from the *Encomium Emmae Reginae*. The encomiast says that Cnut's banner was of 'the plainest and whitest silk', and that a raven, first seen and pointed out by Thorkill the Tall, flapped its wings, assuring victory.

Mass would have been heard in the English camp on the morning of battle. It was St Luke's Day, 18 October. Christian relics were held aloft in the front rank of the army. Cnut and his officers (still heathen by inclination, even if some had been baptised) placed their trust (magical ravens excepted) more firmly in pattern-welded swords, stout iron-bossed shields and sharp-pointed javelins than in religious icons. Mouldering knuckle bones and pitted molars, no matter how splendidly encased, could do them little harm. But, even so, they might rather the saintly relics had remained behind at Ramsey under lock and key, where they belonged.

Churchmen accompanying Edmund's army, having gathered at the battlefield – 'in the English manner' – strongly suggests that rather than a hastily mounted encounter battle, the two armies may have faced each other for some considerable period before hostilities commenced. It would have taken time for the Ramsey monks, along with their abbot and the bishop, to make the journey to the battlefield. Exactly how far they had to travel is of course not known for sure, since there are, as already mentioned, two contending locales in Essex with names that are considered to be etymologically consistent with the Old English place name Assandun – Ashdon

Map of the Assandun campaign showing the main Roan roads and alternative battle sites.

(hill of the ash trees) on the Essex–Cambridgeshire border, and Ashingdon (Assa's hill) beside the Crouch estuary in south-east Essex, near Rochford. The Ramsey monks may have accompanied Edmund throughout the latter stages of his approach march, or have followed on to the battlefield soon after. Possibly the king spent the night at their abbey at some point during the campaign. If so, the battlefield most probably lay close by. Of the two contending battlefield locations, Ashdon lies just 50 miles to the south-east of Ramsey. The alternative site at Ashingdon is twice as far away. Roman roads, following the modern A1307 and A10, would have made for a relatively straightforward journey to Ashdon in the eleventh century, whereas a journey to Ashingdon would have been more problematic, with river systems interposing and no major road systems. (See map of the the Assandun Campaign, p.187).

Once all the preliminaries were over, Florence describes how:

> Cnut very slowly brought his men down to a level ground; but king Edmund, on the contrary, moved his forces as he had arranged them with great rapidity, and suddenly gave the word to attack the Danes. The armies fought obstinately, and many fell on both sides.

Cnut's action displays cautious resolve; Edmund's, a more aggressive impatience – like Alfred at Ashdown – charging rapidly against the enemy. If Florence was merely recycling Asser's description of Alfred's charge at Ashdown then his input is of course worthless. Nevertheless, other contemporary narratives also support the idea of Edmund aggressively launching himself into the fight. Emma's encomiast says that:

> King Edmund led from the front, cutting down the Danes on all sides, and by this example rendered his noble followers more inclined to fight.

The twelfth-century *Ramsey Chronicle* – thought to have been based on eyewitness statements – broadly agrees, stating that Edmund penetrated the enemy line 'with lightning fury'. The *Anglo-Saxon Chronicle* differs somewhat, saying simply that both sides resolutely joined battle.

Like Edmund's purposeful charge, Cnut's abandonment of the higher ground appears to echo the sequence of events at Ashdown. Depending on the steepness of the hill, we can imagine such a manoeuvre might result in putting the Danes into some temporary disorder. Seizing the opportu-

nity to capitalise on this may have persuaded Edmund to rapidly advance
against them. Tradition has it he might even have won the day outright
had not Eadric treacherously intervened, crying, 'Flet Engle, Flet Engle, ded
is Edmund'. The Ramsey Chronicle vividly describes Eadric's actions, stating:

> Eadric, traitor to his country and people, seeing Edmund penetrating the
> enemy line with lightning fury, the cunning contriver of trickery led his
> troop in flight, proclaiming Edmund was dead. Whereupon the remainder
> following in bewilderment and panic; the courage of the Danes increased,
> [and] Edmund abandoned the place of slaughter.

Henry of Huntingdon's account mirrors much of this, saying that
when Edmund realised the Danes were making inroads against his
army, 'fighting more fiercely than usual', he left his command post and
launched a counter attack into the enemy front line. He is said to have
'split the line like a lightning bolt, brandishing a sword worthy of a king.
The enemy front line having been overwhelmed, he then launched another
charge against Cnut's second line, comprising the king's own royal retinue
and lifeguard. With the English looking set for victory, Henry then claims
Eadric betrayed the king by his fateful cry. The men of the Magonsaete
took flight and the whole English nation followed.

William of Malmesbury, Florence and Henry of Huntingdon, all writing some considerable time after the event, all finger Eadric as 'designedly'
giving 'the first example of flight'. William adds – now with echoes of the
Maldon poem – that only a small number of men remained 'mindful of
their former fame' – encouraging each other, forming a compact body and
fighting on before being cut down to a man.

Even after the flight of Eadric's forces, fighting continued on the battlefield until dark. Emma's encomiast alludes to the English beginning
to weary late in the day: even though they outnumbered the Danes, the
enemy appeared to be the more numerous. As a consequence they 'turned
their backs and fled without delay', falling as they did so to Danish blades.
Cnut is honoured for a glorious victory, while Edmund is castigated as a
disgraced, fugitive prince.

By late autumn, darkness would fall at around 5 p.m. Up until then the
battle must have been a grim slogging match, fought out hand-to-hand
between close-packed lines of men armed with spears, swords and axes. The
encomiast's suggestion that the Danes were the less numerous, but fought
bravely – 'choosing death rather than the danger attending flight' – is prob-

The village sign at Ashingdon, Essex.

ably not to be trusted. Very rarely did weaker armies overcome larger ones, especially in early medieval times. Whatever the disparity, Edmund's forces had fared the worse of the two and were forced to retreat. Only the fall of night and unfamiliar terrain prevented a bloody defeat from becoming an overwhelming one.

At some point in the battle, Thorkill and Ulfcytel are recounted in as having clashed in mortal combat. With old scores to settle, they are portrayed, like dualists, diligently seeking each other out from among the mass of participants. When they finally fought hand-to-hand, Thorkill emerged victorious, thus avenging the earlier supposed killing of Thorkill's brother Hemming. If it were not for Snorri Sturluson unaccountably crediting Erik of Lade with the killing of Ulfcytel, we could feel reasonably confident that at least one loose end had been tied up. The reference to Erik by Snorri is the only time the Norwegian is mentioned as having been actually present at the battle. However, various sagas link him with the prosecution of the siege of London, a task presumably delegated to him by Cnut. If so, he had been driven back to the Medway by Edmund earlier in the autumn, and was therefore likely present with his master at Assandun.

In reality, it is of course probable that neither Thorkill nor Erik of Lade killed Ulfcytel. The valiant East Anglian leader more plausibly fell to an unknown assailant's sword or axe at the height of battle or in the rout that followed. Thorkill is reputed to have later married Ulfcytel's widow, and historians sometimes portray her as a trophy bride. But since the tall Dane would later be gifted East Anglia by a grateful Cnut, Thorkill's marriage to one of Aethelred's daughters, like Cnut's later marriage to Aethelred's widow, Emma, owed more to realpolitik than revenge or personal aggrandisement.

In explaining Edmund's defeat we are faced yet again with the medieval mindset of blaming a single individual – Eadric. Though there had been enmity between Edmund and the Mercian in the past, the two men had put these differences aside. That the fighting men of the Magonsaete – of brittle quality and far from home – were the first to break seems clear from all the accounts. But the question remains, were they deliberately spooked? An alleged cry of '*Flet Engle, ded is Edmund*' can be discounted, since it would not have been heard above the din of battle. But a rumour spreading of the king's death would travel fast. Such a thing happened at Hastings in 1066, forcing Duke William to remove his helmet so that his face could be clearly seen by those around him. Something similar may have occurred at Assandun. But it is less credible that the rumour was started deliberately. The way the story of the battle is told in the *Encomium Emmae Reginae*, has Eadric say even before battle commenced: 'Let us flee, oh comrades, and snatch our lives from imminent death, for else we will fall forthwith, for I know the hardihood of the Danes'. The way this is written forms a poetic counterpoint to Thorkill's claims regarding the magic raven – creating a sort of yin-yang effect, good versus bad, black against white. Eadric is said to have 'concealed' his own banner when urging his men to flee, contrasting his behaviour with Thorkill's morale-boosting allusion to the Danish banner and the propitious magic raven.

No mention of treachery is made in Ottar the Black's *Knutsdrapa*; the relevant verse more prosaically praises Cnut's generalship, claiming he fought side by side with his men in the 'shield wall' like a true 'warrior-king, serving up flesh to the raven' – 'the blood-bird' – and winning a great name for himself on the field of Assandun, north of the Dane's Woods.

Aftermath

Edmund escaped to fight another day but left behind him the flower of the English nobility slain on the battlefield. The most prominent among them were:

Aelfric, Ealdorman of the Western Shires
Aethelweard, son of Ealdorman Aethelsige of East Anglia
Eadnoth, Bishop of Dorchester
Godwine, Ealdorman of Lindsey
Ulfcytel of East Anglia
Wulfsige, Abbot of Ramsey

The churchmen's deaths are confirmed in the twelfth-century *Liber Eliensis*, which also mentions the slaying of many monks from Ramsey Abbey caught up in either the battle itself or the subsequent rout. Those that survived the carnage recovered the bodies of Eadnoth and Wulfsige and stayed overnight at Ely Abbey en route back to Ramsey from the battlefield (the monastery at Ramsey lay a further 20 miles away to the north-west of Ely – a full day's march). Conflict erupted the following morning when the Ely monks withheld from them the body of Bishop Eadnoth. The Ramsey monks had intended to transport both bodies back to their own abbey, but were initially prevented from doing so by their acquisitive brethren. The monks of Ely prevailed in the case of Eadnoth – holding on to the body – but only after a heated struggle. Only the corpse of their own bishop – Wulfsige – eventually travelled back to Ramsey. Of even greater import to medieval audiences, the precious relics of the Holy Virgin Wendryth had been abandoned by the Ramsey monks on the battlefield and were for a time thought lost. They were later recovered by the victorious Danes, and Cnut had them confiscated to Canterbury – much to the annoyance of the Ramsey community.

The fight at Assandun may not have been the final military encounter between the contending kings. Although the clash in Essex had destroyed Edmund's army, his will to resist remained undiminished. Tellingly, when forced onto the defensive, the English king fell back into the West to gather strength to meet the Danish onslaught. Earlier in the year, he had done the same – fighting battles at Penselwood and Sherston, the former deep in the heart of Wessex, the latter on its extreme western edge. Now, having suffered a crushing defeat at Assandun, he once again headed west, falling back behind the River Severn on the Welsh borders, determined to renew the fight.

As previously mentioned, Edmund is thought to have allied himself with at least one Welsh king – and possibly others. While many Englishmen deserted him or withheld their support, his Welsh allies may have remained loyal. The Forest of Dean, on the Welsh borders, would have been a relatively secure location to marshal the remaining forces available to him and to fight his last battle. The reference in Ottar's poem to a fight north of the Dane's Woods (*Danoskogar*) could be taken to mean a battle fought there sometime later than Assandun, rather than as a reference to woods of that name south of the battlefield, as is sometimes supposed. No details are known about the clash, if indeed there ever was one. Henry of Huntingdon later stated that the armies faced each other again – confirming that it was this time in Gloucestershire – and that the nobles, fearing that the fight would result in yet another stalemate and further great loss of life, refused to fight, instead urging the rival kings to find some other way of settling their disputes. Another battle, had it been fought, should have favoured Cnut, whose prestige would have grown after his victory in Essex, attracting support. Nevertheless, all sources stress Edmund's strength, resilience and resolve. Cnut, on the other hand, is more modestly portrayed by Emma's encomiast as someone who relied heavily on others, in particular Erik of Lade. If Erik was once more organising an attempt on London, and Thorkill had remained in East Anglia, consolidating his grip on the region after Ulfcytel's death, then Cnut may have been disinclined to risk all on yet another throw of the dice, where death, alone, would be the arbiter. Instead, with both sides worn down after their year-long campaigns, the protagonists were persuaded to meet face-to-face in an attempt to broker a deal.

They came together near Deerhurst in Gloucestershire – an important Anglo-Saxon ecclesiastical centre, 2½ miles south of Tewkesbury, and part of the province of Hwicce, located on the Welsh borders. The region abutted both Mercia and Wessex. Edmund set up camp on the west bank of the River Severn; Cnut, on the east bank. Hostages were exchanged to ensure neither side broke the truce. The rival kings were then conveyed by skiff to Alney Island. Situated in the middle of the river, it was a safe place for them to let down their guard. The settlement may have been overseen by Eadric, now a seasoned intermediary. 'Peace, friendship, and fraternity' were confirmed by agreements made and oaths sworn. The *Anglo-Saxon Chronicle* states that the kings 'came together' – becoming partners – and pledged oaths as blood brothers.

They agreed the level of payment (Heregeld) required for the Danish raiding army, and afterwards – having, apparently, split the country between them – parted amicably. Edmund is said to have gained control of Wessex. Cnut gained an ill-defined region described as 'the north part of the country' by one chronicler – simply Mercia by another. William of Malmesbury confirms a similar split, whereas Simeon of Durham merely states that the kingdom was divided between the two men, without specifying how. Florence takes an altogether different slant, claiming that Wessex, East Anglia, Essex and London were all allotted to Cnut, while the supremacy of the kingdom was to remain with Edmund. If true, Edmund would have become – in effect – Cnut's overlord. Emma's encomiast further muddies the water by failing to mention any agreement at all, other than that the two men – after Edmund had impetuously and unsuccessfully challenged Cnut to settle the matter in single combat – made peace with each other, ominously indicating that conflict would most likely break out again at any time.

For whatever reason, neither the fate of Northumbria nor the northern Danelaw (the Five Boroughs) is mentioned in any of the accounts. The Worcester version of the *Anglo-Saxon Chronicle* comes closest with its vague allusion to the 'north part of the country' being ceded to Cnut. The term Mercia may have served as shorthand for the North in general. Or perhaps the fate of Northumbria and the Five Boroughs was seen as already sealed: it had twice fallen to Danish interlopers in the space of three years and was now administered by the Norseman Erik of Lade.

With both sides exhausted after their year-long campaign, and with many parts of the country devastated by war, a truce of some sort was the sensible outcome. Worcestershire was said to have been particularly badly affected during the conflict. If contemporary accounts can be taken at face value, the litany of harrying and slaughter enacted there in 1016 was considerable, perhaps unprecedented. Later examples of ravaging, where the outcomes are better documented, and have come under close study, reveal substantial and long-standing damage done to the communities affected. The best example is William the Conqueror's 'harrying of the North' in 1069–70 – a protracted campaign of destruction and killing which devastated large tracts of Northumbria – the repercussions of which were still being felt several generations later. Many of the inhabitants of such places must have breathed sighs of relief when Edmund and Cnut embraced as blood brothers, exchanging presents of arms, clothing and hostages. More importantly for the Vikings, Cnut accepted a promised payment to his fleet from Edmund of £70,000.

Although, territorially, what was agreed is far from clear, the broad consensus indicates a division of the country the returned England back to borders last seen in the 880s. Cnut's gaining of Mercia, with East Anglia and Northumbria already under Danish control, would have represented an even more drastic partition than the one agreed between Alfred and Guthrum after the Battle of Ethandun, and was a good deal more favourable to the Danes than the split agreed by Edmund's namesake with Olaf Guthfrithsson in 940. Whether any discussion about succession planning was entered into is unclear, though Cnut would later claim that both men accepted the division would last only until the other died, at which time the whole country would be united under the survivor. No wonder Edmund's death a few weeks later attracted such an abundant crop of medieval conspiracy theories.

Even as late as the eleventh century a unified English state was by no means regarded as inevitable, or even necessarily desirable. Though briefly achieved (and with some aplomb) by the West Saxon royal dynasty during the reign of Edgar (959–75), and more shakily throughout Aethelred's long reign, only the heavy hand of Roman rule had previously held the country together for any extended time. Athelstan had been the first Anglo-Saxon king to successfully enforce his overlordship over much of the country. But his successors Edmund and Eadred had had to fight to assert their authority when challenged by Olaf Guthfrithsson and Eric Bloodaxe. Even after this, between the years 957 and 959, the kingdom was split between Edgar and his brother Eadwig, for a time reinventing the kingdoms of Mercia, Northumbria and Wessex. Having fought each other to a standstill, Edmund and Cnut appear to have accepted a temporary partition of the country as politically expedient – though in Edmund's case –

according to the encomiast – with fingers tightly crossed behind his back. Cnut had better reason to be pleased with the outcome. Denied the kingship of Denmark by his brother Harald, he had now won for himself substantial territories in England.

With the summit concluded, Cnut's army returned to their ships, moored nearby. According to Simeon of Durham, they then loaded their longships with all their plunder before travelling back to their base on the Isle of Sheppey, where Cnut was offered a further £15,000, plus the inducement of winter quarters, by the Londoners if he immediately called off the siege. The stage was set for an uneasy coexistence between Englishman and Dane, with the almost inevitable likelihood of renewed conflict. But it was not to be. Edmund died on 30 November 1016 – just six weeks after Assandun.

9.2

Was it clear at Deerhurst that Edmund was dying? In an age of rudimentary medicine, his death may well have been the result of wounds received in battle. Where he died is not known. London has been suggested, but the fact that his remains were buried at Glastonbury Abbey would tend to support the contention that his death occurred in Wessex. The story told by Henry of Huntingdon, that he died in single combat with Cnut to decide the fate of the country, is of course a fiction. Emma's encomiast, while agreeing that a contest in single combat was considered by Edmund, imagined instead that divine forces had intervened, saying, with biblical insight, 'a kingdom divided cannot long endure'; he added that it was God who very soon led Edmund's spirit forth from his body, 'having compassion on the realm'.

Outlandish stories designed to titillate the credulous circulated later in the century. One recounted how Edmund met his death at the hands of Eadric in typically X-rated fashion, featuring the king shot from below by an arrow while seated at a garderobe – an open-bottomed medieval toilet. Less imaginatively, the German chronicler Adam of Bremen claimed Edmund was villainously poisoned. In Icelandic saga, Eadric was known as 'Heinrekr Strjona', which translates as 'the Regicide'.

After Edmund's death, Cnut was able to consolidate his control over England, and was eventually able to divide the country among his supporters. He took Wessex for himself. Thorkill the Tall was given East Anglia. Eadric retained Mercia. Erik of Lade was confirmed as Earl of Northumbria. Granting substantial earldoms to Thorkill and Eadric was not mere administrative expedience. Both men were powerful warlords in their own right, and likely to oppose Cnut if not assuaged by the trappings of power and wealth.

Edmund was buried alongside his grandfather Edgar at Glastonbury. As pointed out by M.K. Lawson in his short biography of Edmund contained in the *Oxford Dictionary of National Biography*, 'despite strong links with the East Midlands and the North, it had been to Wessex that Edmund first turned for support when he launched his campaign against Cnut – in particular from the counties of Hampshire, Wiltshire, and Dorset'. Lawson adds that Edmund was a determined, skilled and inspiring leader, who drew on the 'deep wells of loyalty to the native royal family in Wessex' – this despite Cnut's terror tactics in forcing the earlier submission of the Wessex nobility and dealing brutally with any intransigence. By insisting on retaining Wessex in the division of the country, then electing to be buried there beside his grandfather, Edmund had made it clear prior to his death that he wished to be associated directly with the region and its line of martial kings.

Cnut visited Edmund's tomb at Glastonbury on the fifteenth anniversary of the English king's death (*c.* 1031) and laid a cloak decorated with peacocks upon it. Peacocks were the symbol of salvation and the resurrection of the flesh. The occasion was no doubt heavily stage-managed. The Dane wished to re-emphasise to the Wessex nobility the bonds of brotherhood that had latterly existed between the two men once peace had been sealed. Nevertheless, he may also have genuinely held Edmund in high regard as a worthy opponent. The Englishman's fighting qualities had come close to denying Cnut victory, echoing the glory days of Alfred the Great and Athelstan. It was therefore probably for personal, as well as for political reasons, that he made the visit to the abbey. Tellingly, when later he founded a new abbey at Bury St Edmunds, he chose the anniversary of Assandun, 18 October, for its consecration.

In 1020, Cnut and Thorkill – with other veterans of Assandun – attended another consecration, this time one held at a minster (now lost) located on the site of the battlefield. The dedication took place in their presence with great pomp and ceremony and was officiated over by Aethelred's one-time critic Wulfstan, the Archbishop of York. Other bishops assisted, including the Church's first prelate, Stigand. After commencing his career as Cnut's chaplain, Stigand would go on to serve six English kings during his long life, before dying in 1072, having attained the sees of both Canterbury and Winchester. Some trace of the minster might be expected to have survived into the twenty-first century, but this is not the case. St Andrew's church at Ashingdon makes a claim to have done so, and a coin depicting Cnut is said to have been discovered there in the past. St Andrew's – known locally as St Andrew's Minster – dates from the fourteenth century, but is built on the foundations of an earlier religious site. The noted A.H. Burne, in his *Battlefields of England*, claimed, not unreasonably, that the nearby hill at Canewdon might be the location of Cnut's position on the day of battle. However, the name Canewdon is thought to derive from an earlier Saxon one, Caningadon, meaning 'hill of the Can people', or 'hill of Cana's people' – the same prefix presumably as Canvey Island in the Thames. Ashingdon, beside it, is thought to mean 'hill of Assa's people', in a similar fashion. The parish church of All Saints at Ashdon also dates from a later era, this time the thirteenth century, though, like St Andrew's, it may have been built on the site of an earlier church. St Botolph's at Hadstock, beside Ashdon, is a nearer fit time-wise, being alleged to have the oldest door in England (more than 1,000 years old), which predates the consecration. There is also good reason for assuming the existence of a former church at Old Church Field at Ashdon, since the Domesday Book makes reference to one. This could be the lost minster. Unfortunately, no trace of the structure exists above ground.

Canewdon church, near Ashingdon, thought by some to be the site of Cnut's camp prior to the Battle of Assandun.

Local field names in the area are also suggestive: 'Bone Croft', 'Danes Croft', 'Long Dane' and 'Short Dane', all at Hadstock. Nearby, the Bartlow Hills – prehistoric burial mounds, predating the Viking age, were for many years associated with the battle, and until quite recently were referred to as the 'battle hills'. The plant known as danewort, with its blood-red berries, was in the past referred to locally as Danes-blood. It is a plant which thrives in disturbed soil, and local tradition tells how it first bloomed after the fatal battle. Though merely a folk tale, the recounting of it, and the reference to 'battle hills' may preserve the memory of a battle fought nearby.

The minster at Assandun was not the only church visited by Cnut in 1020. Determined to atone for past misdemeanours, and to demonstrate his Christian credentials, he rebuilt and reconsecrated the Saxon church of St Martin on the Walls at Wareham in Dorset – which had largely been destroyed by his rampaging war-bands in 1015. Three years later, in 1023, Cnut sanctioned the removal of the remains of Archbishop Aelfheah – who had been murdered by the Danes at Greenwich more than a decade earlier. He had the relics transported under heavy guard from St Paul's in London to Canterbury. The ship carrying the Archbishop's coffin would have passed close to the spot where the brutal murder was committed.

But not all of the new king's activities were as wholesome. Edmund's brother, Eadwig – of whom so little is known – was put to death on Cnut's orders a year after Assandun, having apparently rebelled, been outlawed and then been betrayed by erstwhile friends. The same fate might have befallen Edmund's two sons – Edward and Edmund (the identity of the mother is not known – but if it was Ealdgyth they were still babes in arms, possibly twins). The *Anglo-Saxon Chronicle* (predictably) claims it was Eadric who counselled the Danish king to have Edmund's sons slain, presumably to prevent either of them becoming the focus for future rebellions. Cnut is said to have demurred, realising so heinous a crime would rebound on him to his disadvantage. The high regard he felt for their father may also have influenced him to be merciful. Rather than suffer a secretive death in England, the young boys were sent abroad instead. Edmund's son Edward, known as 'the Exile', later married Princess Agatha, niece of the Holy Roman Emperor, Henry II. The daughter from their union, named Margaret, would one day become a Queen of Scotland. Edward the Exile returned to England in 1057 – ostensibly as Edward the Confessor's heir apparent – but died, suspiciously, soon after making landfall. His son Edgar was but a babe, too young to be considered as Edward the Confessor's successor.

If Cnut did not already have reason enough to distrust Eadric, his wife and consort, Aelfgifu of Northampton, would likely have lobbied for the Mercian's death, to avenge the killings of her kinsmen Morcar and Sigeferth, and, if earlier tales can be believed, also to avenge the assassination of her father, Aelfhelm, and the blinding of her two brothers. Stripped of his lands, the Mercian was beheaded in London in 1017. In keeping with a modest cast list (peculiar not just to TV whodunnits, but medieval morality tales too), the deed was reputedly carried out by Erik of Lade. Eadric's decapitated head is said to have remained on view for some time for all to see – his trunk was thrown over the city wall and left unburied for pigs and crows to devour. The cautionary footnote was that 'contemporaries should learn from the example of Eadric's fall, to be faithful, not faithless, to their kings'.

Like the wavering of Thorkill and the bravery of Edmund, the treachery of Eadric is a common theme running throughout all the accounts of the period. But, as the historian Simon Keynes has pointed out, 'a man's posthumous reputation [especially during medieval times] was determined by those who happened to have occasion to write about him, and not necessarily by those who might have been counted among his friends'. The evidence for Eadric's perfidy comes mainly from the *Anglo-Saxon Chronicle*, though the first instance of his nickname – Streona, the Acquisitive – appeared later in a short history of Worcester Cathedral priory, where the ealdorman was described as 'one who has been set up over the whole kingdom of the English and held dominion as if a sub-king'. Eadric's reputation as an enemy of the Church, though likely well deserved, cannot have helped when the histories of the events were written.

Simon Keynes argues that instead of being the cause of the disasters which occurred during Aethelred's reign, Eadric might have been the willing and loyal instrument by which the king executed his often unpopular policies. He further adds that Eadric's actions throughout could be seen as being to protect the Royal Family's best interests, but that either just before or upon Aethelred's death he was forced to choose between two equally abhorrent options – to serve either Edmund or Cnut. It was a medieval catch-22. Though it may be impossible to rehabilitate Eadric completely, it is much too easy to vilify him. This is especially so considering he lived in a brutal age, where murder, blinding, castration and exile were all seen and executed as accepted political expedients.

Eadric was not the only man targeted for elimination during Cnut's terror of 1017. Three other notables: Northman, son of Ealdorman Leofwine

of Warwickshire; Aethelweard, son of Aethelmaer the Stout from the western shires and Beorhtric, son of Aelfheah of Devonshire, all met similar fates.
Others were exiled. It seems the pious spin attaching to Eadric's execution
masked political expediency. Cnut settled all family business that year in
one fell swoop. He also disbanded the army and agreed to rule the country
justly and abide by the law codes of King Edgar. In doing so, he subtly omit-
ted any reference to Aethelred's more extensive law codes. The year before,
he had held a feast honouring Edward the Martyr, an occasion designed
to more proactively undermine Aethelred's line and thereby the rights of
remaining family members.

Cnut later married Aethelred's widow, Emma; this was an action motivated by a desire not for her but to placate her powerful Norman relatives.
Emma's encomiast fictionalises the manner of Cnut's marital advances,
alleging – implausibly – that the king's emissaries searched far and wide
– 'through realms and cities' – for a suitable bride before at last chanc-
ing upon Emma. Wooers are said to have been sent to Normandy bearing
royal gifts. Despite claims by Thietmar of Merseburg that the Royal Family
remained in London throughout the cataclysmic events of 1016 – as previously asserted – the widowed queen had more likely fled to her brother's
court at Rouen either immediately before or after Aethelred's death, taking
her children with her. It was therefore to the Norman court that the
Danish king's suitors made their approaches. Most likely Cnut had never
laid eyes on Emma before the ceremony took place. The *Encomium Emmae
Reginae* is crammed full of noble sentiment, describing Emma as 'the most
distinguished of the women of her time', and as being 'a great ornament'
conveyed to Cnut from across the English Channel. The occasion of the
marriage was described as being full of rejoicing, both in Gaul (Normandy)
and in England, laying to rest 'the disturbances of war'.

Emma bore Cnut a son named Harthacnut. Her encomiast claims that the
queen laid a condition on her marriage that no other son (by Cnut) from
any other wife than herself should rule after him. If true, it would appear
Emma had presciently sought and given legitimacy to her later struggle to
promote Harthacnut over both Aelfgifu's son by Cnut (Harald Harefoot)
and her own two sons by Aethelred (Edward and Alfred). By insisting that
her firstborn by Cnut should succeed to the throne, she was protecting her
own future interests, while at the same time keeping her husband and her
powerful Norman relatives onside. Little wonder her eldest son, Edward –
having been sidelined in this way – when king in his own right held his

mother to account, banishing her for a time from court; the rivalry engendered between Cnut's two spouses and their sons would (on Cnut's death in 1035) bring the country to the brink of civil war.

9.3

Cnut retained forty longships in commission for the defence of his new kingdom. Even so they could not prevent attacks across the border from Scotland. The Scottish king, Malcolm II, cannily chose this time to reassert himself militarily by restating his claim to southern Lothian. Accompanied by an intruding comet, which appeared in northern skies, Malcolm crossed the border into England mob-handed, having allied himself with the Strathclyde Welsh of Eugene 'the Bald'. The outnumbered English forces were crushed at a battle fought at Carham – an important bridging point on the River Tweed – later the site of Wark Castle. A twelfth-century history relates how 'the whole population from the Tees to the Tweed was almost completely cut down while fighting an infinite multitude of Scots'. The English troops were no match for Malcolm's northern hordes, and reinforcements from York may have arrived too late to influence the outcome.

By this time, the bulk of Cnut's forces had returned to Scandinavia. The unfortunate English were harshly taxed to pay them off. Altogether, an enormous sum of £82,500 was handed over to settle accounts before disbandment, and there is evidence that the English continued to be heavily taxed throughout Cnut's reign. The residual forty ships retained by him imply a force of around 1,600 to 2,000 fighting men – a range of numbers which reoccur throughout the period; Eadric apparently lured forty ships from Aethelred to join Cnut in 1015. Thorkill's fleet, too, numbered around forty ships when in Aethelred's employ.

A discrete body, known as housecarls, akin to Edmund's Optimates, were retained by the new king to act as a royal bodyguard. Their make-up and historicity have often been challenged. Some military historians claim they constituted an elite unit, like the legendary Jomsvikings, dedicated to a Spartan life of war, and disciplined and organised as such. Others claim they were equivalent in rank to thegns, the term housecarl merely being a Scandinavian variant. An early mention of the king's housecarls occurs in 1023, in relation to the removal of Archbishop Aelfheah's relics from London to Canterbury. There was concern that the Londoners would riot when it became known the remains were being moved, and so elaborate measures were taken to avoid a confrontation. London Bridge and the banks of the Thames were lined with armed men – common soldiers –

while a diversion is said to have been staged at the city's outer gates by men who are called the king's housecarls, implying a bodyguard. In 1040, after the death of Cnut's son Harald Harefoot, the powerful Earl Godwine, father of Harold II, the future King of England, presented Harthacnut with an exquisitely wrought longship, manned by eighty specially chosen soldiers. Cnut, too, is reputed to have had a very large warship, known as a *Drakkar*. With ornamented prows and sixty thwarts, or rowers' benches, it boasted a crew of at least 120 men. Florence claimed:

> Each crew member had on each arm a golden bracelet, weighing sixteen ounces, and wore a triple coat of mail and a helmet, partly gilt, and a sword with gilded hilt, and had a Danish battle-axe, adorned with silver and gold, hanging from his left shoulder; whilst on his left hand he held a shield, the nails and boss whereof were also gilded, and in the right arm a lance, in the English tongue called ategar.

Like modern-day guardsmen, soldiers such as these may have been hand-picked for ceremonial duties; but that they were housecarls is less certain. When taxpayers in Worcestershire, one of the most severely ravaged shires in England in 1016, baulked at paying exorbitant sums demanded by Harthacnut in 1041, severe riots are reported as resulting. Two of the king's housecarls, masquerading as tax collectors, were killed. It seems unlikely any of Godwine's eighty hand-picked soldiers, or Cnut's *Drakkar*'s crew, would have been used for such a mundane task.

A short reign of terror, an orchestrated political marriage, the taking of hostages from influential families and an outburst of remorse over past misdeeds against the Church appear to have served to secure Cnut's position in most parts of the country. But some lingering resentment remained in Wessex – also, perhaps, elsewhere. Despite the sobering sight of young men without noses, ears or hands in the streets of Canterbury, Winchester and Sherborne, a number of 'underground' plots were hatched against the new regime. To counter threats such as these, Cnut kept a close personal control over the Wessex region in particular. Edmund's surviving brother, Eadwig, may have been a rallying point for the disaffected; his eventual execution on Cnut's orders was inevitable on this basis. As well as certain hotspots in Wessex, there is also circumstantial evidence to indicate that the Londoners, too, remained a problem for Cnut. One of the reasons Archbishop Aelfheah's remains were whisked away to Canterbury under heavy guard is claimed to have been to pre-vent a cult of Aelfheah – hostile to Danish rule – emerging in London; a threat that leaving one of the saint's fingers at St Paul's was designed to assuage. Instead, Winchester became Cnut's capital.

The earlier four-way division of the country, between Cnut, Eadric, Erik and Thorkill, had represented, in a very real sense, a military occupation. The scant evidence is that Cnut remained an insecure king. Important places such as London, Oxford and Wallingford are known to have been garrisoned by him until quite late on. Winchester, Southampton and Exeter may have been too. Veiled references to Cnut accompanying his fleet to the Isle of Wight in the 1020s imply problems with troublesome pirates, but may – just as likely – have been to guard against organised opposition from across the Channel in Normandy. Likewise, the threat of Welsh attacks from across the Severn may help explain why such a large proportion of Cnut's warriors were settled in the Marches. Like Aethelred, the Viking king routinely employed mercenary troops to control the parts of the country most at risk. The Scottish victory at Carham in 1018 – described by the military historian Richard Brooks as 'typical Dark Age bloodletting with no permanent significance' – may also have resulted in special settle-ment measures being initiated in the North.

In 1021, Cnut unleashed a second wave of purges – this time focused on the Danish old guard. Thorkill was the most prominent of the victims, although Erik of Lade may also have been removed from office at this time. Thorkill was outlawed and banished to Denmark. Erik's end is less certain. One account records him as dying from a massive haemorrhage following a medical procedure. Why Thorkill and Erik were targeted is unclear, although the former's overbearing presence and greed may have had something to do with it. It should not be forgotten that Thorkill and Olaf Haraldsson had at one time been close associates. Cnut – probably with good grounds, as we shall see – feared a wider, hostile Scandinavian coalition emerging; one potentially backed by Thorkill and Olaf, among others. In the circumstances, Thorkill was lucky to escape to Denmark with his life. Briefly reconciled with Cnut a few years later, the giant Dane remained a powerful figure for a time; Cnut must have felt, despite some qualms, that it was more politic to have him on his side rather than other-wise. The dictum 'keep your friends close, but your enemies closer' comes to mind. The two men are said to have shaken hands and exchanged sons as hostages. Thorkill then disappears from the scene – his death, and the manner of it, go unrecorded.

By this time, new, equally ruthless men were emerging to take the place of those toppled by Cnut. Among them was the powerful Saxon nobleman, Godwin of Wessex. Godwin's father, Wulfnoth, was the man who had unaccountably absconded with twenty of Aethelred's ships in 1009. The circumstances surrounding the mutiny are thoroughly obscure. Even so, Aethelred II's biographer Ann Williams has suggested Wulfnoth may have been part of the same anti-Eadric faction at court that saw the downfall of Morcar and Sigeferth. It was Eadric's brother, Brithtric, who had denounced Wulfnoth to the king prior to the mutiny, adding credence to this assertion. Such claims, if true, help underline the complex web of alliances existing between Danes and Englishmen prior to the Danish invasions of 1013 and 1016. Because of his family's estrangement from the Crown, it is quite possible that Godwin fought alongside Cnut at Assandun. Long-standing antipathy to Aethelred's regime may have attracted him to the Danish banner. On the other hand, he may equally well have fought alongside Edmund, and then later risen under Cnut. The Dane is said to have admired loyalty, which appears to have been one of Godwin's strong suits. The Englishman most likely accompanied Cnut on trips to Denmark in 1019 and again in 1023, after that acting as regent during Cnut's later long absences. The capricious nature of Scandinavian politics necessitated Cnut being away from England, campaigning for protracted periods. Large numbers of Englishmen, like Godwin, are said to have fought side by side with the Danes on these occasions.

As a result of Cnut's brother Harald's death or exile around this time, a pressing objective for the young king was to secure Denmark and the other client Scandinavian territories – his birthright. Many of the areas previously under Danish control in Norway lay under the thrall of Olaf Haraldsson, now famously Christianised, and later to be more commonly known as St Olaf. The Norwegian warlord had won back control of his homeland with money earned while in Aethelred's employ, and with the help of his Swedish ally, King Anund Jacob. What is more, a hostile faction had arisen in Denmark led by Cnut's in-laws – Jarl Ulf and Eiglaf – threatening Cnut's security more directly.

To further their own interests – sometime before the year 1026 – the two men appear to have championed Cnut and Emma's son, Harthacnut, in a quest to seize power in Denmark. They allied themselves with Olaf in Norway and Anund Jacob in Sweden. According to the *Knutsdrapa*, Cnut fought them all at a battle known as the Holy River (*c.* 1026). The location of the battle is thought to have been beside the River Helgea, which joins the sea near Kristianstad in southern Sweden, bordering the Danish province of Skane. The nature and outcome of the fight are unclear. The *Anglo-Saxon Chronicle* says that the Swedes had 'the place of slaughter' whereas the *Knutsdrapa* says Cnut threw them back. But if the battle was initially a setback, Cnut's losses were soon replaced. Greater material and financial resources at his command from England tipped the balance in his favour. The Swedes and Norse on the other hand were weakened through losses incurred at the battle and had difficulty in making them up. As a result – with Jarl Ulf killed or executed – Cnut emerged from the struggle victorious. In a letter written to his English subjects he recounted how he had concluded peace with those nations who 'wished to deprive [him] of the kingdom and of life, but could not [do so] since God destroyed their strength'. In the letter, Cnut titles himself 'king of all England and Denmark, and of the Norwegians and of some of the Swedes'. This is the basis of the later grandiose description of him as 'Emperor of the North'.

After the Battle of the Holy River, the energetic Norwegian, Olaf Haraldsson was driven out of Norway by his own people, the Norwegians having been bribed to do so by the English. Later, while attempting a comeback, he would be killed at the Battle of Stiklestad near Trondheim on 29 July 1030. Sanctified for his vigorous Christianising efforts in Norway, Olaf's demise is said to have stemmed from his unpopular habit of having his follower's wives apprehended and executed for sorcery. Like his Norwegian namesake, Olaf Tryggvason, 'rough religion' seems to have appealed to him. Meanwhile, in Britain, Cnut is said to have allied himself with the Hiberno-Norse King of Dublin, Sihtric Silkenbeard, against the troublesome Welsh. Raids into Wales are recorded as occurring in 1030. The skald Ottar the Black even held that Cnut became a king of the Irish at some point. But although Silkenbeard may have submitted to him, it appears unlikely Cnut ever assumed the overall kingship at Dublin.

A major war was also fought in Scotland, with Cnut gaining the upper hand. But nothing is known of the details. Relations between England and Scotland had been mended for a time in the 1020s after an earlier spate of bloodletting when Cnut's wife Emma and her brother Richard, Duke of Normandy intervened. On the second occasion, reconciliation with the Scots took place in 1031 when unnamed Scottish princes 'brought their heads' to Cnut from Fife to buy a peace.

9.4

Cnut died at Shaftesbury in November 1035 after a lengthy illness. He was buried with all the trappings of state in the Old Minster at Winchester; his bones were later transferred with others to the new, prestigious cathedral built by the Normans, which still stands today. Outlines of the Old Minster are still visible, paved over, beside the new one. Cnut's relics now lie jumbled in one or more of six mortuary chests, along with those of other pre-conquest kings and queens. After being disinterred and kicked around by Parliamentarian troops quartered in the cathedral during the early part of the English Civil War, his remains were later gathered and placed in the casks on display at the cathedral today. M.K. Lawson, Cnut's biographer, describes 'England's Viking king' as 'ultimately elusive', summing him up as 'ruthless and good at grasping political opportunities'. He may have been much like other Scandinavian warlords who preyed on the English: men such as Ivar the Boneless and Olaf Guthfrithsson, rivalling the former in cruelty, the latter in ambition. The warriors he led into battle in 1016 had no compunction about trashing Church property, murdering monks, or carrying off nuns. Nevertheless, just before his death, Cnut is said to have expressed genuine contrition over his past crimes; he hoped the gifts he made to the Church would redeem him from his sins, and requested that the religious community at Sherborne should pray daily for his salvation. Even earlier, in 1027, while at Rome on pilgrimage, he had written to his countrymen expressing similar sentiments. The relevant section from the letter reads:

> I have humbly vowed to Almighty God to amend my life from now on in all things, and to rule justly and faithfully the kingdoms and people subject to me and to maintain equal justice in all things and if hitherto anything contrary to what is right has been done through the intemperance of my youth or through negligence I intend to repair it all henceforth with the help of God.

The Roman pilgrimage had been made for political reasons, but more pointedly served to engender a pious image. So too did his visit to the shrine of St Cuthbert at Durham, when he walked the last 5 miles barefoot, like any other pilgrim. The wording of his letter from Rome reiterates pledges made at his coronation, and mirror those made by his predecessor Aethelred in 1014. If he meant what he wrote in 1027, and was genuine when he expressed contrition prior to his death, then his atonement marked a

The 'raven' memorial at Cnut's daughter's grave at Bosham church in West Sussex.

sea change from the violent and unusually cruel youth who cast ashore his mutilated trophy victims at Sandwich in 1014.

Most people today know of Cnut only from the famous folk tale of his attempt to hold back the tide on the seashore: a ruler apparently demonstrating to his subjects the worldly limits of his powers. Cnut's infant daughter is said to have drowned in a millpond at Bosham in West Sussex, where the incoming tide is still a problem for the unwary. The ancient church at Bosham features on the Bayeux Tapestry; it is from where Harold Godwinson, the later King of England, set out on his ill-fated expedition to Normandy in 1065. Arguably, nowhere else in England is more evocative of those times.

Quite long by the standards of the day, Cnut's reign left no indelible legacy on England, merely serving to underline the country's vulnerability. There was no wholesale dispossession of landed estates as occurred after 1066. What is more, upon his death his empire was soon swept away by the tide of events. To all intents and purposes, Norway had been lost while he still lived, falling to Olaf Haraldsson's son, the formidable Magnus Olafsson. Seven years after Cnut's death, Denmark too was lost. Neither of Cnut's sons (Harald Harefoot, d. 1040, or Harthacnut, d. 1042) reigned for long: nor was there any great love lost between them while they did. In 1040, Harthacnut ordered his dead half-brother's remains dug up and thrown into a swamp. Two years later, Harthacnut was seized by a series of fatal convulsions and died soon after.

Unopposed, Aethelred's son Edward, later known as 'the Confessor', became king. He might have done so even earlier had fortune favoured him more kindly. In Cnut's latter years, relations with Normandy had

broken down, and an attempted invasion of England by Edward's supporters had been launched from Fecamp in Upper Normandy, but was beaten
back by a gale. Norman charter evidence shows Edward as being accorded
the title 'King of England' as early as 1033, two years before Cnut's death.
From Normandy, the pretender had even made a formal gift of lands in
Cornwall to the Benedictine abbey of Mont-Saint-Michel in Brittany,
lands which included the lookalike St Michael's Mount, where the aspirant
king hoped to establish a similar order once formally enthroned. Edward
and his younger brother Alfred both separately launched expeditions to
England shortly after Cnut's death, having been encouraged to do so, sup-
posedly, by their mother, Emma. Edward's force was almost immediately
turned back by armed supporters of Harald Harefoot. Alfred's expedition,
however, ended in tragedy. Intercepted on the road to London by Earl
Godwin's troops, he was handed over to Harald's men and taken to Ely,
where he was tortured and blinded. He died shortly afterwards.

Like Cnut's short Danish dominion, the eventual return of Anglo-
Saxon rule in England under Edward the Confessor was to also prove
short-lived. The English king died childless in 1066. Harold Godwinson,
his brother-in-law, and the most powerful man in England, immediately seized the crown. Having no inherited right to do so, his action
provoked a predictable response from other powerful and unscrupulous
men. Armies gathered in Scandinavia and on the Continent – ready to
pounce. Harold's brother Tostig, the deposed Earl of Northumbria, in alliance with Harold Hardrada, the half-brother of Olaf Haraldsson, struck
first. They invaded Northumbria and defeated local English opposition at
the Battle of Fulford in South Yorkshire. Force marching his army from
London, King Harold surprised them at Stamford Bridge, near York, on
25 September and destroyed them. Tostig and Hardrada were killed in the
fighting. Unbeknown at the time, it was to be the last occasion a Viking
army from Scandinavia would ever threaten England. But just days later,
even before the corpses of the dead had been cleared at Stamford Bridge,
a Norman–French army led by Duke William 'the Bastard' was landing on
the Sussex coast, at Pevensey, near Hastings.

Selected Further Reading

The main primary and near-contemporary sources referenced in the narrative – the *Anglo-Saxon Chronicle*, Asser's *Life of King Alfred*, the *Encomium Emmae Reginae*, the twelfth-century histories attributed to Florence of Worcester, Simeon of Durham, William of Malmesbury and Henry of Huntingdon, the *Heimskringla*, and other Icelandic sagas – are all readily available in modern translations. The works listed below represent a short selection of the more important secondary sources consulted. They deal with various aspects of early medieval military history and biography. Several contain extensive bibliographies covering a comprehensive range of relevant academic work.

Aitcheson, Nick. *The Picts and the Scots at War*. 2003
Bridgeford, Andrew. *1066 – The Hidden History of the Bayeux Tapestry*. 2004
Brooks, Nicholas. *Communities and Warfare 700–1400*. 2000
Brooks, Richard. *Cassell's Battlefields of Britain and Ireland*. 2005
Campbell, James. *The Anglo-Saxon State*. 2000
Clements, Jonathan. *A Brief History of the Vikings – The Last Pagans or the First Europeans?* 2005
Davies, Wendy (editor). *From the Vikings to the Normans*. 2003
Delbruck, Hans. *History of the Art of War, Volume II – The Barbarian Invasions*. Trans. Walter J. Renfroe, Jr. 1980
Fletcher, Richard. *Bloodfeud – Murder and Revenge in Anglo-Saxon England*. 2002
Foote, Peter & Wilson, David M. *The Viking Achievement – The Society and Culture of Early Medieval Scandinavia*. 1974
Griffiths, Bill (editor & translator). *The Battle of Maldon*. 1991
Hanson, Victor Davis. *The Western Way of War – Infantry Battle in Classical Greece*. 1989

Hart, Cyril. *The Danelaw.* 1992

Hinde, Thomas (editor). *The Domesday Book – England's Heritage, Then and Now.* 2002

Howard, Ian. *Swein Forkbeard's Invasions and the Danish Conquest of England, 991–1017.* 2003

Keynes, Simon. 'Æthelred II (*c.* 966x8–1016)', *Oxford Dictionary of National Biography*

Keynes, Simon. 'Eadric [Edric] Streona'. *Oxford Dictionary of National Biography*

Laing, Jennifer. *Warriors of the Dark Ages.* 2000

Laing, Lloyd & Laing, Jennifer. *The Picts and the Scots.* 1993

Lavelle, Ryan. *Aethelred II – King of the English.* 2002

Lavelle, Ryan. *Alfred's Wars – Sources and Interpretations of Anglo-Saxon Warfare in the Viking Age.* 2010

Lawson, M.K. *Cnut – England's Viking King 1016–35.* 2011

Lawson, M.K. 'Edmund II – Known as Ironside'. *Oxford Dictionary of National Biography*

Loyn, H.R. *Anglo-Saxon England and the Norman Conquest.* 1991

McGlynn, Sean. *By Sword and Fire – Cruelty and Atrocity in Medieval Warfare.* 2008

Marren, Peter. *Battles of the Dark Ages – British Battlefields AD 410 to 1065.* 2006

Marsden, John. *The Fury of the Northmen – Saints, Shrines and Sea-Raiders in the Viking Age.* 1996

O'Brien, Harriet. *Queen Emma and the Vikings.* 2005

Richards, Julian D. *English Heritage Book of Viking Age England.* 1991

Rodger, N.A.M. *The Safeguard of the Sea – A Naval History of Britain – Volume One 660–1649.* 1997

Siddorn, J. Kim. *Viking Weapons and Warfare.* 2000

Smyth, A.P. *Scandinavian York and Dublin, Volumes 1 & 2.* 1987

Stafford, Pauline. *Unification and Conquest – A Political and Social History of England in the Tenth and Eleventh Centuries.* 1989

Stenton, Frank *Anglo-Saxon England* 1943

Stevenson, I.P. *Viking Warfare.* 2012

Strickland, Matthew (editor). *Anglo-Norman Warfare.* 1992

Sturdy, David. *Alfred the Great.* 1995

Thompson, Logan. *Ancient Weapons in Britain.* 2004

Williams, Ann. *Aethelred the Unready – The Ill-Counselled King.* 200

Wood, Michael. *In Search of the Dark Ages.* 1981

Battle Chronology 796–1016

Place	Year	Shire	Description
Don's Mouth	796	South Tyne	Battle fought near the monastic site at Jarrow
Whalley	798	Lancashire	Norse raiders defeat Northumbrians
Carhampton 1	836	Somerset	Viking raiders defeat King Egbert's West Saxons
Hingston Down	838	Cornwall	King Egbert defeats a coalition of Vikings and Britons
Southampton	840	Hampshire	Ealdorman Wulfheard defeats a large Viking force
Portland	840	Dorset	Ealdorman Aethelhelm killed in battle against Vikings
Romney Marsh	841	Kent	Ealdorman Hereberht killed by victorious Viking raiders
Carhampton 2	843	Somerset	King Aethelwulf's army defeat Vikings
Parrett River	848	Somerset	Men of Dorset and Somerset defeat Viking raiders
Wigborough	850	Somerset	Ealdorman Ceorl's Devon men defeat the Vikings
Aclea	851	Kent	King Aethelwulf and Aethelbald crush a large Viking army

Sandwich	851	Kent	Kentish men capture nine ships in first recorded naval action
Thanet	853	Kent	Two ealdormen killed in fight with Viking raiding army
Winchester	860	Hampshire	Weland's Vikings from the Somme destroyed
York	866	Yorkshire	Ivar defeats Northumbrian kings with great slaughter
Hoxne	870	East Anglia	Ivar defeats and martyrs King Edmund of East Anglia
Englefield	870	Berkshire	Ealdorman Aethelwulf defeats Danes in Berkshire
Reading	871	Berkshire	Ealdorman Aethelwulf killed in follow-up battle
Ashdown	871	Berkshire	Major defeat for Halfdan – Bagsecg killed plus five jarls
Basing	871	Hampshire	Danes victorious against King Aethelred I and King Alfred
Mereton	871	Wiltshire	Aethelred I, mortally wounded, defeated in a hard-fought battle
Wilton	871	Wiltshire	King Alfred defeated by Half-dan and a truce later agreed
Unlocated	875	Wessex coast	Alfred defeats Danes in sea battle
Cynwit / Countisbury	878	Somerset	Danish army led by Ubba destroyed in north Devon
Ethandun/ Edington	878	Wiltshire	Alfred decisively defeats Guthrum in Wiltshire
Unlocated	882	Wessex coast	Alfred defeats Danes in sea battle
River Stour	884	East Anglia	Alfred's fleet clashes with Danes
Farnham	893	Surrey	Edward the Elder defeats Danish army on the march

Benfleet	893	Essex	Mercians from London destroy Danish encampment
Chichester	893	West Sussex	Viking band destroyed at Kingly Vale
Buttington	893	Powys	Haesten's raiding army destroyed near Welshpool
Unlocated	896	South Coast	Alfred's new ships defeat Danish East Anglian squadron
The Holme	903 or 904	East Anglia	Pyrrhic victory for rebels and Danes over Kentish rearguard
Tettenhall	910	Staffordshire	Momentous English victory in Danelaw
Archenfield	914	Herefordshire	Edward the Elder defeats Hroald and Ohtor's army
Corbridge 1	914	Northumberland	Vikings defeat Scots–Bernician coalition
Tempsford	917	Bedfordshire	Edward the Elder destroys Danish fortress on Ouse
Corbridge 2	918	Northumberland	Vikings defeat second Scots–Bernician coalition
Brunanburh	937	Unlocated	Athelstan defeats Olaf Guthfrithsson's coalition
Castleford	948	West Yorkshire	Eric Bloodaxe destroys English rearguard
Stainmoor	954	Durham	Eric Bloodaxe defeated and killed while fleeing to his ships
Watchet	988	Somerset	Goda intercepts, defeats and kills Viking raiders
Maldon	991	Essex	Byrhtnoth killed, defeated by Olaf Tryggvason's army
The Thames	992		Naval debacle, tarnishing the reputation of Aethelred's leaders
Unlocated	993	Northumbria	Flight of the northern thegns when faced by a large Viking army

Aethelingadene	1001	West Sussex	Swein Forkbeard defeats army raised in Hampshire
Pinhoe	1001	Devon	Swein Forkbeard defeats army raised in Devon and Somerset
Thetford	1004	East Anglia	Ulfcytel defeated by Swein's forces in fierce battle
Kennet	1006	Berkshire	Tostig's Vikings defeat English defenders
Ringmere	1010	Norfolk	Ulfcytel defeated by Thorkill (among others) in hard-fought battle
London	1013		Swein's forces repulsed at London
Hemingbrough	1016	Yorkshire	Cnut defeats Northumbrians and marches on York
Penselwood	1016	Somerset	Edmund Ironside and Cnut clash on high ground
Sherston	1016	Wiltshire	Major battle – the outcome favouring Edmund Ironside
Brentford	1016	London	Edmund Ironside raises the siege of London
Otford	1016	Kent	Edmund Ironside drives Cnut's forces back to Sheppey
Assandun/ Ashdon	1016	Essex	Edmund Ironside defeated by Cnut in epochal battle

Source: Richard Brooks. *Cassell's Battlefields of Britain and Ireland*. 2005

The Burhs of the Burghal Hidage

Name of Burh	Hides
Axbridge, Somerset	400
Bath	1,000
Bredy/Bridport, Dorset	760
Buckingham	1,600
Burpham/Arundel, West Sussex	720
Chichester, West Sussex	1,500
Chisbury, Wiltshire	500
Cricklade, Wiltshire	1,400
Eashing, Surrey	600
Eorpeburnan (Appledore?), East Sussex	324
Exeter, Devon	734
Halwell, Devon	300
Hastings, Sussex	500
Langport, Somerset	600
Lewes, Sussex	1,200
Lydford, Devon	140
Lyng, Somerset	100
Malmesbury, Wiltshire	1,200

Pilton, Somerset	360
Portchester, Hampshire	500
Sashes (Cookham?), Berkshire	1,000
Shaftesbury, Wiltshire	700
Southampton, Hampshire	150
Southwark, London	1,800
Twynham/Christchurch, Dorset	470
Wallingford, Berkshire	2,400
Wareham, Dorset	1,600
Warwick, Warwickshire	2,400
Watchet, Somerset	513
Wilton, Wiltshire	1,400
Winchester, Hampshire	2,400
Worcester, Worcestershire	1,200

The West Saxon and English Succession (858–1066)

Name	Died	Reigned (years)	Relationship to predecessor	Succession comments
Aethelwulf	d. 858	19	Son of Egbert	Previously King of Kent for 14 years
Aethelbald	d. 860	2	Son	None
Aethelberht	d. 865	5	Brother	None
Aethelred I	m.w. 871	6	Brother	None
Alfred 'the Great'	d. 899	28	Brother	Assumed power over Aethelred's infant sons at a time of great danger
Edward 'the Elder'	d. 924	25	Son	Civil war with Aethelwold (Aethelred's son) resulted
Aelfweard	d. 924	<1	Son	The circumstances of his death in the same year as his father are obscure
Athelstan	d. 939	13	Half-brother	Historians consider Athelstan may have been responsible for Aelfweard's death

Edmund I	m. 946	9	Half-brother	Allegedly murdered in a drunken brawl, possibly assassinated
Eadred	d. 955	9	Brother	See above
Eadwig	d. 959	4	Son	Shared power with his younger brother Edgar
Edgar 'the Peaceable'	d. 975	6	Brother	See above, otherwise none
Edward 'the Martyr'	m. 978	3	Son	Probably murdered by his stepmother's supporters
Aethelred II	u. 1013	35	Half-brother	His succession was tarnished by the murder of his half-brother Edward.
Swein Forkbeard	d. 1014	<1	None	Gained the kingship by force of arms
Aethelred II	d. 1016	A further 2	None	Regained his kingship by force of arms
Edmund II 'Ironside'	d. 1016	<1	Son	Forced to seize power upon the death of his father despite being the nominated heir
Cnut	d. 1035	19	None	After a protracted armed struggle, gained overall control of England upon the death of Edmund Ironside
Harald 'Harefoot'	d. 1040	5	Son	Succession disputed by his half-brother Harthacnut
Harthacnut	d. 1042	2	Half-brother	Briefly took control of the country upon the death of his half-brother Harald Harefoot

Edward 'the Confessor'	d. 1066	24	Half-brother	None – though earlier attempts to impose himself from Normandy had failed
Harold Godwinson	k. 1066	<1	Brother-in-law	Seized power upon the death of Edward – an act claimed to have been in accord with Edward's death-bed wishes
William 'the Conqueror'	d. 1087	27	None	Gained the kingship by force of arms – he may have been promised the succession by Edward at some earlier stage

Key: d. = died; k. = killed in battle; m.w. = mortally wounded in battle;
     m. = murdered; u. = usurped

Index